OCS Study
MMS 2003-062

Refining and Revising the Gulf of Mexico Outer Continental Shelf Region High-Probability Model for Historic Shipwrecks

I0423564

Final Report

Volume III: Appendices

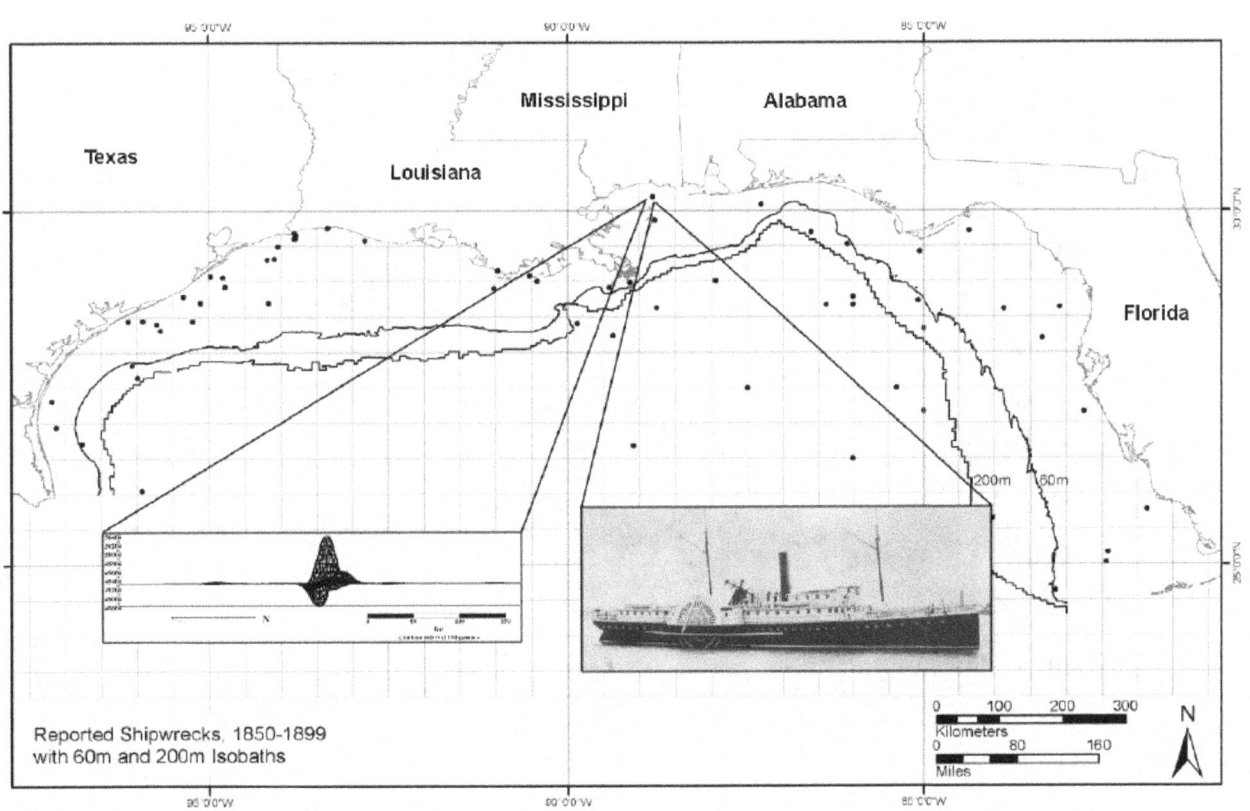

Reported Shipwrecks, 1850-1899
with 60m and 200m Isobaths

U.S. Department of the Interior
Minerals Management Service
Gulf of Mexico OCS Region

OCS Study
MMS 2003-062

Refining and Revising the Gulf of Mexico Outer Continental Shelf Region High-Probability Model for Historic Shipwrecks

Final Report

Volume III: Appendices

Authors

Charles E. Pearson
Stephen R. James, Jr.
Michael C. Krivor
S. Dean El Darragi
Lori Cunningham

Prepared under MMS Contract
1435-01-00-CT-31054
by
Panamerican Consultants, Inc.
Memphis, Tennessee
and
Coastal Environments, Inc.
Baton Rouge, Louisiana

Published by

U.S. Department of the Interior
Minerals Management Service
Gulf of Mexico OCS Region

New Orleans
December 2003

DISCLAIMER

This report was prepared under contract between the Minerals Management Service (MMS), Panamerican Consultants, Inc., and Coastal Environments, Inc. This report has been technically reviewed by the MMS and it has been approved for publication. Approval does not signify that the contents necessarily reflect the views and policies of the MMS, nor does mention of trade names or commercial products constitute endorsement or recommendation for use. It is, however, exempt from review and compliance with the MMS editorial standards.

REPORT AVAILIBILITY

Extra copies of this report may be obtained from the Public Information Unit (Mail Stop 5034) at the following address:

> U.S. Department of the Interior
> Minerals Management Service
> Gulf of Mexico OCS Region
> Public Information Unit (MS 5034)
> 1201 Elmwood Park Boulevard
> New Orleans, Louisiana 70123-2394
>
> Telephone: (504) 736-2519 or
>   1-800-200-GULF

CITATION

Suggested citation:

Pearson, C.E., S.R. James, Jr., M.C. Krivor, S.D. El Darragi, and L. Cunningham. 2003. Refining and Revising the Gulf of Mexico Outer Continental Shelf Region High-Probability Model for Historic Shipwrecks: Final Report. Volume III: Appendices. U.S. Dept. of the Interior, Minerals Management Service, Gulf of Mexico OCS Region, New Orleans, LA. OCS Study MMS 2003-062, 338 pp., 3 volumes.

TABLE OF CONTENTS

PAGE

INFORMATION IN THIS APPENDIX IS NOT AVAILABLE FOR PUBLIC DISCLOSURE

APPENDIX A

THE 1989 SHIPWRECK DATABASE DEVELOPED BY GARRISON ET AL. (1989)

APPENDIX B

DATAFIELD DEFINITIONS: 2001 SHIPWRECK DATABASE

1. RECORD NUMBER: The number of the record in the database.

2. VESSEL ID NUMBER: A unique identification number assigned to each vessel and object in the database during data collection. Duplicate and other irrelevant records have been removed causing gaps in this number. This number remains with each individual record such that it can be tracked, even if records entered before or after it are deleted.

3. CLASSIFICATION: All entries in the database are classified as either a "Vessel" or an "Object." A vessel is any entry that is identified as a vessel, part of a vessel or an item from a vessel. An "Object" is any other type of item on the seafloor, such as pipe, cable, wellhead, etc.

4. VESSEL NAME: Name of vessel or object as provided in the sources examined. In some instances, this might be a descriptive name, such as "24-foot pleasure boat," or "10-foot pipe," "obstruction," or simply "object." If no name or descriptors are available for an entry, the terms "Unknown vessel" or "Unknown object" are used.

5. ALTERNATE NAME: Any other name given in the sources examined for the vessel or the object.

6. 1989 MMS NUMBER: This is the unique number assigned to entries that were included in the 1989 MMS Shipwreck Database. This number is retained for information and reference purposes only.

7. OFFICIAL NUMBER: This is the official registration number assigned to vessels of United States registry.

8. STATE SITE NUMBER: This is the trinomial state site number assigned to a wreck site.

9. DATE OF LOSS: This is the reported date of loss given in month, date, and year, (e.g., 01-11-1950) or year only (e.g., 00-00-1847) if that is all that is provided in sources. If date of loss is unknown, entries are 0's.

10. YEAR OF LOSS: The reported year of loss if known. If the year of loss is unknown, "0" is entered. This field appears in Access Table View only and is included for analysis purposes.

11. CAUSE OF LOSS: This is a two-letter code for the documented cause of loss. The entries are:

AB = abandoned	FO = foundered
BE = beached	GF = gunfire/battle
BU = burned	SC = scuttled
CA = capsized	ST = stranded & swamped
CO = collided	SU = sunk
EX = explosion	UN = unknown

12. MMS LEASE BLOCK: Two- or three-letter code for the MMS lease area and the lease block number within which the entry falls. MMS lease area codes are listed below.

AC = Alaminos Canyon	LS = Lund South
AM = Amery Terrace	LU = Lund
AP = Apalachicola	MA = Miami
AT = Atwater	MC = Mississippi Canyon
BA = Brazos	MI = Matagorda Island
BAA = Brazos A	MIA = Matagorda Island A
BM = Bay Marchand	MO = Mobile
BS = Breton Sound	MP = Main Pass
CA = Chandeleur	MU = Mustang Island
CC = Corpus Christi	MUA = Mustang Island A
CE =Campeche Escarpment	PB = St. Petersburg
CH = Charlotte Harbor	PE = Pensacola
DC = Desoto Canyon	PI = Port Isabel
DD = Destin Dome	PL = South Pelto
DT = Dry Tortugas	PNA = North Padre Island A
EB = East Breaks	PN = North Padre Island
EC = East Cameron	PR = Pulley Ridge
EI = Eugene Island	PSA = South Padre Island A
EL = The Elbow	PS = South Padre Island
EW = Ewing Bank	RK = Rankin
FM = Florida Middle Ground	SA = Sabine Pass (LA)
FP = Florida Plain	SE = Sigsbee Escarpment
GA = Galveston Area	SM = South Marsh Island
GAA = Galveston Area A	SP = South Pass
GB = Garden Banks	SS = Ship Shoal
GI = Grand Isle Area	ST = South Timbalier
GC = Green Canyon	SX = Sabine Pass (TX)
GV = Gainesville	TP = Tarpon Springs
HE = Henderson	TV = Tortugas Valley
HH = Howell Hook	VK = Viosca Knoll
HI = High Island	VN = Vernon
HIA - High Island A	VR = Vermilion
KC = Keathley Canyon	WR = Walker Ridge
KW = Key West	WC = West Cameron
LL = Lloyd	WD = West Delta

13. LATITUDE (DD): The latitude of the entry in decimal degrees.

14. LONGITUDE (DD): The longitude of the entry in decimal degrees.

15. DATUM: The map datum of the coordinates provided in the principal source for a record. These will be NAD27 or NAD83. In a large number of instances, the map datum is not specifically referenced in the sources examined. However, in many of these instances it can be reasonably inferred that the datum is NAD27 and this is entered. In those cases where it is impossible to identify or reasonably infer a datum, "Not reported" is entered. In ArcView mapping, all of the data are mapped to a NAD27 base such that those entries with NAD83 datum coordinates or contain a "Not reported" entry are converted to NAD27. However, in the Access database, the NAD83 and "Not reported" coordinates are maintained in the decimal degree fields (i.e. "Latitude (DD)" and "Longitude (DD)" for information and reference purposes.

16. LORAN 1: The Loran 1 coordinate if provided in the principal source for the record. "UNKNOWN" is entered if no Loran coordinates are available.

17. LORAN 2: The Loran 2 coordinate if provided in the principal source for the record. "UNKNOWN" is entered if no Loran coordinates are available.

18. LATITUDE NAD27: The latitude of the entry in decimal degrees, North American Datum 1927. If NAD27 is the value for the DATUM field the value recorded will be the same as that recorded in LATITUDE (DD). If the value for the DATUM field is NAD83, this value will record the coordinates projected to NAD 1927. This should be the latitude used for mapping purposes.

19. LONGITUDE NAD27: The longitude of the entry in decimal degrees, North American Datum 1927. If NAD27 is the value for the DATUM field the value recorded will be the same as that recorded in LONGITUDE (DD). If the value for the DATUM field is NAD83 this value will record the coordinates projected to NAD 1927. This should be the longitude used for mapping purposes.

20. NEAREST LANDMARK: Includes any reference to a geographic location provided in the principal source of information for the record, such as a landform, port, or community. If no reference to a landmark is contained in the principal source, "None" is entered.

21. NEAREST STATE (2): Two-letter code for the state nearest to the position of the entry. These are: AL   Alabama; FL   Florida; LA   Louisiana; MS   Mississippi and TX   Texas

22. LOCATION RELIABILITY: Reliability of available information on the reported location of loss.

    1. Wreck location is confirmed through physical verification and has been accurately positioned (e.g., with GPS or on an accurate, modern map) or is identified on the basis of accurately positioned remote sensing survey. The location is considered to be very reliable such that a wreck would be easy to relocate using standard DGPS equipment.

    2. A specific location is provided for a wreck or a vessel loss by an informant, reported in the literature or on a map. Included in this category are wrecks or losses whose position is given to at least the nearest actual minute of latitude and longitude, to a specific offshore lease block, and those that have been discovered and positioned using LORAN equipment. The location reliability of these wrecks or losses is considered to be moderate to good. It is anticipated that these wrecks could be discovered, but discovery would require a moderate amount of field survey with remote sensing equipment, plus it may require additional historical research.

    3. A general location for a wreck or a vessel loss is provided by an informant or in the literature. Included in this category are vessels whose locations of loss are given only in degrees of latitude and longitude. Also included in this category are vessels whose general position of loss is provided in relation to a known landmark, such as "10 miles south, southeast of Ship Island." The location reliability of these wrecks or losses is considered to be fair to poor. Discovery of wrecks included in this category could be very difficult and commonly would require a considerable amount of historical research and/or remote sensing survey.

    4. Unreliable or vague location information is provided on a wreck or place of loss of a vessel. Examples would include many early accounts of vessel losses such as reports of vessels lost in hurricanes "near latitude such and such" or other general

indications of loss, such as "30 miles off Padre Island," "off the coast of Louisiana" "south of Galveston," or "between Galveston and New Orleans." Directed searches for these vessels are nearly impossible and their discovery will mainly be by chance. Also included in this reliability category are items that were reported to be "adrift" when there is no evidence to indicate where, or if, they sank as well as those cases where information is unavailable to make any assessment of the reliability of the position given.

23. VESSEL TYPE: Two- or three-letter code of the vessel type, object associated with a vessel, or an aircraft as given on the historical records, or obtained from archaeological data. If type is unknown or unreported, "UNK" is entered.

AIR = aircraft	FRT = freighter	SCH = schooner
ANC = anchor/chain	GBT = gunboat	SDW = sidewheeler
BAR = barque	GLN = galleon	SHM = shrimp trawler
BGE = barge	H/B = hopper barge	SHP = ship
BNK = barkentine	HEL = helicopter	SKI = skiff
BRG = brig	JUB = jack-up barge	SLP = sloop
BRI = brigantine	LDC = landing craft	SPV = supply vessel
BYT = buoy tender	LNS = landing ship	ST =
CCR = cabin cruiser	LST = landing ship,	steamer/steamboat
CLP = clipper	tanks	STW = sternwheeler
CRB = crane barge	LUG = lugger	SUB = submarine
CRW = crewboat	M/V = motor vessel	T/B = tug or tow boat
CUT = cutter	MCH = merchant	TNK = tanker
DES = destroyer escort	MSW = mine sweeper	TOW = tow boat
DIR = drilling rig/ship	P/C = pleasure craft	TPB = torpedo boat
DRE = dredge	PAS = passenger	TRA = trawler
DVT = dive tender	steamer	TUG = tug boat
EXP = exploration	PAT = patrol boat	YCT = yacht
vessel	PDL = paddlewheel boat	
F/V = fishing vessel	SAI = sailboat	UNK = Unknown
FER = ferryboat	SB = schooner/barge	

24. PROPULSION TYPE: Two-letter code for the propulsion system as given in the source for the record. If no information on propulsion is provided, "Unknown" (UN) is entered.

DS = diesel screw	SA = sail	SW = steam
GA = gas	SM = steam	sidewheeler
GS = gasoline screw	SS = steam screw	TW = towed
OR = oar	ST = steam	UN = Unknown
OS = oil screw	sternwheeler	

25. YEAR BUILT: Year in which vessel was built, if known. If the year built is unknown "0" is entered.

26. WHERE BUILT: Two- or three-letter code for the place of build of the vessel, if known. If place of build is unknown "UN" is entered.

ABW = Aberdeen, WA	ALG = Algiers, LA	BBM = Booth Bay, ME
AL = Alabama	APF = Apalachicola, FL	BEL = Belfast, Northern
ALC = Alameda, CA	AST = Astoria, NY	Ireland

BER = Bergen, Norway
BFM = Belfast, ME
BIL = Biloxi, MS
BLZ = Belize
BMD = Baltimore, MD
BME = Birmingham, England
BMT = Beaumont, TX
BNC = Bluefields, Nicaragua
BNY = Brooklyn, NY
BPC = Bridgeport, CN
BRL = Baton Rouge, LA
BRM = Bremen, Germany
BRS = Brashear, LA
BSL = Bay St. Louis, MS
BSM = Boston, MA
BST = Bostock
BTM = Bath, ME
BWT = Brownsville, TX
CAM = Calais, ME
CBN = Caibarien, Cuba
CCT = Corpus Christi, TX
CDS = Cadiz, Spain
CGA = Columbus, GA
CHC = Chicago, IL
CHF = Charlotte Harbor, FL
CHP = Chester, PA
CMM = Campeche, Mexico
CNJ = Camden, NJ
CNO = Cincinnati, OH
CRV = Caracas, Venezuela
CSC = Charleston, SC
CUB = Cuba
DEL = Delaware
DET = Detroit, MI
DRT = Dry Tortugas
DUM = Duluth, MN
EBM = East Boston, MA
ECM = Ecorse, MI
ENG = England
EPA = E. Pascagoula, MS
EPR = East Providence, RI
ESM = Essex, MA
EVW = Everett, WA
FLA = Florida
FMF = Ft. Meyers, FL
FTM = Frontera, Mexico
GAL = Galveston, TX
GLS = Glasgow, Scotland
GPM = Gulfport, MS
GPN = Gravelly Point, NJ
GRC = Groton, CN

GRN = Granville, Nova Scotia
GUA = Guatemala
HAM = Hamburg, Germany
HOB = Hoboken, NJ
HON = Honduras
HOT = Houston, TX
HPA = Hog Island, PA
HRP = Harriman, PA
HTI = Haiti
HVN = Havana, Cuba
JFL = Jacksonville, FL
KIJ = Kingston, Jamaica
KKF = Knights Key, FL
KWF = Key West, FL
LA = Louisiana
LAC = Los Angeles, CA
LAK = Lake Charles, LA
LAN = Lancaster, England
LFL = Lafitte, LA
LON = London, England
LPE = Liverpool, England
MAF = Marco, FL
MAT = Matagorda, TX
MEX = Mexico
MFD = Millard, DL
MGC = Morgan City, LA
MIA = Miami, FL
MLD = Maitland, DL
MNW = Manitowoc, WI
MOA = Mobile, AL
MRF = Marseille, France
MS = Mississippi
NBC = New Bedford, CN
NBM = Nobleboro, ME
NBP = Newburyport, MA
NC = North Carolina
NCE = Newcastle, England
NIC = Nicaragua
NLC = New London, CN
NO = New Orleans, LA
NOC = Noank, CN
NOF = Norfolk, VA
NOR = Norway
NPM = Neponset, MA
NPN = Newport News, VA
NY = New York
NYC = New York City, NY
OAK = Oakland, CA
ORB = Orebic
ORT = Orange, TX
OSL = Oslo, Norway
PA = Pennsylvania

PAM = Pascagoula, MS
PAN = Perth Amboy, NJ
PAT = Port Arthur, TX
PCF = Panama City, FL
PDK = Paducah, KY
PDS = Port Eads, AL
PEN = Pensacola, FL
PJN = Port Jefferson, NY
PLD = Philadelphia, PA
PLW = Port Ludlow, WA
PSF = Port Sutton, FL
PTC = Puerto Cortez
PTI = Point Isabel, TX
PTL = Portland, ME
PTO = Portland, OR
QUM = Quincy, MA
RI = Rhode Island
RIC = Richmond, CA
RIO = Rio de Janeiro, Brazil
ROM = Rockland, ME
SAB = Sabine, TX
SAF = St. Augustine, FL
SAV = Savannah, GA
SGM = St. George, ME
SHE = South Hampton, Eng.
SHP = Ship Island, MS
SMF = St. Marks, FL
SMK = Smithland, KY
SNF = San Francisco, CA
SPA = Spain
SPC = San Pedro, CA
SPM = South Portland, ME
SPN = Summers Point, NJ
SPR = San Juan, Puerto Rico
STL = Seattle, WA
SUP = Superior, WI
TAB = Tabasco, Mexico
TAR = Tarpon Springs, FL
TMM = Thomaston, ME
TMP = Tampico, Mexico
TNN = Tottenville, NY
TPF = Tampa, FL
TRN = Trondheim, Norway
US = United States
VCM = Vera Cruz, Mexico
WHV = Wheeling, VA
WID = Wilmington, DL
WNC = Wilmington, NC

UN = Unknown

27. HULL MATERIAL: General description of the material that the hull of the vessel was built as reported in source of information. Two-letter codes are:

    AL = aluminum
    CM = composite (iron/steel hull, some wood framing)
    CN = concrete
    FG = fiberglass
    IR = Iron
    MT = metal
    ST = steel
    WD = wood
    UN = Unknown

28. VESSEL LENGTH: Measured length of vessel to 10th of a foot, if known. Object lengths are provided, if known.

29. VESSEL BEAM (width): Measured beam of vessel to 10th of a foot, if known.

30. DEPTH HOLD: Measured depth of hold of vessel to 10th of a foot, if known.

31. DRAFT: Measured draft of vessel to 10th of a foot, if known.

32. TONNAGE (gross): Total or gross tonnage (burden), if known; to the nearest ton.

33. TONNAGE (net): Net tonnage (burden), if known; to the nearest ton.

34. NUMBER OF MASTS: Number of masts, if known.

35. NUMBER OF DECKS: Number of decks, if known.

36. BOW SHAPE: Three-letter code for the shape or profile of bow if given in sources for record. "UNK" is entered if bow shape is unknown.

    CLP = "clipper" bow
    CRP = curved and plumb
    CRR = curved and raked
    HRK = hollow curved and raked
    RKS = straight and raked
    STP = straight and plumb
    TRR = transom and raked
    TRS = transom and straight
    UNK = unknown

37. STERN SHAPE: Three-letter code for the shape or profile of the stern if given in sources for record. "UNK" is entered if bow shape is unknown.

    PKS = "pink" stern
    RDS = round stern
    TKS = "tucked" stern
    TRS = transom or flat stern
    UNK = unknown

38. BUILDER: Name of person or firm who built hull, if known.

39. OWNER: Name of person or firm who owned vessel when lost, if known.

40. MAIN ENGINE TYPE: Three-letter code for type of main engine(s), if known. "UNK" is entered if engine type is unknown.

DEI = diesel engine
GAS = gasoline engine
STH = high pressure steam engine
STL = low pressure steam engine
STM = steam engine
TUR = turbine
UNK = unknown

41. HORSEPOWER: Horsepower for main engine(s), if known

42. NUMBER OF CYLINDERS: Number of cylinders in main engine(s), if known.

43. CYLINDER SIZE (inches): Diameter of engine cylinder(s) in inches, if known.

44. STROKE (feet): Length of piston stroke in feet for main engine, if known.

45. YEAR ENGINE BUILT: Year main engine(s) was built, if known.

46. ENGINE BUILDER: Name of person or firm who built main engine(s), if known.

47. NUMBER OF BOILERS: Number of boilers, if known

48. BOILER TYPE: Three-letter code for type of boiler(s), if known. "UNK" is entered if unknown.

COR = cornish boiler
CYB = cylinder boiler
FLU = flue boiler
LAN = lancashire boiler
LOC = locomotive or fire-box boiler
MTB = marine tubular boiler
NRB = north river boiler
SCT = scotch boiler
TUB = tubular boiler, also called fire tube boiler
VFT = vertical fire tube boiler
WTB = water tube boiler
UNK = unknown

49. VESSEL USE: A two-letter code for the manner in which the vessel was most commonly used, if known.

CC = cargo carrier
DS = dive support vessel
EX = exploration vessel
FV = fishing vessel (includes shrimpers)
PC = passenger carrier
PL = pleasure/recreation craft
PS = patrol ship
PT = packet boat (combined passenger and cargo carrier)
SV = supply vessel
TA = tanker
TU = tug or tow boat
WA = warship
UN = Unknown

50. HOMEPORT: Two- or three-letter code for the city, town, state, etc., identified as vessel's homeport, if known. See Field 26 for list of abbreviations.

51. NATIONALITY: Three-letter code for the flag under which vessel was operating when lost, if known.

ARG = Argentina	MEX = Mexico
BRI = Britain/England	NIC = Nicaragua
CAN = Canada	NOR = Norway
CUB = Cuba	PAN = Panama
ELS = El Salvador	RUS = Russia/Soviet Union
FRA = France	SPA = Spain
GER = Germany	USA = United States of America
HON = Honduras	YUG = Yugoslavia
LIB = Liberia	

52. DESTINATION: Two- or three-letter code for port of destination when vessel was lost, if known. See Field 26 for list of abbreviations.

53. CARGO: Cargo carried by vessel when lost, if known.

54. ARMAMENT: If armed, number of guns carried by vessel when lost, if known.

55. VALUE: Value of vessel when lost, in denomination provided in historical records, if known.

WRECK SITE INFORMATION

56. WATER DEPTH: Depth of water in feet at site of sunken vessel or object when the reported depth is confirmed or considered reliable.

57. SITE SIZE: Site size in square feet, based on measurements obtained from remote-sensing records, diver assessments or if otherwise indicated in source of information.

58. BOTTOM TYPE: Two-letter code for bottom type at site of loss, if reported. If unknown "UN" is entered.

CL = clay
SA = sand
UN = unknown

59. WRECK CONDITION: Condition of the wreck as determined by physical examination or as derived from an assessment of available remote-sensing records.

1 = good, much of hull present and articulated (over 50 percent of hull present)
2 = fair, partially intact (25 to 50 percent of hull present)
3 = poor, deteriorated (less than 25 percent of hull present, little articulated)
4 = unknown

60. EXPOSURE: Degree and nature of exposure of the wreck as derived from physical examination or an assessment of available remote-sensing records.

1 = Mostly or entirely exposed (over 50 percent of vessel exposed)

2 = partially buried by sediment (less than 50 percent of vessel exposed)
3 = entirely buried
4 = unknown

61. MATERIAL COLLECTED: Two-letter code for the four most common types of remains reported to have been collected from the wreck site. If no material is known to have been recovered, "NA" is listed

BO = bone
CE = ceramics
GL = glass
ME = metal
LE = leather
WO = wood
NA = not available

DOCUMENTATION

62. UNPUBLISHED DATA: Two-letter code for the type of unpublished information available for wreck site.

AD = artifact description
FN = field notes
PH = photographs
SM = sketch maps
TI = taped interviews
NA = not available

63. DATA DEPOSITORY: Name of the physical location of unpublished data records and/or artifacts, if known. "MMS-New Orleans" is listed as depository when information is derived from GOMR remote-sensing surveys.

64. PUBLISHED REFERENCES: Published references from which information on the entry has been collected. Author and year of publication are provided and full citations are found in "2001 SHIPWRECK DATABASE REFERENCES" included with the technical report accompanying this database. Although not strictly considered published references, where information on an entry was obtained from records or databases maintained by a specific agency or organization, the entity is identified. If an agency or database file record number for an entry was recorded during data collection, this is included in parentheses. A listing of these references is also included in "2001 SHIPWRECK DATABASE REFERENCES" noted above. When information was obtained from reports of MMS-mandated offshore remote-sensing surveys the author, date and a brief title are listed, where this information is available. Survey reports are also specifically identified with a reference number found in the data field "MMS SURVEY REFERENCE NO." These survey reports are on file at the MMS, Gulf of Mexico Region office in New Orleans.

65. MMS SURVEY REFERENCE NO: The MMS reference number for the lease block or pipeline survey that contains record of the sunken vessel or object.

66. VESSEL PHOTOGRAPHS: Notes the existence and reference source for photographs of a vessel or wreck. Selected examples are attached to records.

67. MAGNETOMETER DATA: Notes if magnetometer data are available for the sunken vessel or object. Magnetic intensity and duration in feet are given where available.

68. SIDE SCAN SONAR RECORDS: Notes if side scan sonar records of the sunken vessel or object are available. Selected examples are attached to records.

69. COMMENTS: Any pertinent comments relevant to the vessel or wreck derived from the sources examined.

70. RECORDER: Name of the individual completing the record.

71. DATE RECORDED: Date when record was completed; given as Month, Day, and Year.

72. INFORMATION SOURCE: Includes a code for the principal source(s) of information for the record, most specifically the source that provided information on the location of the vessel or object. These entries are listed below. Other sources providing information on entries are shown in Datafield 64, PUBLISHED REFERENCES and included in the References section of the technical report.

ANC	Archives des Colonies. n.d. *Archives des Colonies, Series C13A, C13B, and C13C.* Microfilm Copies, Special Collections, Howard-Tilton Library, Tulane University, New Orleans.
ARNOLD	Arnold, J.Barto III; J.L. Goloboy, A.W. Hall; R.A. Hall and J.D. Shively, 1998. *Texas' Liberty Ships: From World War II Working Class Heroes to Artificial Reefs.* Bulletin No. 99-1. Texas Parks and Wildlife, Austin.
AWOIS	Automated Wrecks and Obstructions Information Service files maintained by the National Oceanic and Atmospheric Administration (NOAA).
BERG	Berg, Daniel and Denise Berg 1991. *Florida Shipwrecks: The Diver's Guide to Shipwrecks Around the State of Florida & the Florida Keys.* Aqua Explorers, Inc., East Rockaway, New Jersey.
BERMAN	Berman, Bruce D. 1972. *Encyclopedia of American Shipwrecks.* The Mariners Press, Boston.
CEI	Coastal Environments, Inc. 1977. *Cultural Resources Evaluation of the Northern Gulf of Mexico Continental Shelf.* 3 volumes. Prepared by Coastal Environments, Inc., for the Bureau of Land Management, U.S. Department of the Interior, New Orleans Outer Continental Shelf Office. National Technical Information Service, Springfield, Virginia.
CHURCH	Church, R.A. 2002. Unraveling the Mystery: The Discovery of the German Submarine *U 166.* Paper presented at The Minerals Management Service 2002 Information Transfer Meeting, January 8-10, Kenner, La.
CIPRA	Cipra, David C. 1997. *Lighthouses, Lightships, and the Gulf of Mexico.* Cypress Communications, Alexandria, Virginia.
COWLES	Cowles, D.D. (compiler) 1983. *The Official Military Atlas of the Civil War.* Reprint. New York, New York: The Fairfax Press.
EVANS	Evans, Joseph. n.d. *State and Federally Funded Artificial Reefs of Florida, 1985 1995.* Designed and Produced by the author.
FAC	Shipwreck records maintained by the Florida Bureau of Archaeological Research, Tallahassee.
FDMF	Database of artificial reefs off the coast of Florida maintained by the Artificial Reef Program, Florida Division of Marine Fisheries, Florida Fish and Wildlife Conservation Commission, Tallahassee.
GARRISON	Garrison, E.G., C.P. Giammona, F.J. Kelly, A.R. Tripp and G.A. Wolff. 1989. *Historic Shipwrecks and Magnetic Anomalies of the Northern Gulf of Mexico:*

	Reevaluation of Archaeological Resource Management Zone 1. 3 volumes. The Texas A&M Research Foundation, College Station, Texas, MMS Contract 14-12-0001-30330. U.S. Department of the Interior, Minerals Management Service, Gulf of Mexico OCS Regional Office, New Orleans.
GSMFC	Database of artificial reefs in the Gulf of Mexico maintained by the Gulf States Marine Fisheries Commission, Ocean Springs, Mississippi.
HO	Hangs and Obstructions files formerly maintained by the U.S. Navy, Hydrographic Office but now maintained by the National Imagery and Mapping Agency (NIMA). Information derived from Garrison et al. 1989 (see GARRISON)
HOYT	Hoyt, S.D. 1993. *Offshore Underwater Investigations, Houston Galveston Navigation Channels, Texas Project. Galveston, Harris, Liberty and Chambers Counties, Texas.* Espey, Huston & Associates, Inc., Austin, Texas. Prepared for the U.S. Army Corps of Engineers, Galveston District.
IRION	Irion, J.B. and R.J. Anuskiewicz. 1999. *MMS Seafloor Monitoring Project: First Annual Technical Report, 1997 Field Season.* OCS Report, MMS 99-0014. U.S. Department of the Interior, Minerals Management Service, Gulf of Mexico OCS Region, New Orleans, La..
LLOYDS	Data from *Lloyd's Missing Vessel Books, 1873 1954; Lloyd's Marine Loss Records, 1873 1954; or Lloyd's Weekly Casualty Reports*, published by Lloyd's of London. Records examined at the Mariners Museum, Newport News, Virginia, or derived from Garrison et al. 1989 (see GARRISON).
LOCHHEAD	Lochhead, John L. 1954. Disasters to American Vessels, Sail and Steam, 1841-1846. Compiled from the New York Shipping and commercial list. Mariners Museum, Newport News, Virginia.
MACMILLAN	MacMillan, Bruce, Roger C. Smith and James Miller. 1996. *U.S. Navy and Confederate Shipwrecks in Florida: The Florida Navy Legacy Project Phase One: Historical & Archival Compilation, Volume Two: Florida Shipwreck Database.* Submitted to Naval Historical Center, Washington, DC. Bureau of Archaeological Research, Florida Division of Historical Resources, Tallahassee.
MBT	MBT Divers, Pensacola, Florida, webpage (www.mbtdivers.com/NUMBERSH.htm)
MMS	Refers to information obtained from offshore lease block and pipeline surveys provided by MMS, New Orleans.
MOORE	Moore, Arthur R. 1990. *A Careless Word...a Needles Sinking: A History of the Staggering Losses Suffered by the U.S. Merchant Marine, Both in Ships and Personnel, During World War II.* 5th edition. American Merchant Marine Museum, Kings Point, New York.
MVUS	*Merchant Vessels of the United States.* United States Government Printing Office, Washington DC. Published by various agencies (United States Bureau of Customs, 1868-1880; United States Department of the Treasury, 1881-1935; United States Bureau of Marine Inspection and Navigation; 1936-1941; and United States Coast Guard; 1941-) .
NIMA	Non-submarine Contact Database maintained by the National Imagery and Mapping Agency (NIMA), Washington DC.
PEARSON	Pearson, Charles E. and Paul E. Hoffman. 1995. *The Last Voyage of El. Nuevo Constante: The Wreck and Recovery of an Eighteenth Century Spanish Ship off the Louisiana Coast.* Baton Rouge: Louisiana State University Press.
RINEHART	Rinehart, Captain Laney. 1998. *The Captain's Guide to Wrecks and Reefs*, Privately printed by the author.
SINGER	Singer, Steven D. 1992. *Shipwrecks of Florida.* Pineapple Press, Inc., Sarasota, Florida.
TAC	Data obtained from the Texas Antiquities Committee Shipwreck Files, Austin, Texas.
USCG	Data obtained from electronic database of wrecks, hazards and obstructions maintained by the United States Guard.
USCGCR	Data obtained from United States Coast Guard Marine Board Casualty Reports (www.uscg.mil/hq/g-m/moa)

USLS	U.S. Life-Saving Service. var years. Annual Reports of the Operations of the U.S. Life-Saving Service. Derived from Garrison et al. 1989 (see GARRISON).
WADES	Wades Pages webpage (www.wadespage.com).
WPA	Works Progress Administration [WPA]. 1938. *Wreck Reports A Record of Casualties to Persons and Vessels on the Mississippi River, Its Tributaries, on Lakes and Other Waterways of the U.S. Customs District, Port of New Orleans, 1873 1924.* Unpublished manuscript on file, Louisiana State Museum, New Orleans.

73. RECORD UPDATE-RECORDER'S NAME: Name of the individual updating the record.

74. RECORD UPDATE-DATE OF UPDATE: Date when record was updated; given as Month, Day, and Year.

75. IMAGE: Refers to any images that are attached.

APPENDIX C

**SHIPWRECK HIGH PROBABILITY LEASE BLOCKS
IDENTIFIED FROM THE 1989 MODEL**

GOMR Lease Blocks Requiring Archaeological Survey For Historic Shipwrecks
LEASE BLOCKS REQUIRING 50-M SURVEY INTERVAL

AP0079	AP0466	AP0592	BA0478	CA0029	DT0117
AP0080	AP0485	AP0593	BA0479	CA0030	DT0118
AP0081	AP0486	AP0594	BA0489	CH0725	DT0119
AP0123	AP0495	AP0595	BA0490	CH0726	DT0120
AP0124	AP0496	AP0596	BA0491	CH0727	DT0121
AP0125	AP0497	AP0597	BA0509	CH0769	DT0122
AP0167	AP0498	AP0598	BA0510	CH0770	DT0123
AP0168	AP0499	AP0599	BA0511	CH0771	DT0129
AP0169	AP0500	AP0628	BA0514	CH0813	DT0130
AP0253	AP0503	AP0629	BA0515	CH0814	DT0131
AP0254	AP0504	AP0630	BA0516	CH0815	DT0157
AP0255	AP0505	AP0632	BA0536	DD0008	DT0158
AP0292	AP0506	AP0633	BA0537	DD0009	DT0159
AP0293	AP0507	AP0634	BA0538	DD0010	DT0160
AP0294	AP0508	AP0635	BA0545	DD0048	DT0161
AP0297	AP0509	AP0641	BA0546	DD0049	DT0162
AP0298	AP0510	AP0642	BA0547	DD0050	DT0163
AP0299	AP0529	AP0643	BM0002	DD0092	DT0164
AP0334	AP0530	AP0994	BM0003	DD0093	DT0165
AP0336	AP0539	AP0995	BM0004	DD0094	DT0166
AP0337	AP0540	AP0996	BM0005	DD0136	DT0167
AP0338	AP0541	BA00366	BS0024	DD0137	DT0202
AP0341	AP0542	BA0335	BS0025	DD0138	DT0203
AP0342	AP0543	BA0341	BS0039	DD0300	DT0204
AP0343	AP0544	BA0342	BS0040	DD0301	DT0205
AP0377	AP0545	BA0364	BS0041	DD0302	DT0206
AP0378	AP0546	BA0365	BS0042	DD0344	DT0207
AP0380	AP0547	BA0367	BS0043	DD0345	DT0208
AP0381	AP0548	BA0375	BS0044	DD0346	DT0209
AP0382	AP0549	BA0376	BS0053	DD0388	DT0210
AP0419	AP0550	BA0377	BS0054	DD0389	DT0211
AP0420	AP0551	BA0378	BS0055	DD0390	DT0247
AP0421	AP0552	BA0396	CA0001	DD0478	DT0248
AP0422	AP0553	BA0397	CA0003	DD0522	DT0249
AP0441	AP0554	BA0398	CA0004	DD0566	DT0250
AP0442	AP0555	BA0399	CA0005	DT0041	DT0251
AP0451	AP0583	BA0415	CA0008	DT0042	DT0252
AP0452	AP0584	BA0416	CA0009	DT0043	DT0253
AP0453	AP0585	BA0417	CA0014	DT0085	DT0254
AP0454	AP0586	BA0430	CA0015	DT0086	DT0255
AP0461	AP0587	BA0431	CA0016	DT0087	DT0280
AP0462	AP0588	BA0432	CA0017	DT0113	DT0281
AP0463	AP0589	BA0448	CA0026	DT0114	DT0282
AP0464	AP0590	BA0449	CA0027	DT0115	DT0292
AP0465	AP0591	BA0477	CA0028	DT0116	DT0293

GOMR Lease Blocks Requiring Archaeological Survey For Historic Shipwrecks
LEASE BLOCKS REQUIRING 50-M SURVEY INTERVAL

DT0294	EC0022	EI0058	FM0784	GA0269	GA0347
DT0295	EC0023	EI0059	FM0785	GA0270	GA0352
DT0296	EC0024	EI0060	FM0786	GA0271	GA0353
DT0297	EC0025	EI0067	FM0828	GA0272	GA0354
DT0298	EC0026	EI0068	FM0829	GA0273	GA0359
DT0299	EC0033	EI0069	FM0830	GA0274	GA0360
DT0324	EC0034	EI0070	GA0103	GA0275	GA0361
DT0325	EC0035	EI0071	GA0104	GA0280	GA0362
DT0326	EC0036	EI0072	GA0144	GA0281	GA0363
DT0336	EC0037	EI0079	GA0145	GA0282	GA0379
DT0337	EC0038	EI0080	GA0150	GA0283	GA0380
DT0338	EC0039	EI012A	GA0151	GA0284	GA0381
DT0339	EC0040	EI0138	GA0152	GA0286	GA0382
DT0340	EI0009	EI0139	GA0180	GA0287	GA0383
DT0341	EI0010	EI0140	GA0181	GA0288	GA0460
DT0342	EI0011	EI0143	GA0182	GA0289	GA0461
DT0343	EI0012	EI0144	GA0190	GA0295	GA0462
DT0368	EI0018	EI0145	GA0191	GA0296	GA0464
DT0369	EI0019	EI0146	GA0192	GA0297	GA0465
DT0370	EI0020	EI0149	GA0209	GA0298	GA0503
DT0371	EI0021	EI0150	GA0210	GA0301	GAA0009
DT0372	EI0022	EI0151	GA0220	GA0302	GAA0010
DT0373	EI0023	EI0160	GA0221	GA0303	GAA0011
DT0374	EI0024	EI0161	GA0222	GA0304	GAA0017
DT0375	EI0025	EI0162	GA0223	GA0305	GAA0018
DT0376	EI0026	EI0165	GA0224	GA0311	GAA0019
DT0377	EI0027	EI0166	GA0226	GA0312	GAA0023
DT0378	EI0028	EL0347	GA0227	GA0313	GAA0024
DT0459	EI0029	FM0026	GA0237	GA0314	GAA0025
DT0460	EI0030	FM0027	GA0238	GA0315	GAA0030
DT0503	EI0031	FM0028	GA0239	GA0316	GAA0031
DT0504	EI0032	FM0070	GA0240	GA0319	GAA0032
EC0002	EI0033	FM0071	GA0241	GA0320	GAA0057
EC0003	EI0034	FM0072	GA0242	GA0321	GAA0082
EC0008	EI0035	FM0211	GA0243	GA0323	GAA0083
EC0009	EI0037	FM0212	GA0244	GA0324	GAA0128
EC0010	EI0038	FM0213	GA0250	GA0325	GAA0129
EC0011	EI0039	FM0255	GA0251	GA0330	GAA0158
EC0012	EI0040	FM0256	GA0252	GA0331	GAA0180
EC0013	EI0041	FM0257	GA0253	GA0332	GAA0181
EC0014	EI0042	FM0299	GA0254	GA0333	GAA0182
EC0015	EI0048	FM0300	GA0255	GA0334	GI0015
EC0016	EI0049	FM0301	GA0256	GA0343	GI0016
EC0017	EI0050	FM0740	GA0257	GA0344	GI0017
EC0020	EI0056	FM0741	GA0267	GA0345	GI0018
EC0021	EI0057	FM0742	GA0268	GA0346	GI0019

GOMR Lease Blocks Requiring Archaeological Survey For Historic Shipwrecks
LEASE BLOCKS REQUIRING 50-M SURVEY INTERVAL

GI0020	GV0673	HI0023	HI0138	HIA0121	MI0520
GI0021	GV0674	HI0031	HI0139	HIA0122	MI0526
GI0022	GV0675	HI0032	HI0140	HIA0123	MI0527
GI0023	GV0707	HI0033	HI0141	HIA0132	MI0528
GI0024	GV0708	HI0034	HI0142	HIA0133	MI0556
GI0025	GV0709	HI0035	HI0143	HIA0134	MI0557
GI0026	GV0716	HI0036	HI0153	HIA0482	MI0558
GI0027	GV0717	HI0037	HI0154	HIA0483	MI0564
GI0037	GV0718	HI0038	HI0155	HIA0506	MI0565
GI0044	GV0719	HI0039	HI0156	HIA0507	MI0566
GI0045	GV0760	HI0047	HI0157	HIA0508	MI0567
GI0046	GV0761	HI0048	HI0158	HIA0509	MI0589
GI0053	GV0762	HI0049	HI0159	KW0001	MI0590
GI0054	GV0763	HI0050	HI0160	KW0002	MI0591
GI0055	GV0764	HI0051	HI0164	KW0003	MI0592
GI0056	GV0804	HI0053	HI0175	KW0004	MI0599
GI0057	GV0805	HI0054	HI0176	KW0005	MI0600
GI0058	GV0806	HI0055	HI0177	KW0006	MI0601
GI0083	GV0807	HI0063	HI0178	KW0007	MI0602
GI0084	GV0808	HI0065	HI0179	KW0008	MI0603
GI0085	GV0849	HI0066	HI0193	KW0009	MI0621
GI0086	GV0850	HI0067	HI0194	KW0012	MI0622
GV0045	GV0851	HI0089	HI0195	KW0015	MI0623
GV0089	GV0852	HI0090	HI0196	KW0045	MI0624
GV0133	GV0853	HI0091	HI0197	KW0046	MI0625
GV0355	GV0893	HI0092	HI0202	KW0047	MI0626
GV0356	GV0894	HI0093	HI0203	KW0048	MI0631
GV0357	GV0895	HI0094	HI0204	KW0049	MI0632
GV0399	GV0896	HI0095	HI0205	KW0050	MI0633
GV0400	GV0897	HI0096	HI0206	KW0051	MI0634
GV0401	GV0937	HI0097	HI0207	KW0089	MI0635
GV0443	GV0938	HI0098	HI0208	KW0090	MI0654
GV0444	GV0939	HI0105	HI0228	KW0091	MI0655
GV0445	GV0940	HI0106	HI0232	KW0092	MI0656
GV0584	GV0941	HI0107	HI0236	KW0093	MI0657
GV0585	GV0981	HI0108	HIA0007	KW0133	MI0658
GV0619	GV0982	HI0109	HIA0018	KW0134	MI0663
GV0620	GV0983	HI0110	HIA0019	KW0135	MI0664
GV0621	GV0984	HI0111	HIA0020	KW0177	MI0665
GV0628	GV0985	HI0112	HIA0021	KW0178	MI0666
GV0629	GV0986	HI0113	HIA0022	MA0969	MI0686
GV0630	GV0987	HI0114	HIA0023	MA0970	MI0687
GV0663	HI0019	HI0134	HIA0024	MA0971	MI0688
GV0664	HI0020	HI0135	HIA0106	MA0972	MI0689
GV0665	HI0021	HI0136	HIA0107	MA0973	MI0690
GV0672	HI0022	HI0137	HIA0108	MI0519	MI0698

GOMR Lease Blocks Requiring Archaeological Survey For Historic Shipwrecks
LEASE BLOCKS REQUIRING 50-M SURVEY INTERVAL

MI0699	MO0871	MO0992	MU0745	MU0864	PB0354
MI0700	MO0872	MO0993	MU0750	MU0865	PB0370
MO0765	MO0873	MO0994	MU0751	MU0878	PB0371
MO0766	MO0874	MO0995	MU0757	MU0879	PB0372
MO0767	MO0897	MO0996	MU0758	MU0880	PB0373
MO0778	MO0898	MO0997	MU0759	MUA0001	PB0374
MO0779	MO0899	MO0998	MU0761	PB0018	PB0375
MO0809	MO0900	MO0999	MU0762	PB0019	PB0375
MO0810	MO0901	MO1000	MU0763	PB0020	PB0375
MO0811	MO0904	MO1001	MU0770	PB0062	PB0397
MO0812	MO0905	MO1002	MU0775	PB0063	PB0398
MO0813	MO0906	MP0006	MU0776	PB0064	PB0414
MO0814	MO0907	MP0007	MU0783	PB0109	PB0415
MO0815	MO0908	MP0017	MU0784	PB0151	PB0416
MO0816	MO0909	MP0018	MU0792	PB0152	PB0417
MO0817	MO0910	MP0019	MU0793	PB0153	PB0418
MO0818	MO0911	MP0020	MU0798	PB0193	PB0419
MO0819	MO0912	MP0027	MU0799	PB0194	PB0459
MO0820	MO0913	MP0028	MU0809	PB0195	PB0460
MO0821	MO0914	MP0029	MU0810	PB0196	PB0461
MO0822	MO0915	MP0030	MU0811	PB0197	PB0462
MO0823	MO0916	MP0038	MU0815	PB0198	PB0463
MO0824	MO0917	MP0043	MU0816	PB0237	PB0503
MO0826	MO0942	MP0044	MU0821	PB0238	PB0504
MO0827	MO0943	MP0055	MU0822	PB0239	PB0505
MO0828	MO0944	MP0056	MU0823	PB0240	PB0506
MO0829	MO0945	MP0057	MU0827	PB0241	PB0507
MO0830	MO0946	MP0061	MU0828	PB0242	PB0508
MO0853	MO0948	MP0062	MU0829	PB0243	PB0547
MO0854	MO0949	MP0063	MU0830	PB0281	PB0548
MO0855	MO0950	MP0064	MU0831	PB0282	PB0549
MO0856	MO0951	MP0065	MU0832	PB0283	PB0550
MO0857	MO0952	MP0068	MU0833	PB0284	PB0551
MO0858	MO0953	MP0069	MU0837	PB0285	PB0552
MO0859	MO0954	MP0071	MU0838	PB0286	PB0592
MO0860	MO0955	MP0072	MU0842	PB0287	PB0593
MO0861	MO0956	MP0090	MU0843	PB0309	PB0594
MO0862	MO0957	MP0091	MU0844	PB0310	PB0595
MO0863	MO0958	MP0092	MU0848	PB0325	PB0596
MO0864	MO0959	MP0103	MU0849	PB0326	PB0629
MO0865	MO0960	MP0114	MU0850	PB0327	PB0630
MO0866	MO0961	MP0115	MU0851	PB0328	PB0631
MO0867	MO0987	MP0116	MU0852	PB0329	PB0636
MO0868	MO0988	MP0117	MU0853	PB0330	PB0637
MO0869	MO0989	MP0126	MU0858	PB0331	PB0638
MO0870	MO0990	MP0127	MU0859	PB0353	PB0639

GOMR Lease Blocks Requiring Archaeological Survey For Historic Shipwrecks
LEASE BLOCKS REQUIRING 50-M SURVEY INTERVAL

PB0640	PE0845	PL0010	PN0954	PN1020	PS1152
PB0673	PE0846	PL0011	PN0955	PN1021	PS1153
PB0674	PE0847	PL0014	PN0956	PN1022	PS1164
PB0675	PE0848	PL0016	PN0957	PNA0060	PS1165
PB0681	PE0849	PL0025	PN0958	PR0077	PS1166
PB0682	PE0850	PN0894	PN0959	PR0078	SA0003
PB0683	PE0851	PN0895	PN0964	PR0079	SA0005
PB0717	PE0852	PN0896	PN0965	PR0121	SA0006
PB0718	PE0853	PN0897	PN0966	PR0122	SA0007
PB0719	PE0854	PN0898	PN0967	PR0123	SA0008
PB0862	PE0886	PN0904	PN0968	PR0165	SA0009
PB0863	PE0887	PN0905	PN0969	PR0166	SA0010
PB0864	PE0888	PN0906	PN0970	PR0167	SA0011
PB0906	PE0889	PN0907	PN0972	PR0691	SA0012
PB0907	PE0890	PN0908	PN0973	PR0692	SA0014
PB0908	PE0891	PN0909	PN0974	PR0693	SA0015
PB0909	PE0892	PN0910	PN0975	PR0735	SA0016
PB0950	PE0893	PN0913	PN0976	PR0736	SM0207
PB0951	PE0896	PN0914	PN0977	PR0737	SM0208
PB0952	PE0897	PN0915	PN0978	PR0779	SM0209
PB0953	PE0898	PN0916	PN0979	PR0780	SM0210
PE0751	PE0931	PN0917	PN0980	PR0781	SM0211
PE0752	PE0932	PN0918	PN0985	PR1009	SM0212
PE0753	PE0933	PN0919	PN0986	PR1010	SM0213
PE0754	PE0934	PN0924	PN0987	PR1011	SM0214
PE0764	PE0940	PN0925	PN0988	PS1073	SM0215
PE0793	PE0941	PN0926	PN0989	PS1074	SM0216
PE0794	PE0942	PN0927	PN0990	PS1075	SM0217
PE0795	PE0976	PN0928	PN0991	PS1080	SM0218
PE0796	PE0977	PN0929	PN0993	PS1081	SM0222
PE0797	PE0978	PN0930	PN0995	PS1082	SM0223
PE0798	PI0945	PN0933	PN0996	PS1093	SM0224
PE0801	PI0946	PN0934	PN0997	PS1094	SM0225
PE0802	PI0947	PN0935	PN0998	PS1095	SM0226
PE0803	PI0989	PN0936	PN0999	PS1123	SM0227
PE0804	PI0990	PN0937	PN1000	PS1124	SM0228
PE0805	PI0991	PN0938	PN1001	PS1125	SM0229
PE0806	PL0001	PN0939	PN1006	PS1126	SM0237
PE0807	PL0002	PN0944	PN1007	PS1130	SM0238
PE0808	PL0003	PN0945	PN1008	PS1131	SM0239
PE0837	PL0004	PN0946	PN1009	PS1132	SM0240
PE0838	PL0005	PN0947	PN1010	PS1133	SM0241
PE0839	PL0006	PN0948	PN1011	PS1144	SS0002
PE0842	PL0007	PN0949	PN1012	PS1145	SS0008
PE0843	PL0008	PN0950	PN1014	PS1146	SS0009
PE0844	PL0009	PN0953	PN1019	PS1151	SS0010

GOMR Lease Blocks Requiring Archaeological Survey For Historic Shipwrecks
LEASE BLOCKS REQUIRING 50-M SURVEY INTERVAL

SS0011	SS0094	ST0046	TP0018	TP0360	TP0986
SS0012	SS0096	ST0047	TP0019	TP0361	TP0987
SS0013	SS0097	ST0048	TP0020	TP0367	TP0988
SS0014	SS0098	ST0052	TP0021	TP0368	VK0020
SS0015	SS0103	ST0053	TP0055	TP0369	VK0021
SS0016	SS0104	ST0054	TP0056	TP0371	VK0022
SS0024	SS0109	ST0055	TP0057	TP0372	VK0029
SS0025	SS0110	ST0056	TP0062	TP0373	VK0031
SS0026	SS0111	ST0057	TP0063	TP0403	VK0032
SS0027	SS0113	ST0062	TP0064	TP0404	VK0033
SS0028	SS0114	ST0065	TP0065	TP0405	VK0065
SS0029	SS0115	ST0066	TP0099	TP0411	VK0066
SS0030	SS0116	ST0067	TP0100	TP0412	VR0011
SS0031	SS0127	ST0068	TP0101	TP0413	VR0012
SS0035	SS0139	ST0069	TP0102	TP0455	VR0015
SS0036	SS0140	ST0070	TP0103	TP0456	VR0016
SS0037	SS0143	ST0073	TP0104	TP0457	VR0017
SS0038	SS0144	ST0074	TP0106	TP0458	VR0018
SS0049	SS0145	ST0075	TP0107	TP0459	VR0019
SS0050	SS0158	ST0076	TP0108	TP0460	VR0020
SS0051	SS0159	ST0079	TP0109	TP0499	VR0021
SS0060	SS0160	ST0080	TP0146	TP0500	VR0022
SS0061	SS0167	ST0081	TP0147	TP0501	VR0023
SS0062	SS0168	ST0082	TP0148	TP0502	VR0024
SS0063	SS0169	ST0083	TP0190	TP0503	VR0025
SS0064	ST0009	ST0084	TP0191	TP0504	VR0026
SS0065	ST0010	ST0095	TP0192	TP0545	VR0027
SS0066	ST0011	ST0096	TP0267	TP0546	VR0028
SS0067	ST0016	ST0097	TP0268	TP0547	VR0029
SS0068	ST0017	ST0098	TP0269	TP0548	VR0030
SS0069	ST0018	ST0100	TP0283	TP0589	VR0031
SS0070	ST0019	ST0101	TP0284	TP0590	VR0032
SS0071	ST0020	ST0102	TP0285	TP0591	VR0033
SS0072	ST0021	ST0109	TP0311	TP0592	VR0034
SS0073	ST0022	ST0110	TP0312	TP0667	VR0035
SS0074	ST0023	ST0111	TP0313	TP0668	VR0036
SS0080	ST0024	SX0017	TP0315	TP0669	VR0037
SS0085	ST0028	SX0018	TP0316	TP0711	VR0038
SS0086	ST0029	SX0040	TP0317	TP0712	VR0039
SS0087	ST0030	TP0011	TP0327	TP0713	VR0046
SS0088	ST0031	TP0012	TP0328	TP0755	VR0047
SS0089	ST0032	TP0013	TP0329	TP0756	VR0048
SS0090	ST0033	TP0014	TP0355	TP0757	VR0054
SS0091	ST0034	TP0015	TP0356	TP0942	VR0055
SS0092	ST0035	TP0016	TP0357	TP0943	VR0056
SS0093	ST0036	TP0017	TP0359	TP0944	VR0138

GOMR Lease Blocks Requiring Archaeological Survey For Historic Shipwrecks
LEASE BLOCKS REQUIRING 50-M SURVEY INTERVAL

VR0139	WC0036	WC0065	WC0098	WC0291	WD0049
VR0140	WC0037	WC0066	WC0099	WC0292	WD0050
VR0143	WC0038	WC0067	WC0100	WD0016	WD0056
VR0144	WC0039	WC0068	WC0109	WD0017	WD0057
VR0145	WC0040	WC0069	WC0110	WD0018	WD0058
VR0158	WC0041	WC0070	WC0111	WD0019	WD0059
VR0159	WC0042	WC0071	WC0112	WD0020	WD0070
VRO160	WC0043	WC0073	WC0113	WD0021	WD0071
WC0017	WC0044	WC0074	WC0114	WD0022	WD0072
WC0018	WC0045	WC0075	WC0115	WD0023	WD0077
WC0019	WC0046	WC0076	WC0116	WD0024	WD0078
WC0020	WC0047	WC0077	WC0117	WD0025	WD0079
WC0021	WC0048	WC0078	WC0118	WD0026	WD0080
WC0022	WC0049	WC0079	WC0132	WD0027	WD0081
WC0023	WC0053	WC0080	WC0133	WD0028	WD0085
WC0024	WC0054	WC0081	WC0134	WD0029	WD0086
WC0025	WC0055	WC0082	WC0147	WD0030	WD0092
WC0026	WC0056	WC0083	WC0148	WD0031	WD0093
WC0027	WC0057	WC0090	WC0149	WD0032	WD0094
WC0028	WC0058	WC0091	WC0165	WD0033	WD0095
WC0029	WC0059	WC0092	WC0166	WD0034	WD0096
WC0030	WC0060	WC0093	WC0167	WD0035	WD0098
WC0031	WC0061	WC0094	WC0186	WD0036	WD0099
WC0033	WC0062	WC0095	WC0187	WD0037	WD0100
WC0034	WC0063	WC0096	WC0188	WD0047	
WC0035	WC0064	WC0097	WC0189	WD0048	

GOMR Lease Blocks Requiring Archaeological Survey For Historic Shipwrecks
LEASE BLOCKS REQUIRING 300-M SURVEY INTERVAL

AT0039	DC0392	DDO749	EB0242	FM0235	GAA0246
AT0040	DC0411	DDO793	EB0243	FM0275	GAA0247
AT0041	DC0412	DDO837	EB0244	FM0276	GAA0248
BAA133	DC0413	DDO939	EL0018	FM0277	GBO255
CC0350	DC0455	DDO940	EL0019	FM0278	GI0087
CC0351	DC0456	DDO941	EL0020	FM0279	GI0088
CC0394	DC0457	DDO983	EL0347	FM0319	GI0114
CC0395	DC0498	DDO984	EL0391	FM0320	HE0242
DC0018	DC0499	DDO985	EL0406	FM0321	HE0243
DC0019	DC0500	DDO999	EL0407	FM0590	HE0244
DC0020	DC0542	DT0001	EL0408	FM0591	HE0286
DC0034	DC0543	DT0316	EL0414	FM0592	HE0287
DC0036	DC0544	DT0317	EL0415	FM0634	HE0288
DC0078	DC0586	DT0318	EL0416	FM0635	HE0289
DC0079	DC0587	DT0360	EL0435	FM0636	HE0290
DC0080	DC0588	DT0361	EL0450	FM0678	HE0291
DC0096	DC0755	DT0362	EL0451	FM0679	HE0300
DC0097	DC0756	DT0404	EL0452	FM0680	HE0301
DC0098	DC0757	DT0405	EL0458	FM0769	HE0302
DC0140	DC0799	DT0406	EL0459	FM0770	HE0330
DC0141	DC0800	DT0547	EL0460	FM0771	HE0331
DC0142	DC0801	DT0548	EL0494	FM0813	HE0332
DC0184	DC0843	DT0591	EL0495	FM0814	HE0333
DC0185	DC0844	DT0592	EL0496	FM0815	HE0334
DC0186	DC0845	DT0705	EL0502	FM0857	HE0335
DC0295	DD1000	DT0706	EL0503	FM0858	HE0344
DC0296	DD1001	DT0749	EL0504	FM0859	HE0345
DC0297	DDO429	DT0750	EL0939	FM0942	HE0346
DC0303	DDO430	DT0808	EL0940	FM0943	HE0377
DC0304	DDO431	DT0809	EL0941	FM0944	HE0378
DC0320	DDO459	DT0810	EL0983	FM0986	HE0379
DC0339	DDO460	DT0852	EL0984	FM0987	HE0388
DC0340	DDO461	DT0853	EL0985	FM0988	HE0389
DC0341	DDO473	DT0854	EW0304	GAA0195	HE0390
DC0346	DDO474	DT0896	EW0305	GAA0196	HE0435
DC0347	DDO475	DT0897	EW0347	GAA0197	HE0436
DC0348	DDO503	DT0898	EW0348	GAA0210	HE0437
DC0367	DDO504	DTO793	EW0349	GAA0211	HE0479
DC0368	DDO505	DTO794	FM0189	GAA0212	HE0480
DC0369	DDO517	EB0154	FM0190	GAA0216	HE0481
DC0383	DDO518	EB0156	FM0191	GAA0217	HE0523
DC0384	DDO519	EB0156	FM0231	GAA0218	HE0524
DC0385	DDO547	EB0198	FM0232	GAA0219	HE0525
DC0390	DDO548	EB0199	FM0233	GAA0220	HE0925
DC0391	DDO549	EB0200	FM0234	GAA0221	HE0926

GOMR Lease Blocks Requiring Archaeological Survey For Historic Shipwrecks
LEASE BLOCKS REQUIRING 300-M SURVEY INTERVAL

HE0927	LL0460	LU0497	MC0427	MUA0066	PSA0027
HE0969	LL0492	LU0498	MC0428	MUA0083	PSA0028
HE0970	LL0493	LU0626	MC0429	MUA0084	PSA0029
HE0971	LL0494	LU0627	MC0430	MUA0085	PSA0030
HH1030	LL0495	LU0628	MC0454	MUA0100	PSA0039
HH1031	LL0496	LU0670	MC0455	MUA0101	PSA0041
HH1032	LL0502	LU0671	MC0456	MUA0102	PSA0041
HHO552	LL0503	LU0672	MC0498	MUA0105	RK0040
HHO553	LL0504	LU0714	MC0499	MUA0106	RK0041
HHO554	LL0546	LU0715	MC0500	MUA0107	RK0042
HHO597	LL0547	LU0716	MC0542	MUA0126	RK0746
HHO598	LL0548	LU0730	MC0543	MUA0127	RK0747
HHO599	LL0710	LU0731	MC0544	MUA0151	RK0790
HHO642	LL0711	LU0732	MC0750	MUA0152	RK0791
HHO643	LL0712	LU0774	MC0751	MUA0163	RK0834
HHO644	LL0754	LU0775	MC0752	PI0517	RK0835
HHO671	LL0755	LU0776	MC0753	PI0518	SP0032
HHO672	LL0756	LU0818	MC0794	PNA0060	SP0033
HHO716	LL0798	LU0819	MC0795	PNA0061	SP0034
HHO717	LL0799	LU0820	MC0796	PNA0062	SP0035
HHO761	LL0800	MC0063	MC0797	PNA0071	SP0036
HHO762	LU0123	MC0245	MC0838	PNA0072	SP0037
HHO985	LU0124	MC0246	MC0839	PNA0073	SP0038
HHO986	LU0125	MC0247	MC0840	PNA0074	SP0044
HHO987	LU0167	MC0287	MC0841	PNA0083	SP0045
KC0872	LU0168	MC0288	MC0963	PNA0084	SP0046
KC0873	LU0169	MC0289	MC0964	PNA0085	SP0047
KC0874	LU0211	MC0290	MC0965	PNA0086	SP0048
KC0916	LU0212	MC0291	MC1007	PNA0087	SP0049
KC0917	LU0213	MC0331	MC1008	PNA0096	SP0053
KC0918	LU0299	MC0332	MC1009	PNA0097	SP0054
KC0960	LU0300	MC0333	MIA0005	PR0618	SP0055
KC0961	LU0301	MC0334	MIA0006	PR0661	SP0057
KC0962	LU0343	MC0335	MUA0009	PR0662	SP0058
LL0404	LU0344	MC0340	MUA0010	PR0668	SP0059
LL0405	LU0345	MC0341	MUA0015	PR0669	SP0060
LL0406	LU0387	MC0342	MUA0016	PR0670	SP0061
LL0407	LU0388	MC0375	MUA0017	PR0705	SP0066
LL0408	LU0389	MC0376	MUA0018	PR0706	SP0067
LL0448	LU0408	MC0377	MUA0052	PR0712	SP0070
LL0449	LU0409	MC0383	MUA0053	PR0713	SP0072
LL0450	LU0410	MC0384	MUA0054	PR0714	SP0073
LL0451	LU0452	MC0385	MUA0055	PR0756	VK0781
LL0452	LU0453	MC0386	MUA0063	PR0757	VK0782
LL0458	LU0454	MC0387	MUA0064	PR0758	VK0783
LL0459	LU0496	MC0426	MUA0065	PSA0026	VK0785

GOMR Lease Blocks Requiring Archaeological Survey For Historic Shipwrecks
LEASE BLOCKS REQUIRING 300-M SURVEY INTERVAL

VK0786	VK0869	VK0913	VK0958	VN0016	VN0435
VK0825	VK0870	VK0914	VK0986	VN0017	VN0436
VK0826	VK0871	VK0942	VK1000	VN0347	WD0109
VK0827	VK0873	VK0943	VK1001	VN0348	
VK0829	VK0874	VK0956	VK1002	VN0391	
VK0830	VK0912	VK0957	VN0015	VN0392	

INFORMATION IN THIS APPENDIX IS NOT AVAILABLE FOR PUBLIC DISCLOSURE

APPENDIX D

LEASE BLOCKS IN 1989 SHIPWRECK DATABASE THAT HAVE BEEN SURVEYED AND RESULTS

INFORMATION IN THIS APPENDIX IS NOT AVAILABLE FOR PUBLIC DISCLOSURE

APPENDIX E

2001 GOMR SHIPWRECK DATABASE

APPENDIX F

MAGNETOMETER TECHNOLOGY AND EMPLOYMENT IN THE GOMR

F.1. Marine Magnetics: The Competing Technologies

Magnetometers have been employed for over forty years in detecting and locating various ferromagnetic materials on land and in marine environments. They have been of interest to marine archaeologists and geophysicists since initial experiments by Aitken in 1958 as perhaps the most effective and most versatile of a number of electronic instruments with which it is possible to locate buried cultural features. The principle of magnetic detection and location of ferromagnetic material originates from the localized magnetic field variations that these objects produce. Variations from normal Earth magnetic field conditions are the result of specific characteristics of ferrous material (iron and steel). Magnetometers measure the strength of the Earth's magnetic field and the distinctive disturbances or variations in the strength of the magnetic field known as anomalies caused by ferrous elements. In a marine environment this is particularly important as objects are generally covered by sediments, and many times the environment provides poor visibility during physical searches by divers. In some cases it is possible to determine some of the significant parameters of the targets, such as size and shape, characteristics along with, at times, relative depth of burial.

F.1.1. The Earth's Magnetic Field

The Earth's magnetic field can be described roughly by field lines coming out of the Earth's north magnetic pole, which is in the Southern Hemisphere, and going into the Earth towards its south magnetic pole in the Northern Hemisphere. Such a field is known as a dipole field. The intensity of the Earth's magnetic field is 60,000 gammas at the poles and 30,000 gammas at the magnetic equator, i.e., 0.6 gauss and 0.3 gauss, respectively. One more aspect of the Earth's magnetic field that must be considered is the so-called diurnal variation. Because of ionic currents in the atmosphere, as well as for a number of other reasons, the Earth's magnetic field is not constant in time. It exhibits a slow annual change of 0.1 to 0.3 percent in various geographical areas. The field has a slow annual change in direction as well. The general trend is a diurnal variation, dropping down during the middle of the day. Superimposed on this are short time fluctuations whose severity may be sizeable during periods of magnetic storms. The Earth's magnetic field is within the influence of the sun's comparatively gigantic magnetic field. The space outside the magnetic field of the Earth is dominated by the sun's field and by a constant stream of free ions and electrons that flows from the sun, called the solar wind. Changes in the sun's magnetic field affect the Earth's field dramatically. The sun's influence is apparent at the Earth's surface as low frequency variations that can have high amplitude. Different levels of solar activity can result in changes of several hundred gammas in the course of a few hours; however, diurnal effects do not significantly alter the localized magnetic gradients. So magnetometers collecting data within a local area as small as 30-50 miles will show the same diurnal influence.

F.1.2. Induced Magnetism

This is the principal phenomenon that makes most ferrous material detection and location possible with magnetic surveys. The earth's magnetic field establishes a secondary magnetic field surrounding the ferrous object. This disturbance is measurable when a sensor is within the area of the object's magnetic signature or duration. The intensity and range of the local magnetic field alteration is based on the magnetic susceptibility as well as the size and shape of the object. Since induced magnetism is the combined effects of the magnetic property of the material, the Earth's magnetic field, and the shape and orientation of the object in the Earth's magnetic field, if this magnetic susceptibility value is very high the material is described as being ferromagnetic, which is true for most types of ordinary iron or steel or even iron-rich clay material deposited out of suspension in a marine environment. These factors cause the material to act as a magnet in the presence of the Earth's magnetic field. In addition, the shape and the orientation of an object also tend to enhance induced magnetism: longer objects that are orientated parallel to the Earth's magnetic field produce stronger magnetic fluctuations than shorter ones.

F.1.3. Permanent Magnetization

Permanent magnetization is the property of the material which is related only to the object, not to the Earth's magnetic field, nor the orientation or the shape of the object. Permanent magnetization, also referred to as permeability, is a property of the metallurgy and the thermal and mechanical history of the object; usually the harder the metal, the higher the permeability. Some objects become more magnetized if sufficiently mechanically shocked in the presence of the Earth's magnetic field or simply by remaining at a fixed orientation in the Earth's magnetic field over a long period of time. Alternately, some objects will lose their permeability if heated. For most objects of a search, the permanent magnetism is much greater than induced magnetism. In actual practice, the magnetic disturbance or anomaly which is observed on the magnetometer will be the sum of both the permanent and induced magnetism effects.

F.2. Magnetometer Types

Since early experiments with magnetometers in the late 1950s, the technology and development of these instruments have been nothing short of profound. From the early Varian models such as the V-85 followed by the SeaMag series, Barringer, and the Geometrics 816 and 806, to today's sophisticated optically pumped and computer-driven magnetometers, performance, reliability and accuracy have greatly improved. In order to fully discuss these instruments we must subdivide them into two categories based on performance and principle of operation: 1) vector magnetometers, which detect and measure magnetic fluctuations in a specific direction or vector in a three-dimensional space, and 2) quantum magnetometers, which measure the magnitude of the vector passing through the sensor regardless of direction. Quantum magnetometers are the instruments mostly utilized in geophysical and archaeological surveys as well as search and recovery surveys.

Quantum magnetometers are in turn subdivided into three categories based on the method used in the polarization of subatomic particles such as nuclei or outer electrons. There are three different methods of polarization used in quantum magnetometers. These three methods are:

1- Introduction of a strong magnetic field.

2- Transferring the natural polarization from electrons to nuclei (proton).

3- Optical pumping and de-pumping of electrons.

Each polarization method produces a different instrument with varying degrees of performance level as characteristic limitations. The three primary resulting magnetometers are called free precession or proton precession magnetometers, Overhauser magnetometers, and Cesium magnetometers. As was discussed earlier each magnetometer sensor design and technology has some advantages and disadvantages. The only way to objectively compare them is to study the technical specifications of each manufacturer and each model. This is somewhat confusing, as there are no set standards of system performance parameters that are followed by all manufacturers. Therefore one has to study the individual technical data sheets of each make and compare things like sensor sensitivity, sampling rate, resolution, and susceptibility of the design to dead zones and heading errors. To that end, there are several terms that manufacturers use to describe the specifications of their instruments; we shall attempt to define some of these terms as they relate to marine magnetics.

1-Resolution: This term defines the smallest change in a given magnetic field that a magnetometer can detect. For example, a magnetometer that has a resolution of 0.001 can measure a magnetic fluctuation between 48927.639 and 48927.640. It is obvious that the higher the resolution, the more the instrument is able to detect even the smallest targets.

2-Noise: Noise is defined as the change in a magnetic measurement, which is not caused by variations in a specific magnetic field. Noise is typically reported as the number of gammas per square root hertz.

3-Heading Errors: This term refers to the variation of the strength of the magnetic field resulting from a change in the orientation of the magnetometer sensor.

4-Dead Zones: A Dead Zone is the angle between the magnetic field and the axis of the magnetometer sensor (Figure F-1). If the sensor does not detect any magnetic variations, the sensor is referred to as being in a "dead zone."

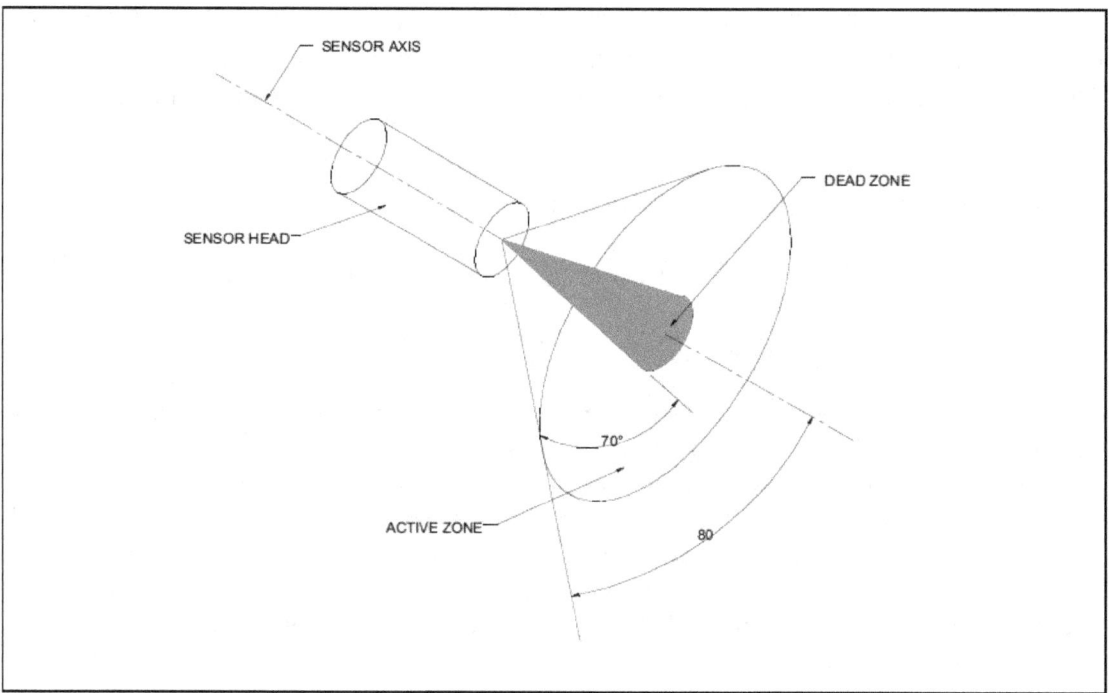

Figure F-1. Schematic of a magnetometer's dead zone. This drawing was obtained from a Geometrics technical report titled *Cesium Optically Pumped Magnetometers, Basic Theory of operation,* written by Kenneth Smith in February 1997.

F.2.1. Proton Magnetometers

There are two types of proton magnetometers in use, the free precession and the Overhauser magnetometer. Although their polarization methods are very different, the common denominator between proton magnetometers is the use of the nuclear properties of hydrogen nuclei or protons contained within a sample of hydrocarbon fluid. The hydrogen proton properties of charge, atomic mass and spin allow for the accurate calculation of the gyromagnetic ratio to within ten parts per billion. The proton gyromagnetic ratio is 2.67515341 x 10(8) Radians/sec/Tesla with a standard error of 0.00000011 x 10 (8) Radians/sec/Tesla. A constant of 23.48719622nT/Hz is used to convert frequencies to magnetic field values.

Free precession proton magnetometers. For decades the standard for marine oil exploration magnetometers has been the proton precession technology. Such instruments have proven robust under demanding field conditions, but data has been subject to limitation in resolution due to a combination of measurement technology, external noise sources and sampling limitations. The theory of operation of these devices is quite simple: a magnetic field is created by introducing a strong electric current through a wire coil immersed in a sample rich in hydrogen. This field, which is more intense than the Earth's own magnetic field at that point, polarizes the hydrogen protons away from their normal alignment with the earth's magnetic field. When the polarizing current is turned off, the protons begin to spin away from this temporary artificial alignment and into their normal alignment within the Earth's magnetic field. This spinning movement generates a weak electrical current referred to as a precession signal, which is received by the same polarizing coils in the sensor. The frequency at which these protons precess is directly proportional to the intensity of the magnetic field in which this polarization occurs. The precession signal is measured from less than .01 to two seconds and allows sensitivities of up to .05 gamma and a sampling rate of up to two readings per second.

One of the pitfalls of this method is that if the polarization occurs in a single coil system, a blind spot or a dead zone will appear when the coil's axis is aligned with the magnetic field vector. This problem can be rectified with the use of three omni-directional coils arranged at 120 degrees from each other. One of the most significant limitations of this early sensor design which is found in both the Geometrics 801 and 866 models is that they will not physically sink below 225 feet below the water surface, regardless of how much tow cable is deployed. This does not allow the sensor to be within the MMS specification of being within six meters of the seafloor, which prohibits good data collection in deeper waters. Most models of proton magnetometers such as the G-866, which was employed in Task 3 (Figure F-2), are comprised of a hydrocarbon-filled sensor, a tow cable, and a topside console where signal processing and amplification is achieved. An external printer is utilized to print the collected data. The G-866 is probably the most well-known and widely used magnetometer of this type and vintage.

Figure F-2. While not completely obsolete, the G-866 is no longer being produced and is being replaced with newer models by many companies.

Improvements in digital and computer technology have resulted in the production of advanced models of proton magnetometers such as the G-886 and G-877. The most significant features of these latter units, in addition to their ability to "fly" closer to the seafloor, is that the signal is processed internally in the sensor and transmitted to a top-side computer where it can be stored along with the navigation data. Since the signal processing and amplification is done in the sensor prior to being sent up through the tow cable, it significantly reduces external noise from ship engines and electronics. In addition, the utilization of a computer to store navigation data allows subsequent interpretation of the data and particularly pinpointing the geographic locales where magnetic anomalies or fluctuations were detected. Employed in Task 3, the G-877 illustrated below is the company's shallow water proton precession replacement for the G-866 that employs these design features (Figure F-3).

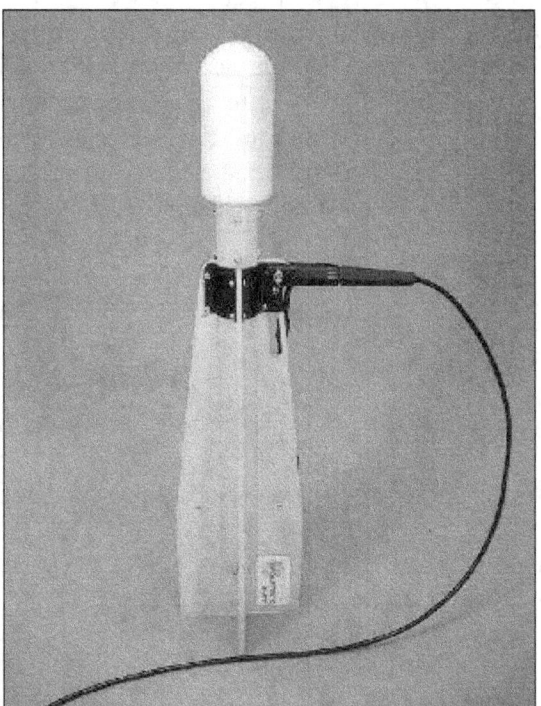

Figure F-3. Geometrics' G-877 proton precession marine magnetometer used in Task 3.

Proton precession magnetometers are relatively accurate instruments; however, they have very limited sampling rate capabilities (no more than twice per second). Their low price and maintenance cost have prolonged their useful life span; they are still in use world-wide for a variety of ferromagnetic detection surveys. Proper care should always be exercised during the disposal of the hydrocarbon fluid in the sensor in order to avoid contamination of the surrounding environment.

Overhauser effect proton magnetometers. The only difference between these magnetometers and free precession magnetometers is the method of polarization. A high frequency RF signal provides the energy to get the protons processing and keep them processing. This method produces a continuous signal, allowing a much faster repetitive rate (up to five readings per second) when compared to the free precession magnetometers.

Because of the physical nature of the proton, there is an error in the field strength measurements of approximately 25 gammas; however, this can be corrected through careful design of the electronics. The band width and noise performance will be slightly better than that of the free precession magnetometer, but about a factor of 100x poorer than the cesium magnetometer. The frequency of the signal produced in the cesium magnetometer is over 80x higher than that produced by the Overhauser effect (between 900 Hz to 4000 Hz). This low frequency is in large part responsible for the poorer performance of the Overhauser. In addition, both free precession and Overhauser magnetometers are subject to noise caused by Doppler shift of the pick-up coils with respect to the processing protons in the operating fluid.

Good examples of Overhauser effect magnetometers are the current production models from GEM Systems and Marine Magnetics of Ontario, Canada. The latter's SeaSPY® marine magnetometer was employed in Task 3 and is illustrated below (Figure F-4). The tow fish contains the digitizing electronics where signal processing and amplification takes place, which means that the signal is measured at its peak and is immune from external noise sources. They are very sensitive (.015 gamma) and by virtue of their sensor design, have virtually no heading errors or dead zones; in addition, they do not display any temperature drift.

Figure F-4. Marine Magnetics' "SeaSPY" Overhauser effect marine magnetometer used in Task 3.

F.2.2. Optically Pumped Magnetometers

This group can be subdivided into swept magnetometers and self-oscillating magnetometers. Both classes utilize the properties of the electron from one of four active materials: potassium, rubidium, cesium, and helium. Although similar in theory of operation, the performance of these magnetometers depends on the material used. This discussion will be limited to the cesium version since the production and use of the other materials in the marine environment is very limited and rare. Ideal for both marine and airborne surveys, the cesium units offer very good sensitivity with high resolution.

The cesium atom contains a single electron in its outermost orbit. Electrons are a subatomic particle with a spin and a negative electrical charge and thus a very small magnetic movement or resonance. This movement allows for variability in the energy of the electron depending on the direction of its spin axis as it relates to a given surrounding magnetic field vector. The theory of optically pumped magnetometers, including cesium vapor units, relies on these physics principles. The strength of that magnetic field equals the change in the electron energy divided by an atomic constant. In the case of cesium there are only nine possible orientations with associated energy levels. The difference in these energy levels will always be proportional to the strength of the present magnetic field. Optically pumped magnetometers typically operate on much higher frequencies than proton magnetometers (70 to 350KHZ versus 0.9K to 4.5KHZ). These higher frequencies should provide faster repetitive rates (up to 10 readings per second) and accurate signal processing. It is worth noting that the cesium utilized in these magnetometers is non-radioactive and has no health hazard risks.

The pitfalls in the cesium magnetometers, however, lie in their inherent susceptibility to natural heading errors and dead zones (polar and equatorial). Dead zones occur when the ambient magnetic field passes through the magnetometer sensor at an angle between zero and 10 degrees. This phenomenon is very prominent at the equatorial and polar regions. Due to the physics of the measuring process in optically pumped magnetometers, they all suffer from phenomenon referred to as heading errors. This occurs when the angle of the magnetic field passes through the sensor head. There are many highly technical causes for this phenomenon; however, their discussion is beyond the scope of this document. Heading errors in cesium magnetometers have been corrected through the development of better optics as well as the readjustment of the alignment of the optical component. These techniques have reduced heading errors to less than 0.1 gamma.

Geometrics produces two cesium magnetometer models: the G-880 is designed for deeper water (up to 10,000 feet), and the G-881 shown in Figure F-5 and employed in Task 3, primarily targeted for shallower water operation. Both systems consist of a sensor fish, coaxial tow cable and a topside computer for data storage and interpretation.

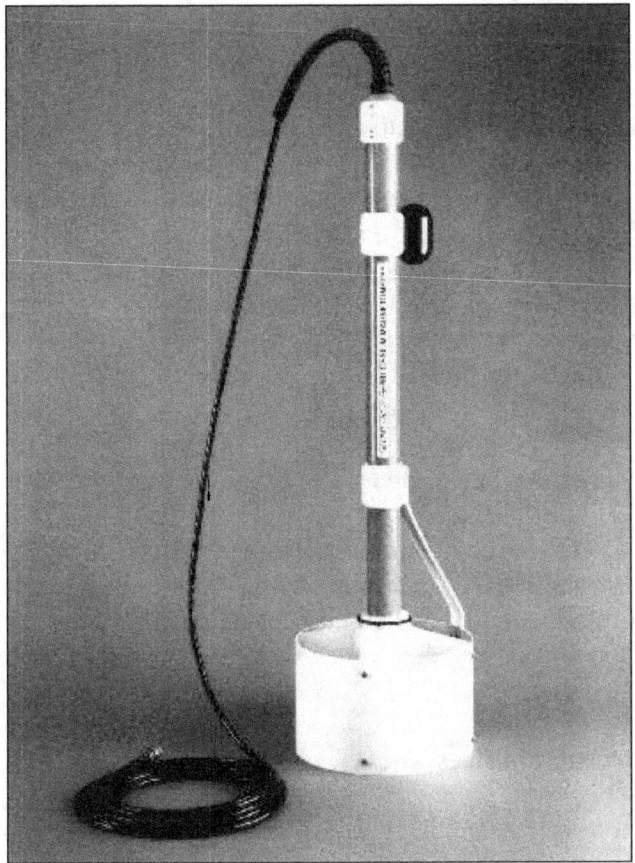

Figure F-5. Geometrics' 881 cesium marine magnetometer employed in Task 3.

F.3. Employment of Magnetometers in the Gulf's Oil and Gas Industry

There are many different makes and models of magnetometers available to the various survey groups and oil and gas companies who actively work across the Gulf of Mexico. In an effort to determine which instruments were and are being employed by the industry, several groups were contacted to see which instruments they own and operate for the many different types of survey projects they conduct in the Gulf. After discussions with some of these companies it became apparent that, as with any other type of business, there are certain philosophical positions as well as practical factors that determine which survey equipment each group prefers to use. It should be stated that not all groups or survey companies were contacted, but the ones that were offered a very homogenous understanding of past, current and future magnetometer types that are and will be employed in the Gulf.

F.3.1. John Chance and Associates (FUGRO)

Currently this company employs several Geometrics proton precession magnetometers, including the G-801/803 and the G-866. These instruments have been used by this company throughout its history with very satisfactory results. The availability of in-house spare parts, the familiarity of the company's technicians of these models and their unique repair predecessors, and the offshore staff's experience and knowledge of how to best deploy and operate them have all contributed to the relatively long period of deployment of these units. Mr. Ted Hampton with FUGRO Geoservices has indicated, however, that his company will be replacing some of its aging proton precession units with newer Overhauser proton magnetometers from GEM systems. This decision was based in part on the fact that Geometrics will no longer support the G-801 series consoles with spare parts, although parts for the tow system, including the sensor, will continue to be available. In addition, the G-866, which was mainly used in shallow water in smaller vessels due to its compact size, was phased out and parts are no longer are available, particularly the plastic gears used in its printer head which required frequent replacement.

F.3.2. C &C Technologies, Inc.

This company has been on the forefront of the cesium technology since its inception during the mid-1990s. According to Mr. Arlen Lejune, his company owns and operates twelve Geometrics model G-880 and G-881 cesium magnetometers. They have collected excellent magnetometer data in all water depths, from a few feet deep to full ocean depth.

F.3.3. Gulf Ocean Services, Inc.

This contractor performs block clearances and pipeline preliminary surveys across the shelf edge. All of the magnetometer data is collected utilizing a Geometrics 801/803 proton precession magnetometer. Mr. Donald Trout, the general manager of Gulf Ocean Services, indicated that this instrument has been able to meet all MMS specifications regarding noise levels of +/-1.5 gammas. In addition, the survey crew's familiarity of the maintenance and repair of this magnetometer have all contributed to its continued use.

F.3.4. Cochrane Technologies, Inc.

Cochrane Technologies currently owns and operates four Geometrics 801/803 proton precession magnetometers. In addition, a Geometrics G-866 magnetometer is utilized in shallow water work on smaller vessels. However, in recent projects the company has opted to deploy a G-881 cesium magnetometer. According to Mr. Kevin Burdeaux, his company is going to make the transition to cesium magnetometers because of the superior data quality his offshore crews have been able to obtain with these instruments.

F.3.5. Racal/NCS/KC Offshore

Until their recent merger, these two firms operated several Geometrics G-801 proton precession magnetometers.

F.3.6. Harvey-Lynch

Harvey-Lynch serves offshore and other related industries by providing equipment sales, rentals, as well as repairs and refurbishment of a variety of instrumentation. These instruments include (but are not limited to) acoustic positioning equipment, bathymetric equipment, echo sounders, GPS, magnetometers, sidescan sonar, and telemetry systems.

The first question posed to Harvey-Lynch concerned the current use, if any, of the G-866. Mentioned above, the G-866 was the longtime favorite for all types of magnetometer surveys in the GOMR. Asked about the current use of the G-866, Harvey-Lynch stated that they have not shipped out one of these instruments in almost a year, although they have some in their rental pool (Larry Stephenson, personal communication June 2002). While a couple of these units have recently been sold to third-world countries due to their low cost (around $5,000 for a used system), their use in the industry today has been eclipsed by advancements in magnetometer technology.

As with any antiquated system, the G-866 has had its share of problems. When asked about the most common problem with the G-866, Harvey-Lynch responded that cable problems were the most prevalent. Other less prevalent problems include console and/or electrical trouble. It should be addressed here that numerous problems with the G-866 occurred during the current investigations. The first problem occurred prior to running the grid lines over the *Rhoda* site. While configuring the Hypack system at the dock the towfish heated up, expanding the fluid inside, resulting in blown bulkheads on either end. While this can be attributed to operator error and not the equipment itself, it illustrates the potential for problems in the field. The blown bulkheads needed to be pulled out and replaced, resulting in the loss of one day of work.

Besides the blown bulkheads, the G-866 has had numerous console problems. Console problems usually consist of electrical malfunctions or print head failure. While the more modern magnetometers are computer-driven, the G-866 relies on a stand-alone console complete with all electronics, resulting in the potential for more problems, especially in a marine environment.

Noise within the data is yet another problem with the G-866. While the newer magnetometers are accurate within tenths of gammas, the data collected by the G-866 tended to be much noisier (±5 gammas) depending on the direction of the track line. While running north-south track lines over the *Josephine,* the data collected was much noisier running north (into the swell) versus that collected running south (with the swell). Noisy data can often result in difficulty identifying smaller anomalies. While it is possible to reduce noise to some extent (i.e., grounding the console, extending the tow cable, filling the towfish with adequate amounts of fluid), the problem illustrates yet another limitation when dealing with antiquated equipment.

In summary, magnetometer development over the last ten to fifteen years has benefited greatly from the recent advancements in electronic circuitry innovations, computer programs, as well as the global positioning accuracy. These advances have resulted in better sensors and processors. Not only have the sensing capabilities of these instruments improved, signal processing and subsequent data interpretation have also been enhanced. The digital collection and storing of magnetometer data, along with precise navigation data, allows for very accurate post-processing of anomalies and therefore the locating of ferromagnetic material. A summary of the features and recommended applications of quantum magnetometers follows:

1- Although optically pumped magnetometers can be produced by using four electron resonance vapors (cesium, potassium, rubidium, and helium), we concentrated on the cesium version since it accounts for most of the production of this sensor technology. These units offer very good sensitivity with high resolution and fast repetitive rate (up to ten readings per second). They are ideal for both marine and airborne magnetometer surveys.

2- Overhauser magnetometers produced by GEM Systems and by Marine Magnetics offer nearly the same sensitivity as the cesium magnetometers, particularly at moderate speeds. In addition, this sensor design produces very accurate readings and is inherently immune to dead zones and heading errors. Simple design and low cost are additional benefits of this system of magnetic detection. Marine and archaeological surveys, as well as oil and gas development surveys, are some of the applications Overhauser magnetometers are well suited for.

3- Proton precession magnetometers are very simple to operate and maintain; however, their sensor design is affected by heading errors, noise caused by the sensor head swimming or wobbling down the survey line, and they have lower sensitivity than both the Overhauser and cesium sensors with relatively slow sampling rates. Even with these limitations this sensor design continues to evolve, as evidenced by the multitude of newer models being marketed by firms such as Geometrics and JW Fisher. Proton precession magnetometers are generally placed at the end of competing magnetometer technology, and are best suited for low-speed ground surveys and shallow water marine surveys where the low cycling rate will not be a problem.

APPENDIX G

TASK 3 SURVEY EQUIPMENT

G.1. Survey Equipment

Trimble AgGPS 132 Receiver. Providing sub-meter differential GPS accuracy for offshore surveys, the Trimble AgGPS™ 132 differential GPS receiver utilizes The Choice™ technology (Figure G-1). This technology combines a GPS receiver, a beacon differential receiver and a satellite differential receiver in the same housing. These receivers use a combined antenna with a single antenna cable. This configuration greatly improves the accuracy, reliability and availability of differential GPS corrections. The medium frequency (MF) beacon receiver uses the broadcasts from government-established navigation beacon reference stations around the world. The L-band satellite differential correction receiver requires a subscription to a differential correction service and provides multiple vendor support. A built-in virtual reference station (VRS) permits the satellite corrections to be uniformly accurate over the entire satellite coverage area, without the degradation in accuracy associated with increasing distance from fixed reference stations.

The AgGPS 132 combination DGPS receiver with The Choice™ technology status of DGPS corrections can be determined easily for either of the two built-in differential correction receivers, or from an external differential correction source. To ensure that the AgGPS 132 can be powered from the machine's power system, it operates over an input voltage range of 10 to 32 volts. The AgGPS 132 is easy to install and connects to a wide range of precision maritime equipment.

Figure G-1. Trimble AgGPS™ 132 differential GPS receiver used during the Task 3 survey (courtesy of Trimble).

The receiver can output industry-standard NMEA 0183 messages. The user-selectable outputs include position, velocity, navigation, and status information. The standard configuration outputs positions once per second with very low latency. For applications on faster-moving vehicles, the AgGPS 132 can optionally output 10 positions per second, with latency of less than 100 ms.

The L-band satellite receiver uses a Trimble-developed sensitive design to provide coverage across the entire satellite footprint. The MF beacon differential correction receiver built into the AgGPS 132 is a dual channel, all-digital, low noise design allowing it to receive corrections at distances of hundreds of miles from the reference stations.

The AgGPS 132 includes a high accuracy 12-channel GPS engine with improved ionosphere and troposphere models. It provides sub-meter differential position accuracy and offers differential speed accuracy of better than 0.1 mile per hour (0.16 kph), thus eliminating the need for an external speed sensor. The positions are computed using robust differential processing techniques, allowing operation to begin a few seconds after switching on the machine.

SG Brown Meridian Gyrocompass. The SG Brown Meridian is an accurate gyrocompass, which is easy to use and simple to integrate into navigation systems (Figure G-2). Outputs include RS232, RS422, 20mA Current Loop, Stepper and Synchro. Latitude and speed compensation can be entered either by the top panel controls or from a navigation computer via the RS232 interface. The Meridian is also IMO Wheelmark and HSC certified.

Figure G-2. The SG Brown Meridian gyrocompass.

The heart of the Meridian gyroscope is its element, which is a dynamically tuned gyrosphere (DTG). Used for many applications, the DTG incorporates high precision technology, allowing for accuracy, reliability, and shock resistance. The accuracy of the unit is realized through specialized, high-quality engineering and sophisticated high speed post-processing. The result provides an exceedingly stable heading and the ability to follow a high turn rate of up to 200° per second.

Hypack MAX. Hypack® is PC-based Windows software for planning, conducting, editing and publishing hydrographic surveys. Hypack® MAX contains tools to quickly design a survey and display results. Its powerful drawing engine can display background files in DXF, DGN, TIF, S-57, BSB raster, C-Map, and VPF files at any rotation and scale. Design tools allow the user to quickly create planned lines (Figure G-3). Hypack® MAX automatically stores information to a project directory, allowing the user to set up new surveys or to quickly switch to an existing survey.

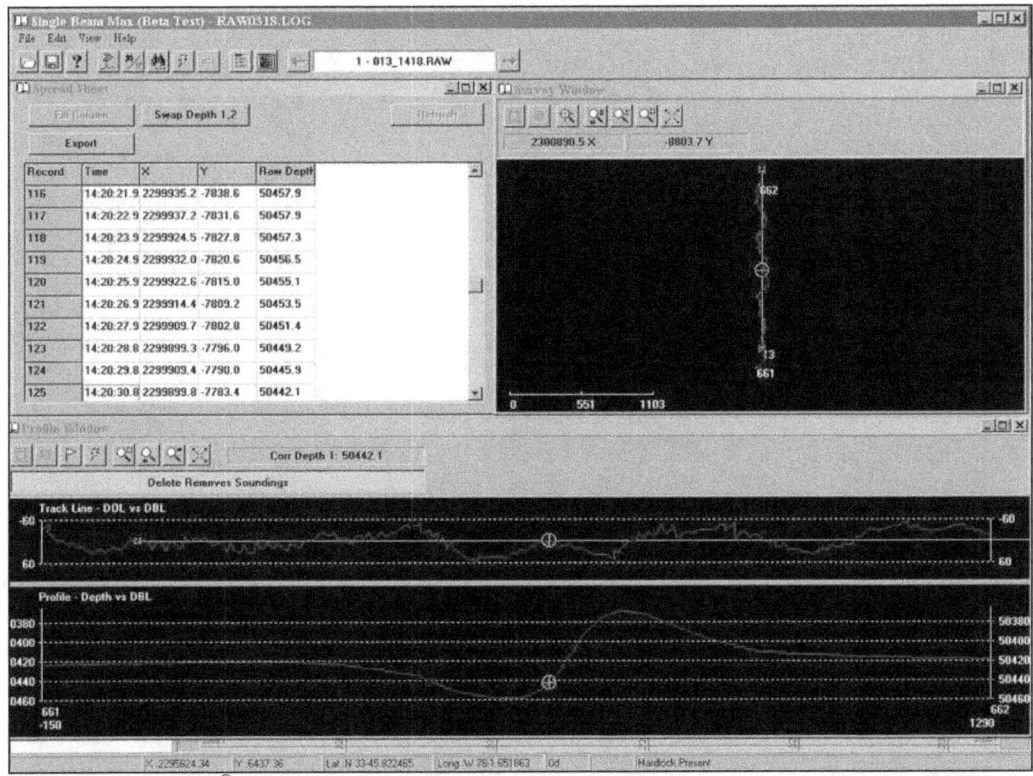

Figure G-3. Hypack® MAX allows for the quick placement of tracklines with the correct offsets.

Hypack® MAX's SURVEY program supports GPS, Range-Azimuth, and Range-Range navigation systems. It supports single beam, dual frequency, multiple transducer, and multi-beam echosounders, along with gyros, magnetometers, telemetry tide gauges, and other survey devices. The SURVEY program can be configured to display and track single vessels, multiple vessels, or the main vessel and ROVs or towfish.

Hypack® MAX's graphical editing routines allow quick editing of survey data. Water level corrections can be automatically determined using RTK GPS water level techniques, telemetry tide gauges, manual observations, or downloaded from NOAA web sites. Sound velocity corrections can be applied. Users can quickly review and edit individual points or blocks of data. Hypack® MAX's "Field to Finish" process allows the user to automatically remove data spikes, perform final sounding selection, and generate smooth sheets or export info to CAD before going into the field.

Hypack® MAX has a variety of final product programs. The Cross Section and Volume program is the standard used by the U.S. Army Corps of Engineers for calculation of dredge volume quantities throughout the USA. The Surface Modeling program generates 3-D models, contours, and also computes volumes between surfaces for beach erosion studies. The Export program allows users to import Hypack® MAX data into CAD and GIS packages in either DXF or DGN format.

INFORMATION IN THIS APPENDIX IS NOT AVAILABLE FOR PUBLIC DISCLOSURE

APPENDIX H

GRID TRANSECT COORDINATES FOR THE *JOSEPHINE* AND *RHODA*

APPENDIX I

STRIPCHARTS BY LINE FOR EACH INSTRUMENT
***JOSEPHINE* 25-METER SURVEY INTERVAL GRID**

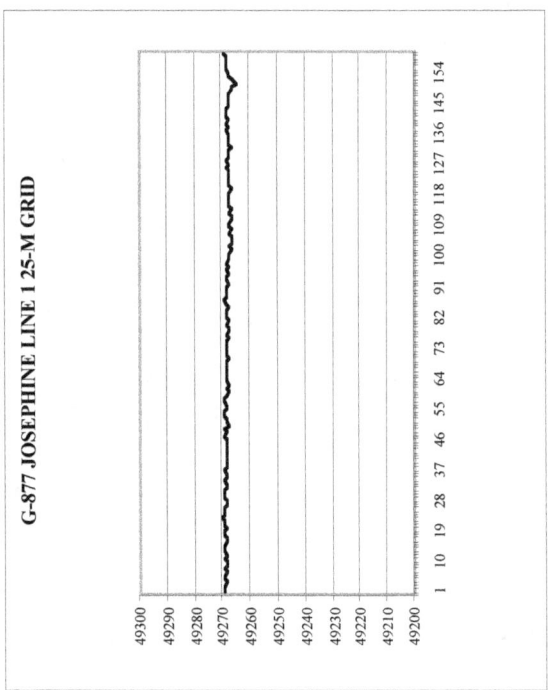

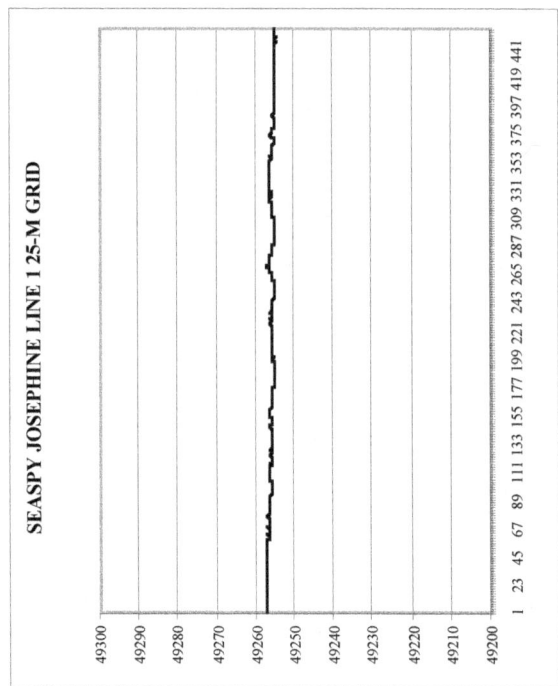

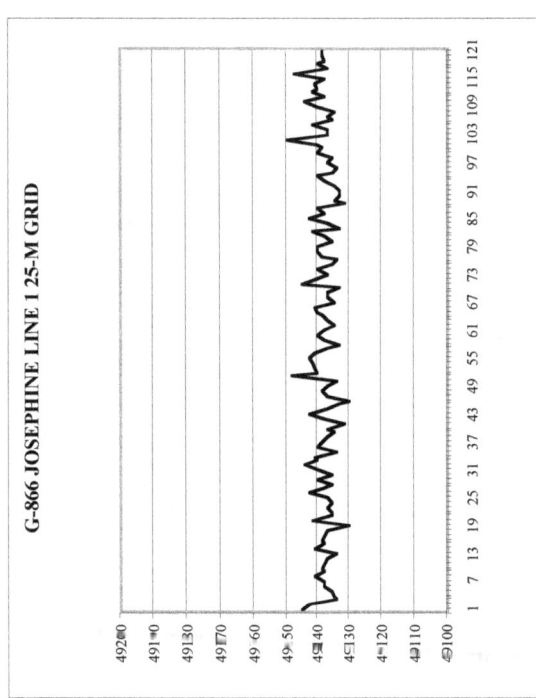

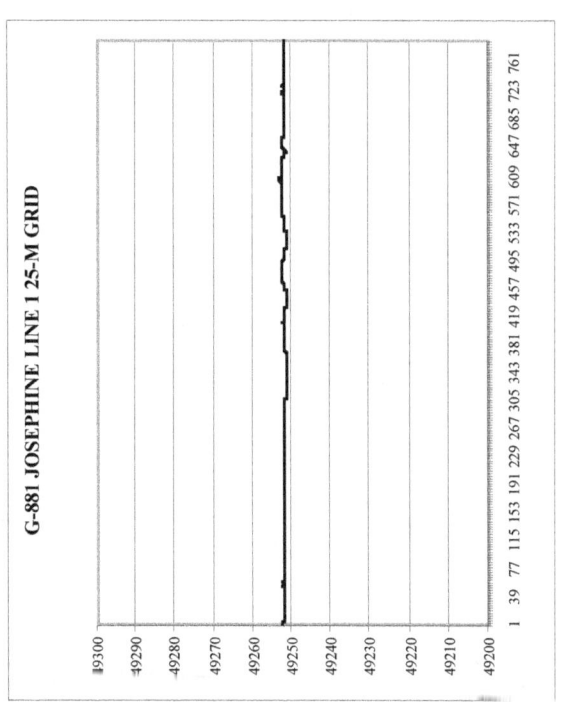

Josephine 25-Meter Survey Interval Grid Strip charts. Y-axis is the gamma scale, X-axis is the sampling rate.

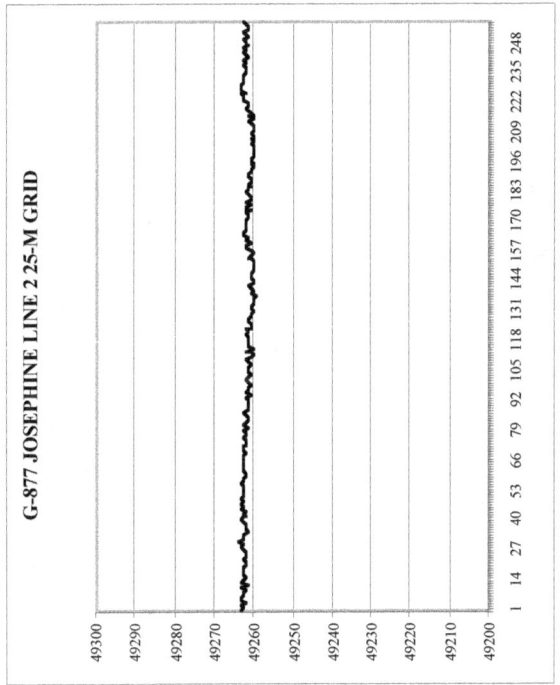

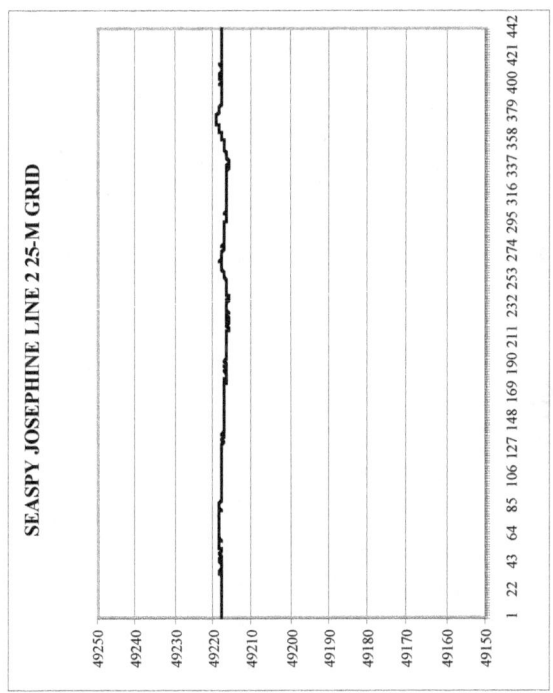

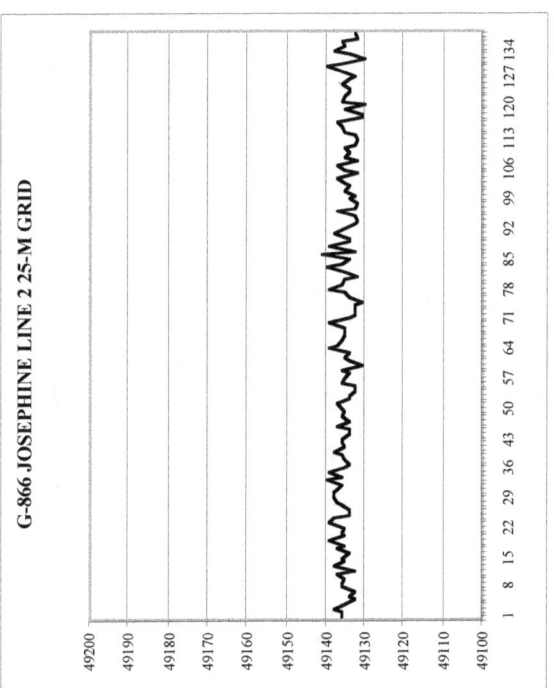

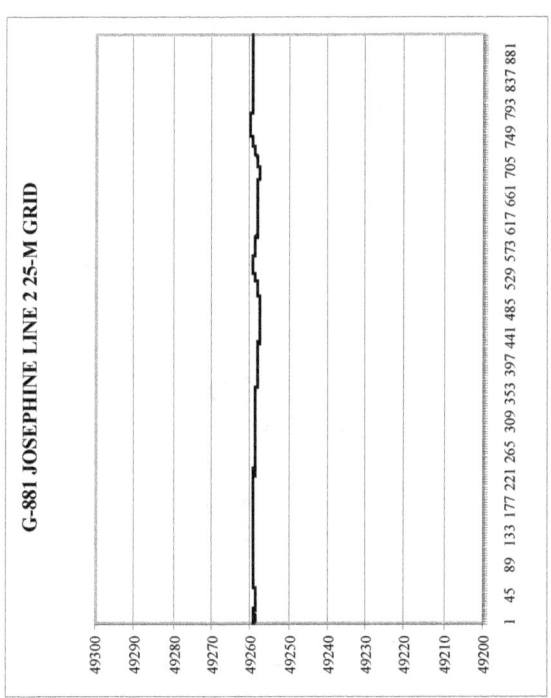

Josephine 25-Meter Survey Interval Grid Strip charts. Y-axis is the gamma scale, X-axis is the sampling rate.

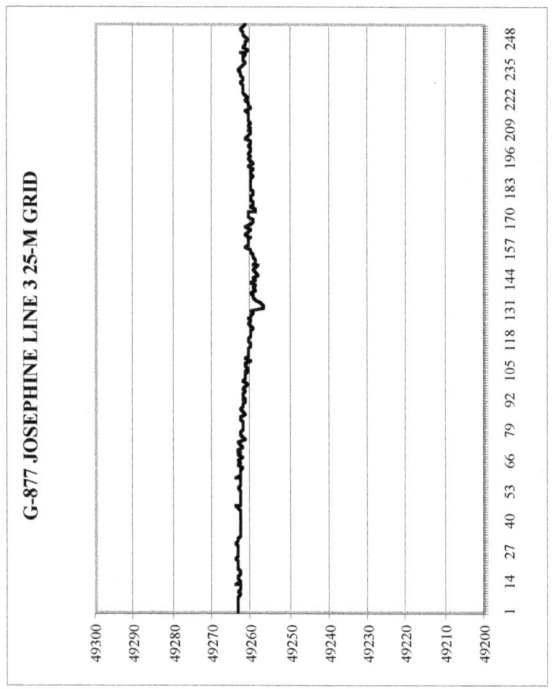

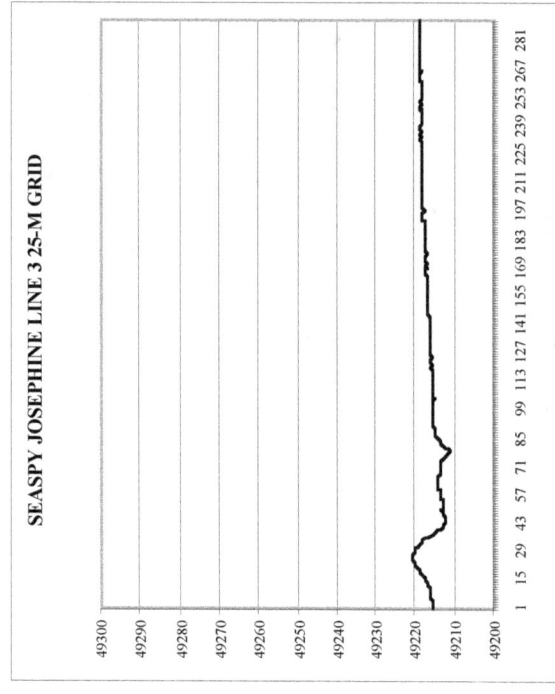

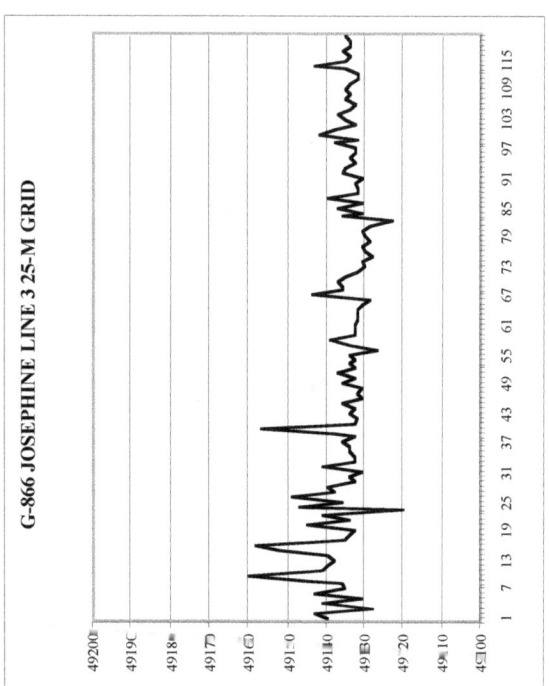

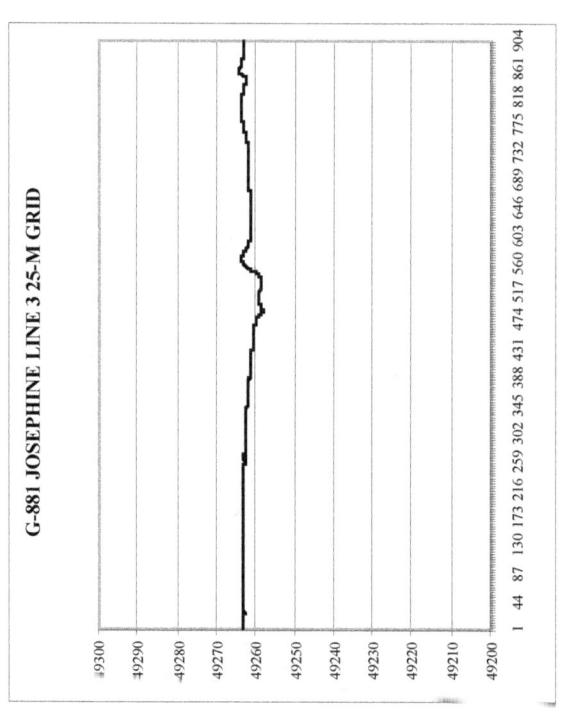

Josephine 25-Meter Survey Interval Grid Strip charts. Y-axis is the gamma scale, X-axis is the sampling rate.

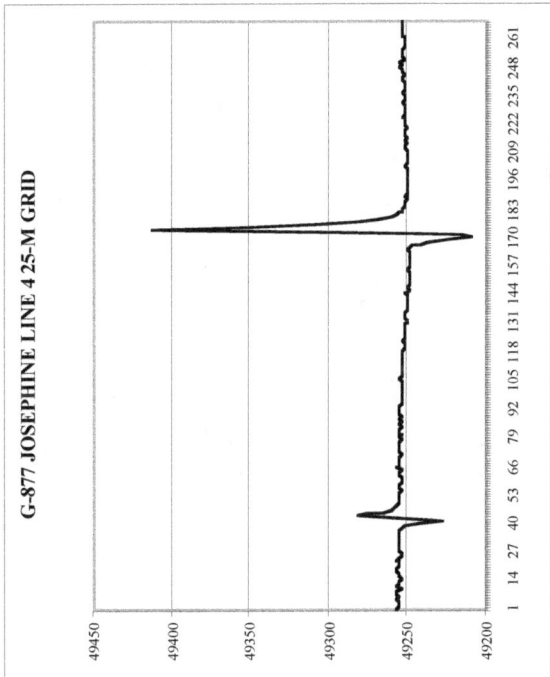

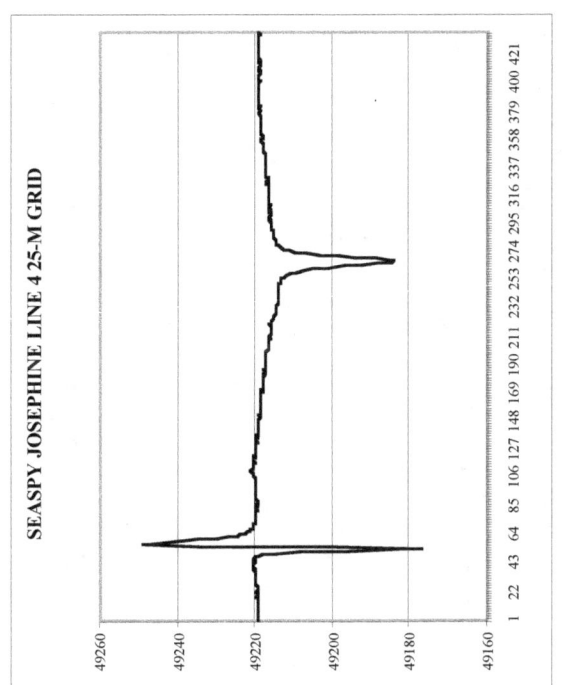

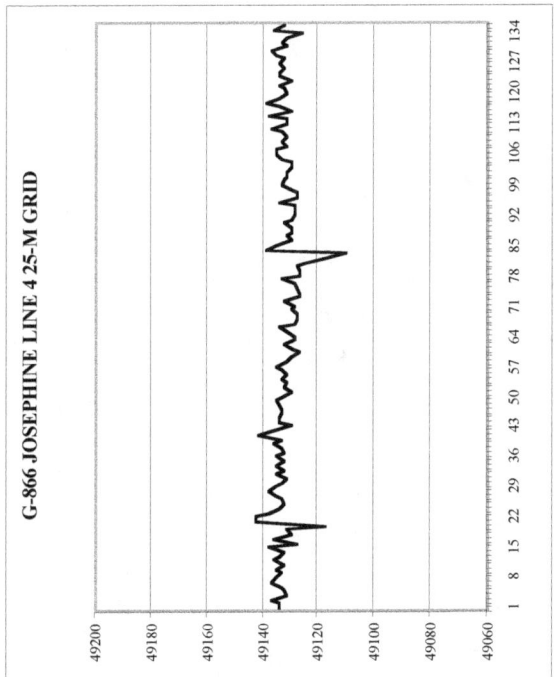

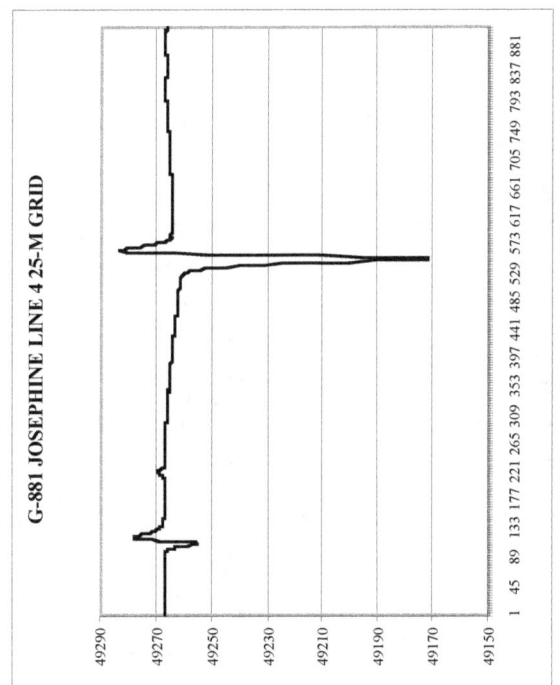

Josephine 25-Meter Survey Interval Grid Strip charts. Y-axis is the gamma scale, X-axis is the sampling rate.

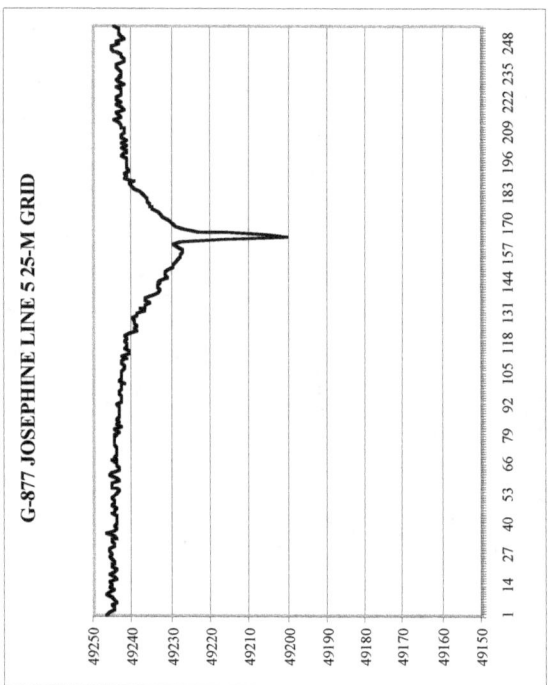

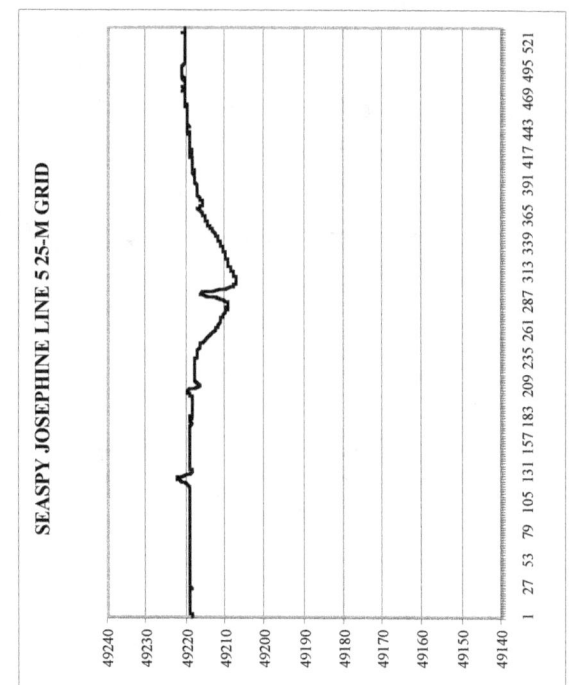

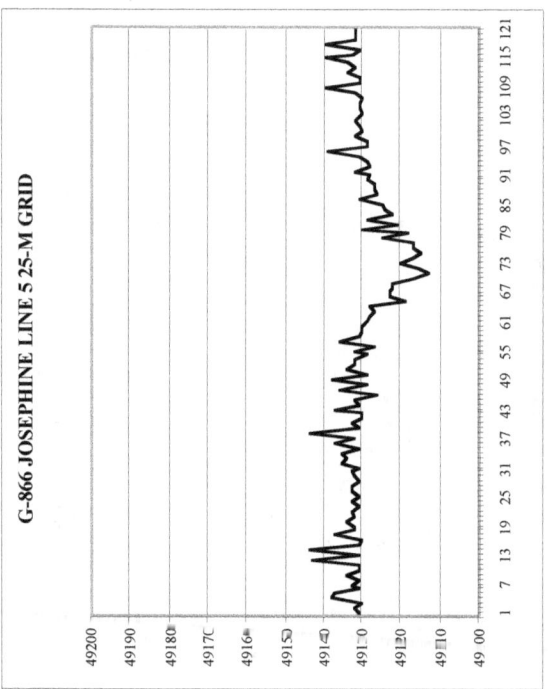

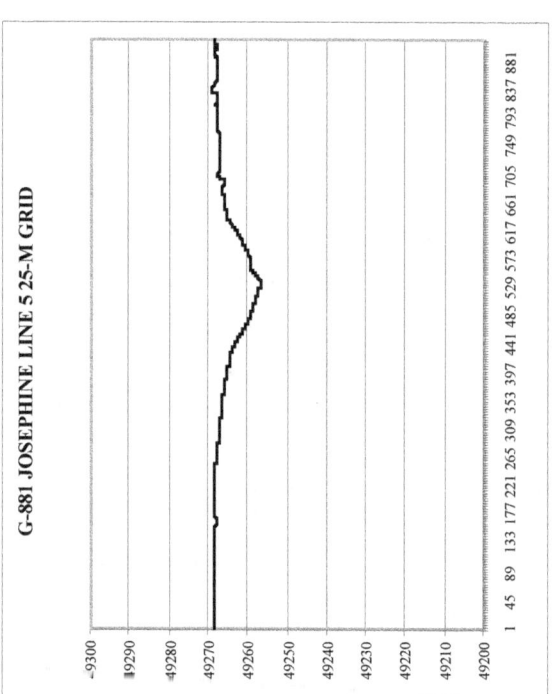

Josephine 25-Meter Survey Interval Grid Strip charts. Y-axis is the gamma scale, X-axis is the sampling rate.

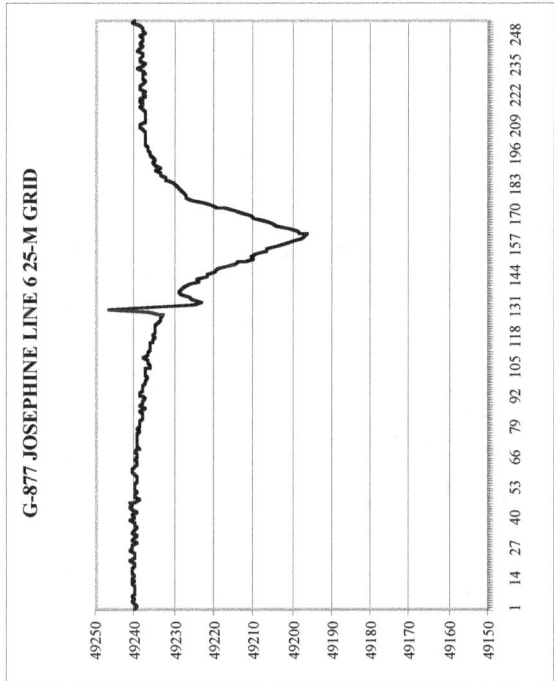

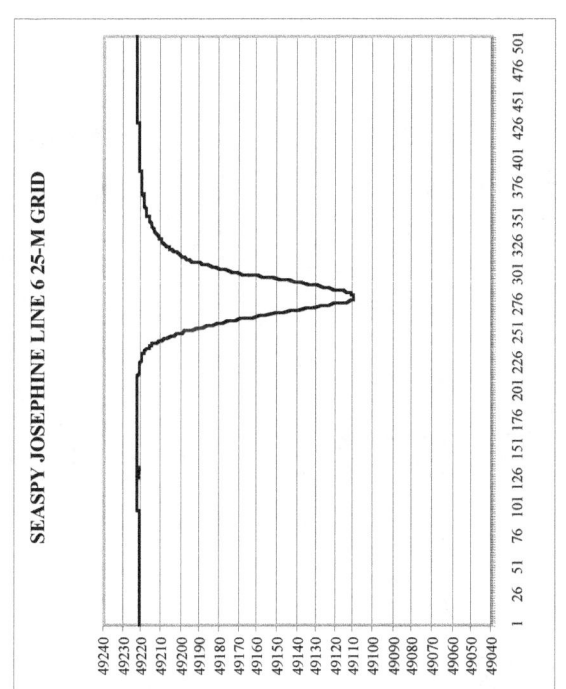

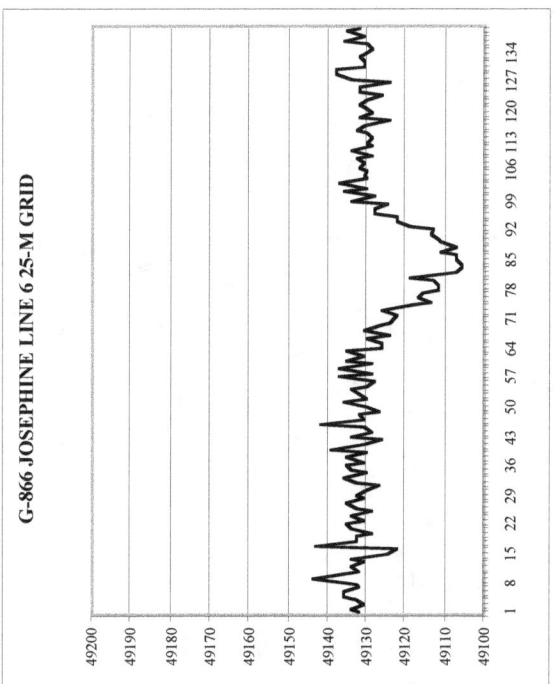

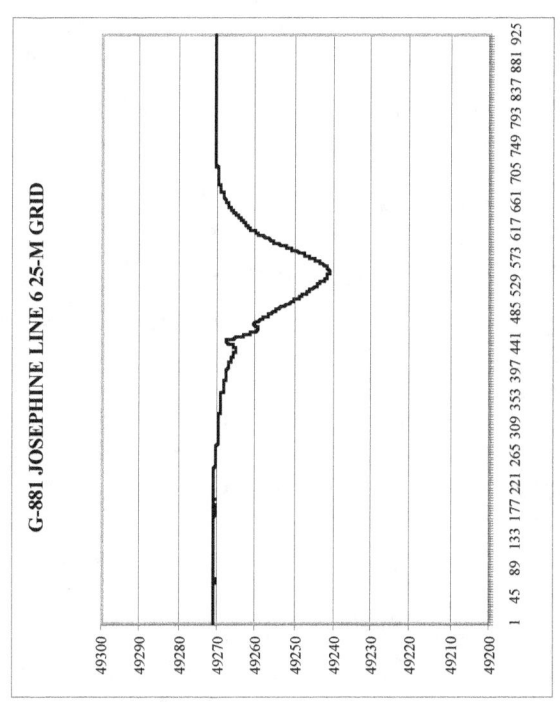

Josephine **25-Meter Survey Interval Grid Strip charts. Y-axis is the gamma scale, X-axis is the sampling rate.**

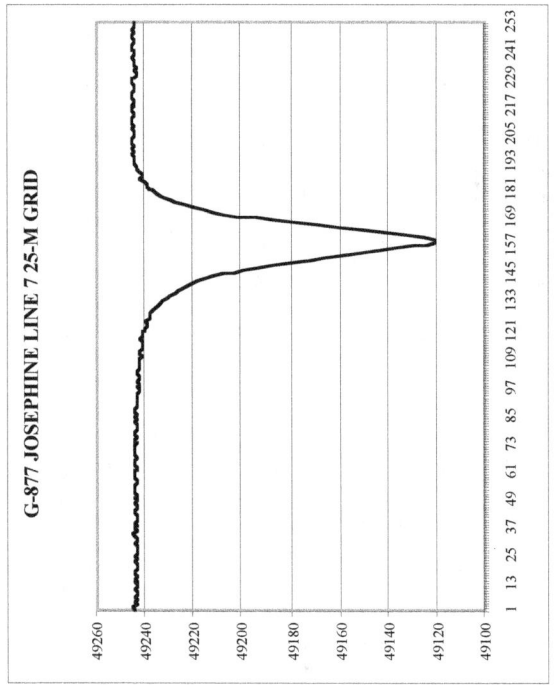

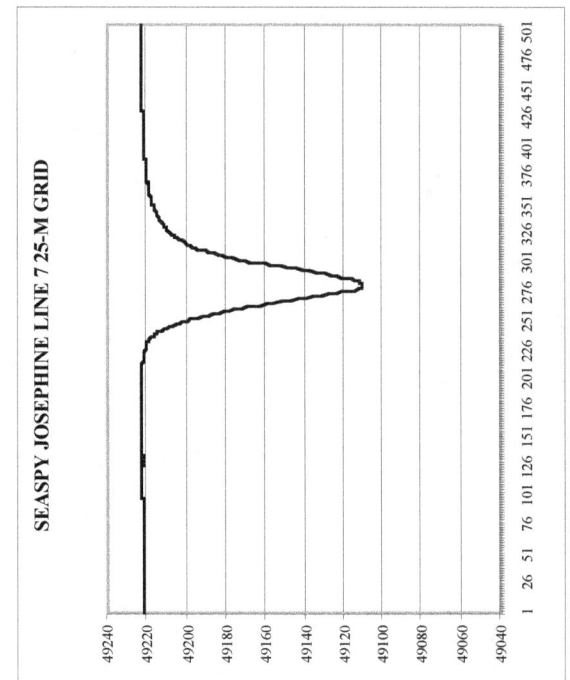

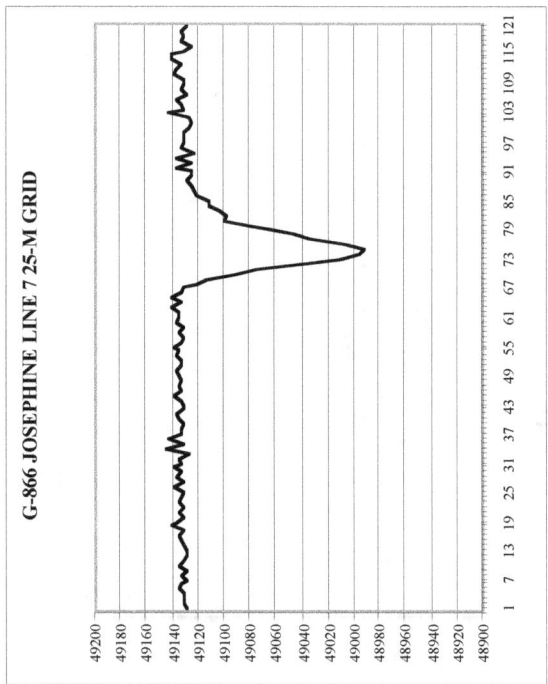

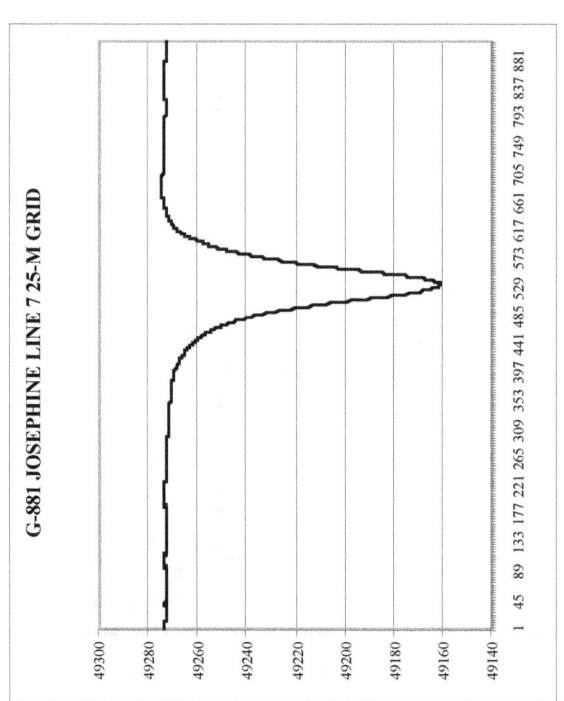

Josephine 25-Meter Survey Interval Grid Strip charts. Y-axis is the gamma scale, X-axis is the sampling rate.

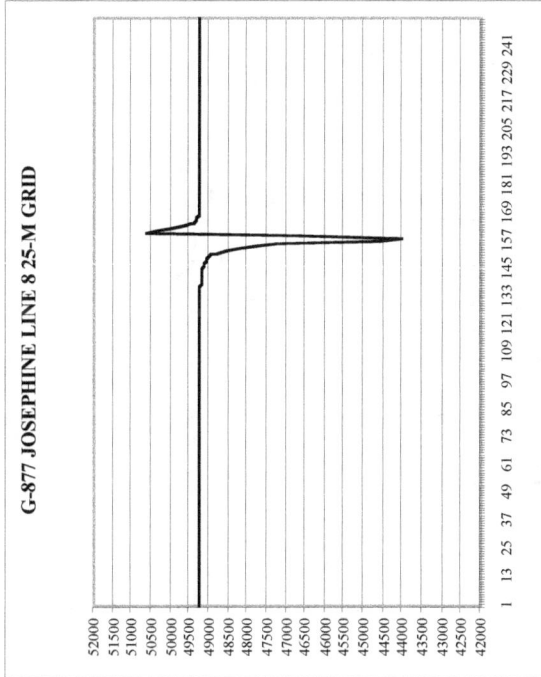

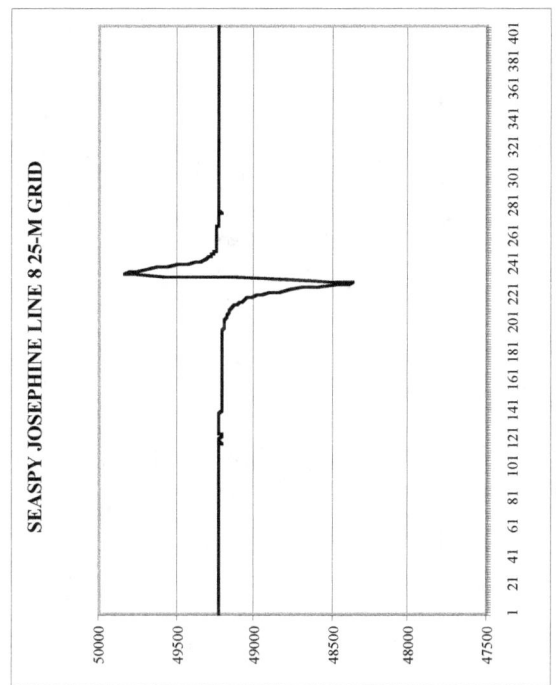

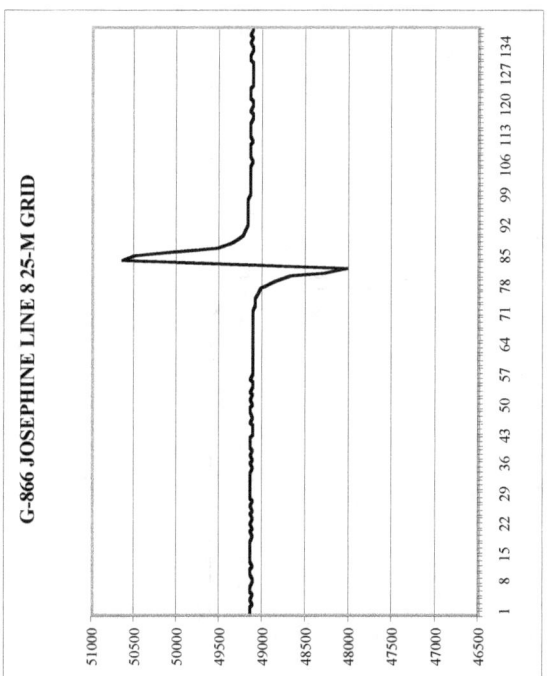

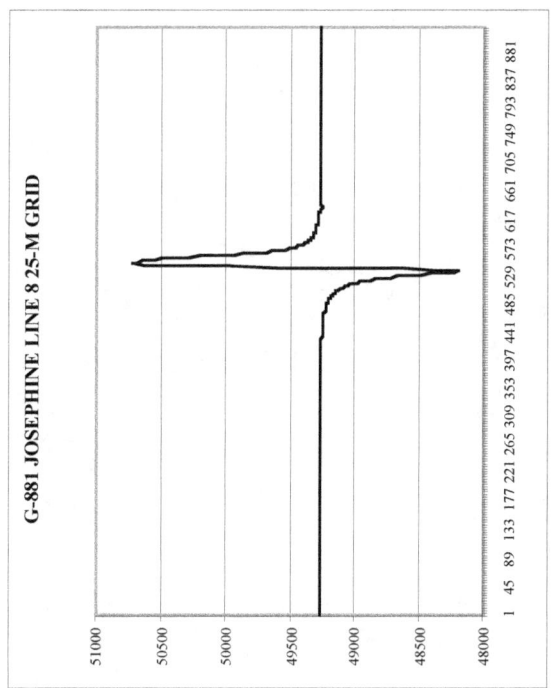

Josephine 25-Meter Survey Interval Grid Strip charts. Y-axis is the gamma scale, X-axis is the sampling rate.

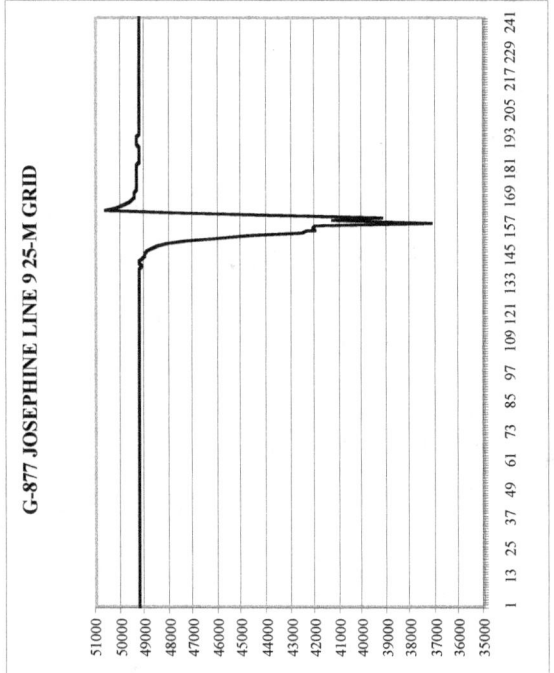

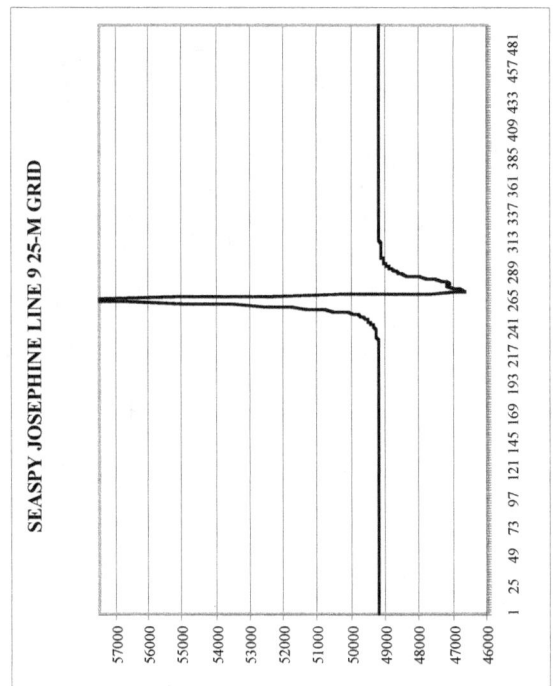

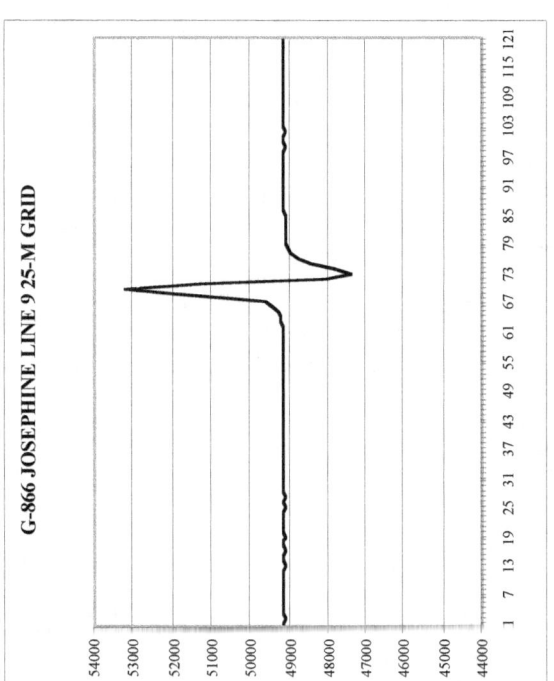

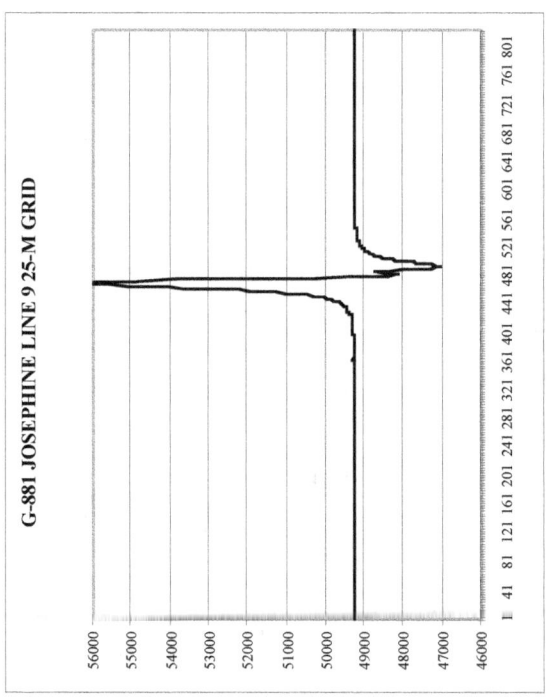

Josephine 25-Meter Survey Interval Grid Strip charts. Y-axis is the gamma scale, X-axis is the sampling rate.

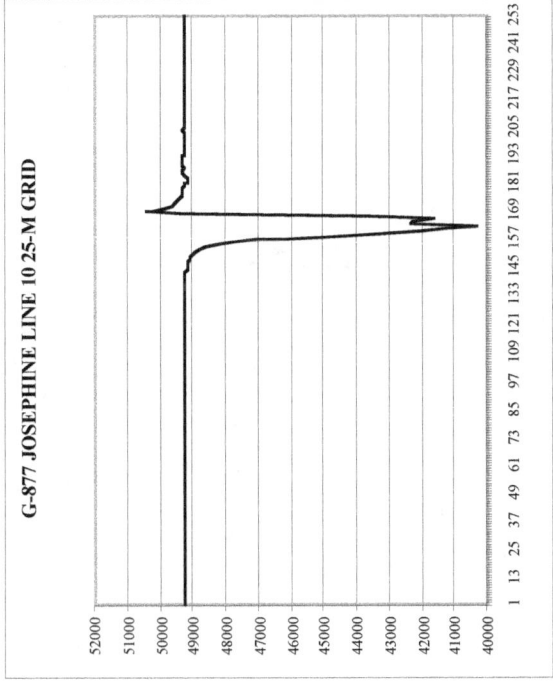

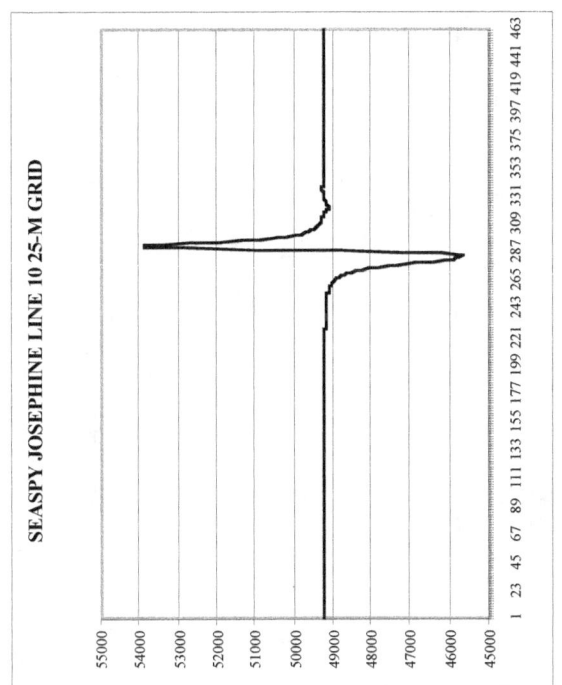

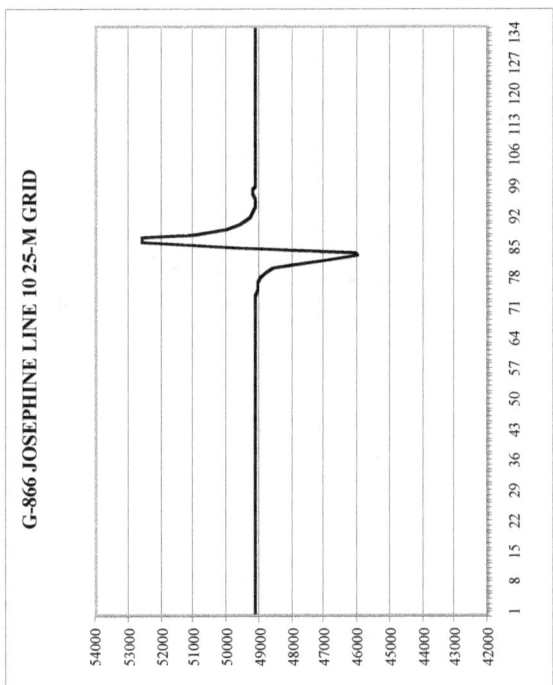

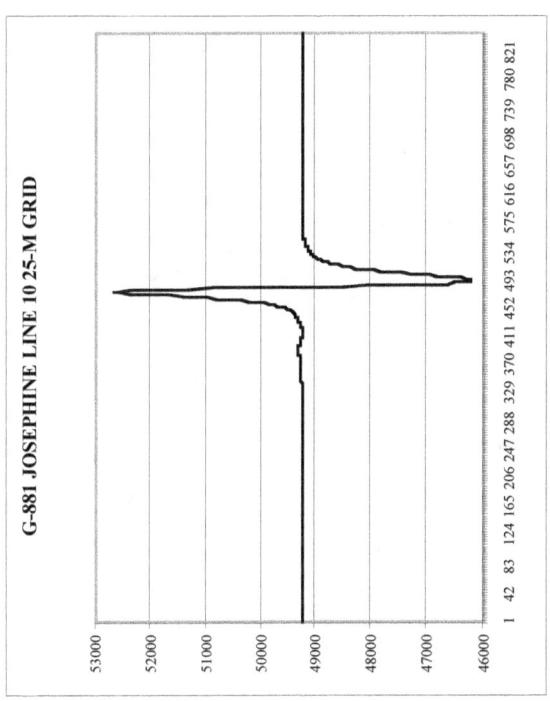

Josephine 25-Meter Survey Interval Grid Strip charts. Y-axis is the gamma scale, X-axis is the sampling rate.

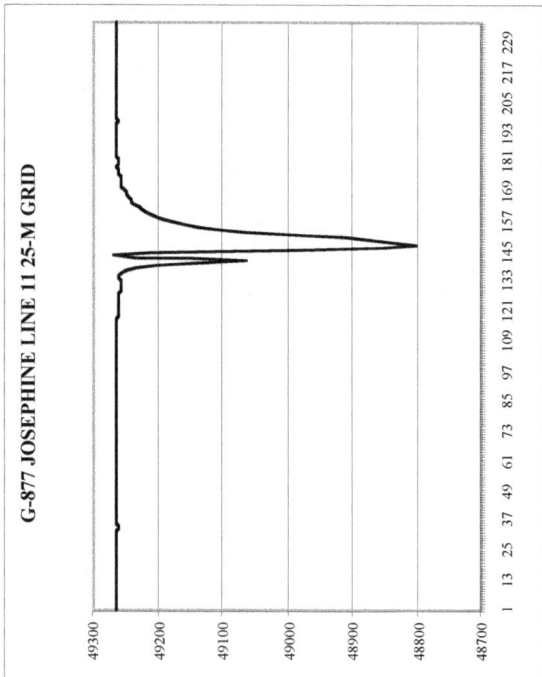

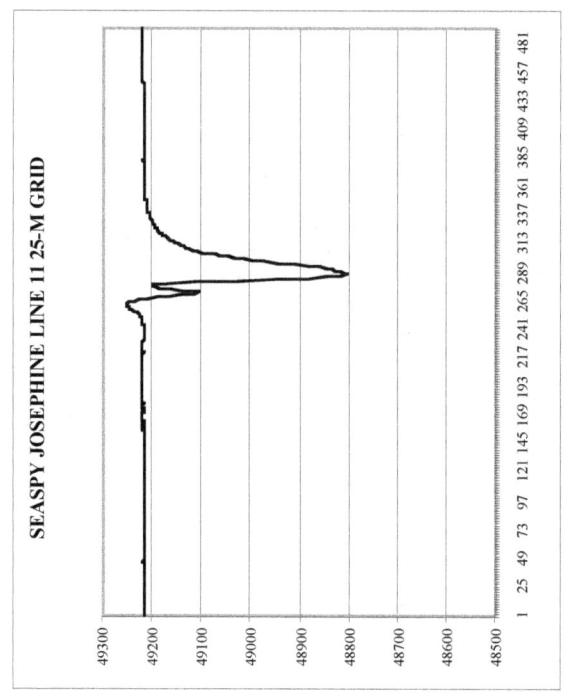

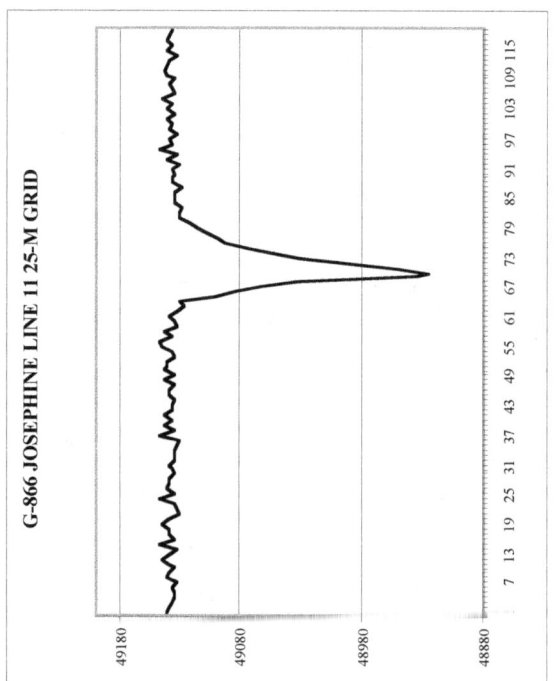

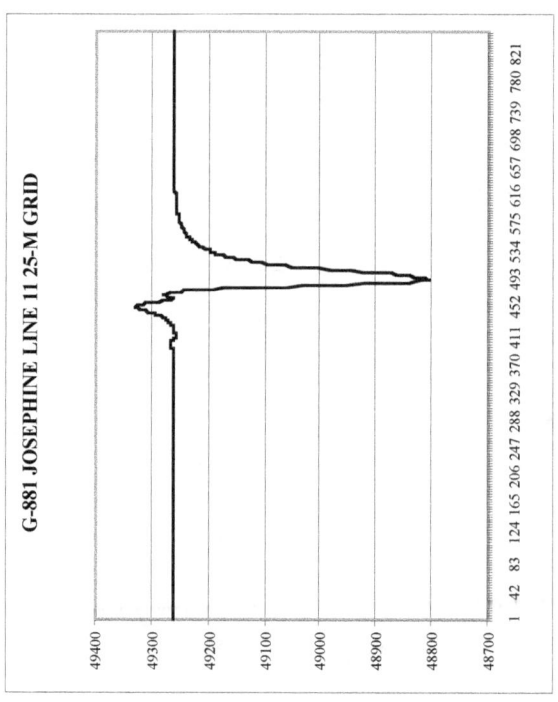

Josephine 25-Meter Survey Interval Grid Strip charts. Y-axis is the gamma scale, X-axis is the sampling rate.

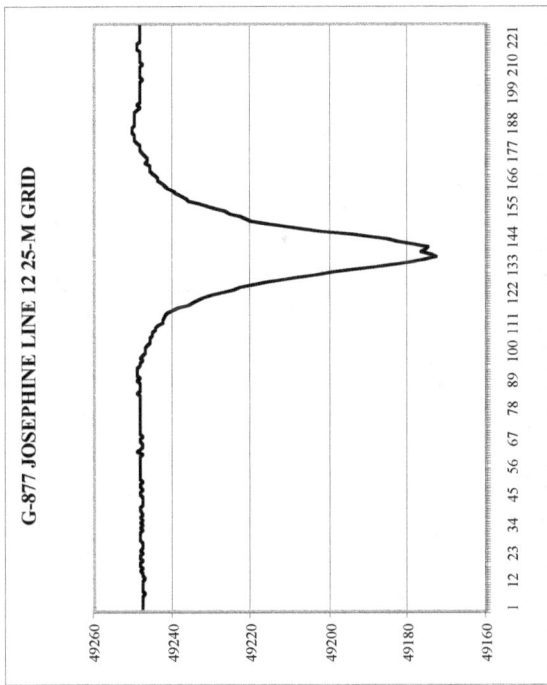

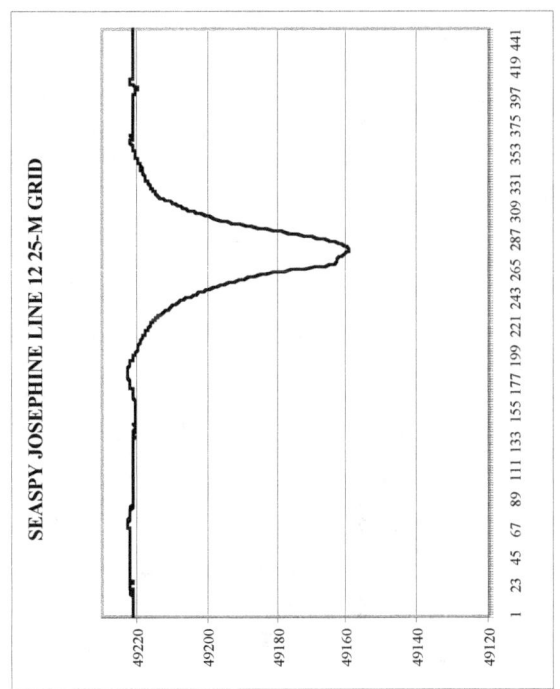

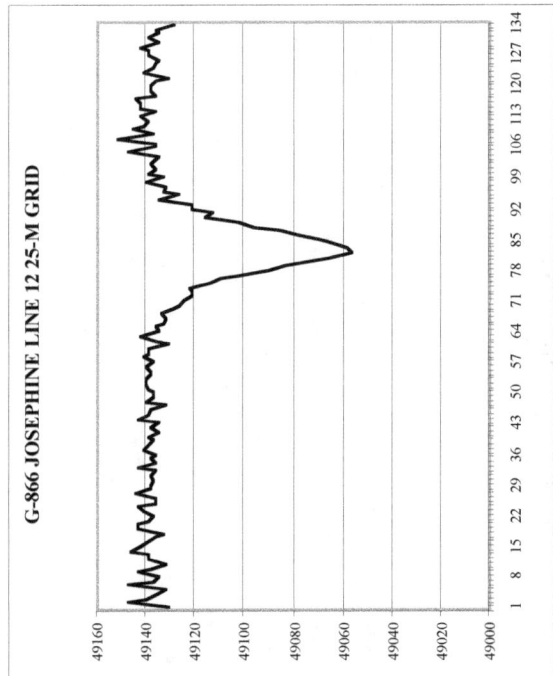

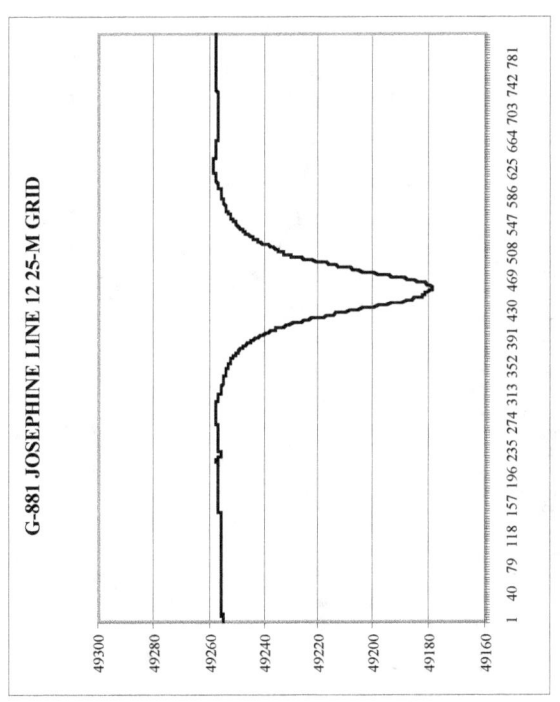

Josephine 25-Meter Survey Interval Grid Strip charts. Y-axis is the gamma scale, X-axis is the sampling rate.

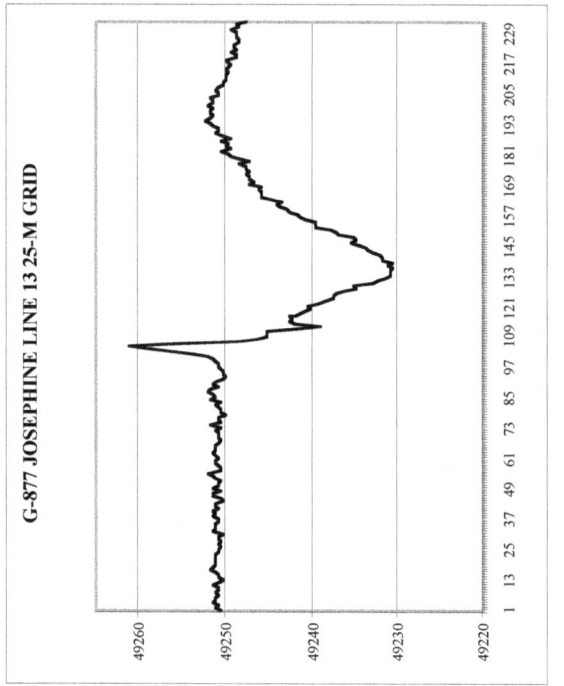

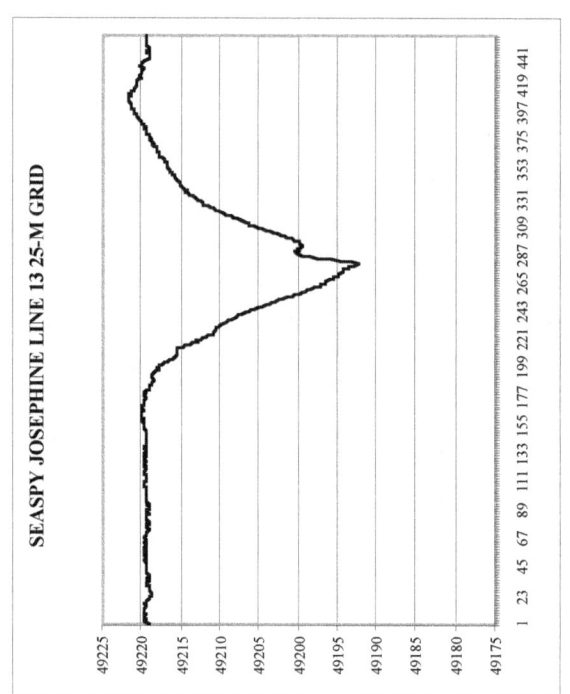

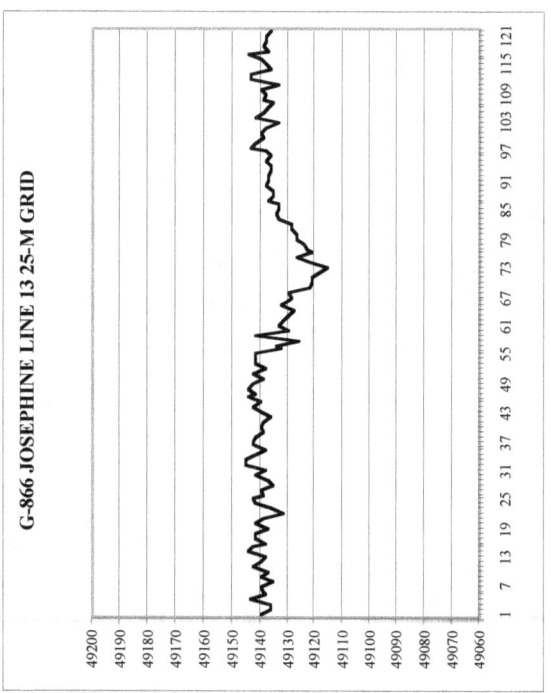

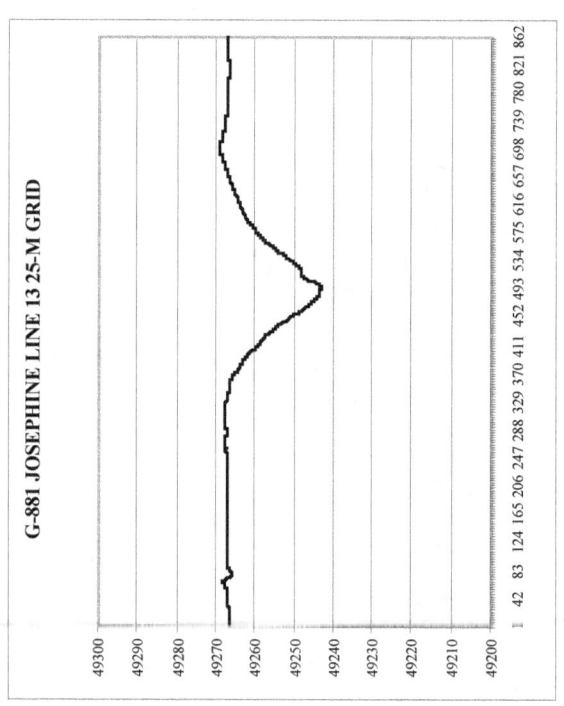

Josephine 25-Meter Survey Interval Grid Strip charts. Y-axis is the gamma scale, X-axis is the sampling rate.

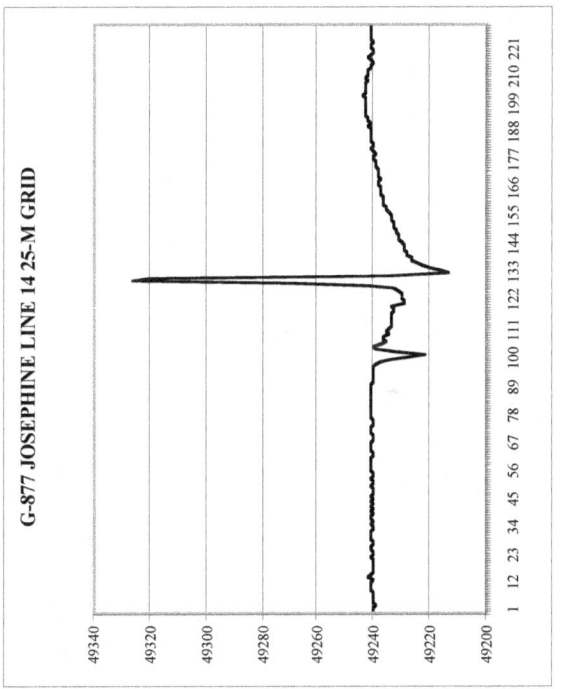

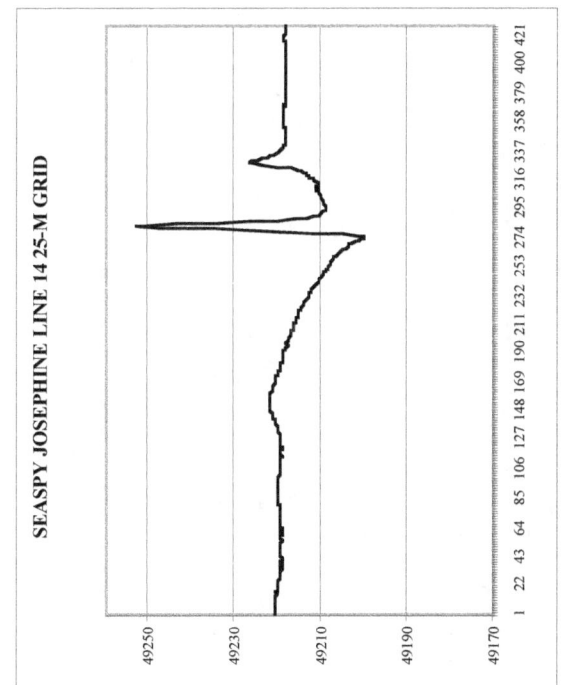

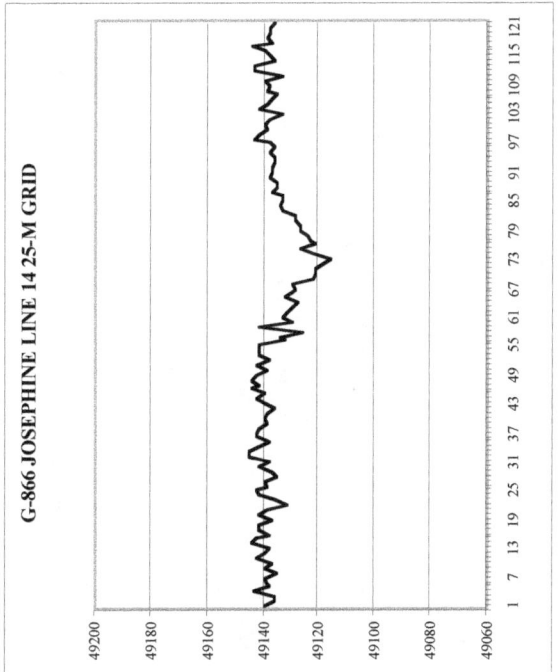

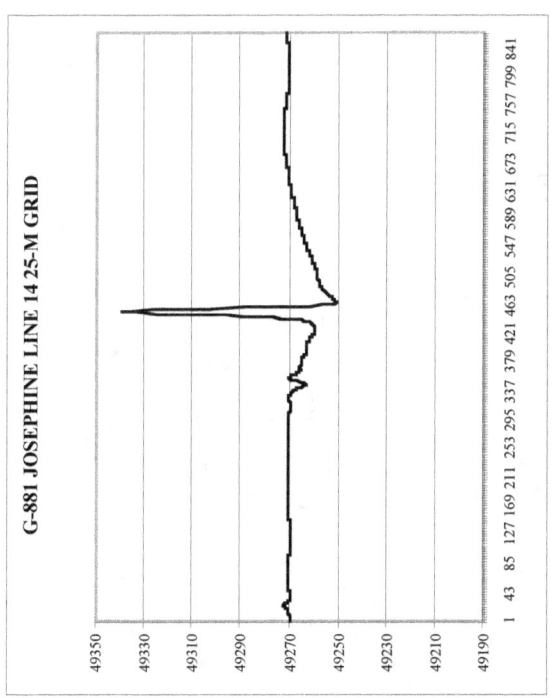

Josephine 25-Meter Survey Interval Grid Strip charts. Y-axis is the gamma scale, X-axis is the sampling rate.

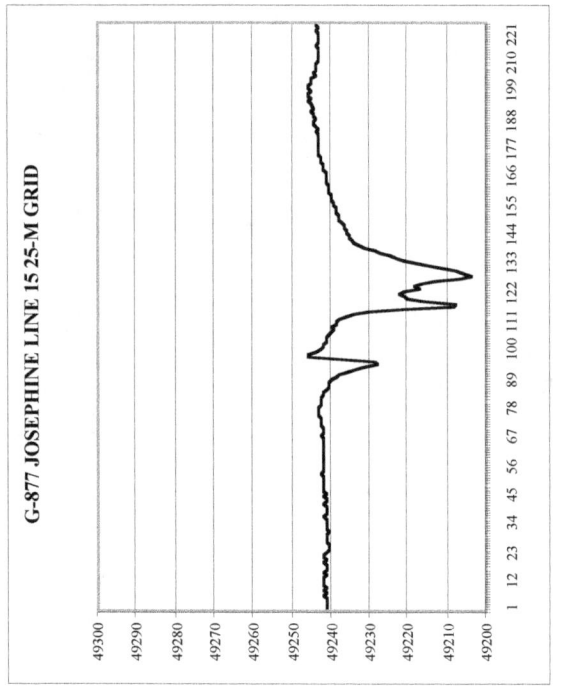

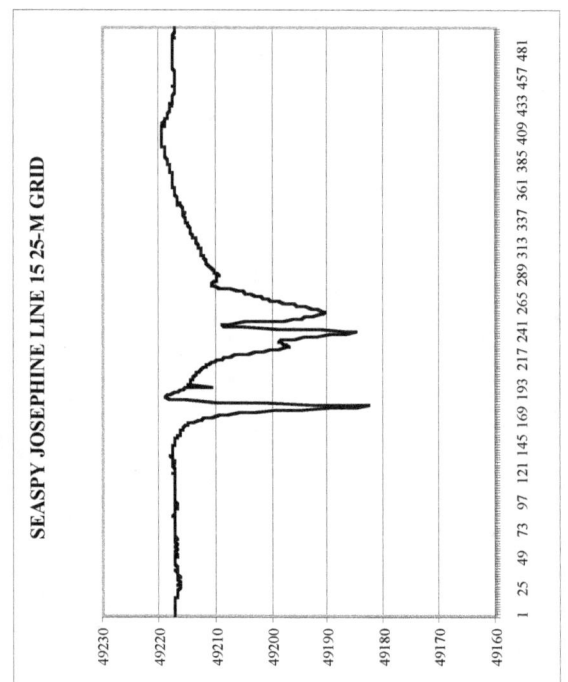

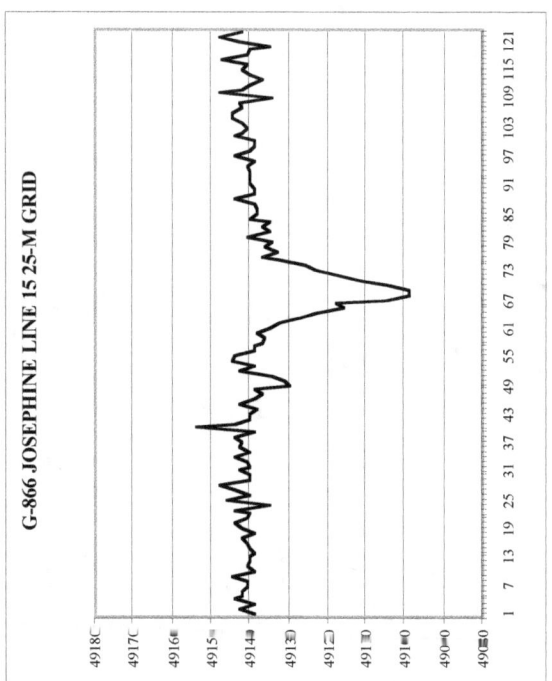

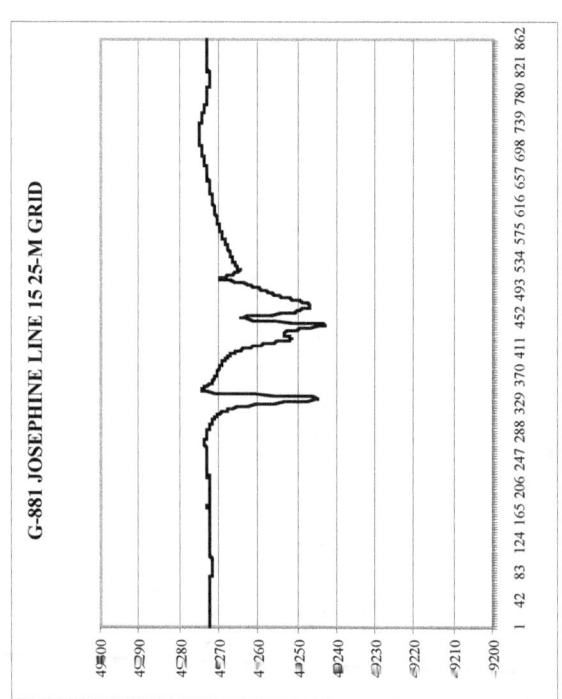

Josephine 25-Meter Survey Interval Grid Strip charts. Y-axis is the gamma scale, X-axis is the sampling rate.

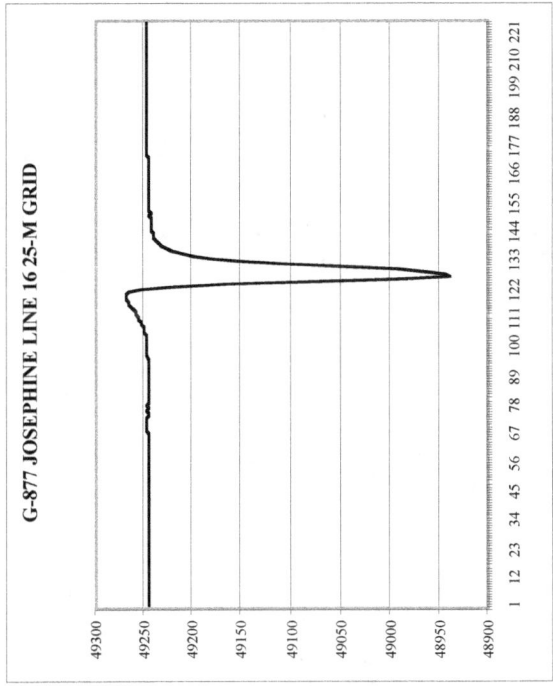

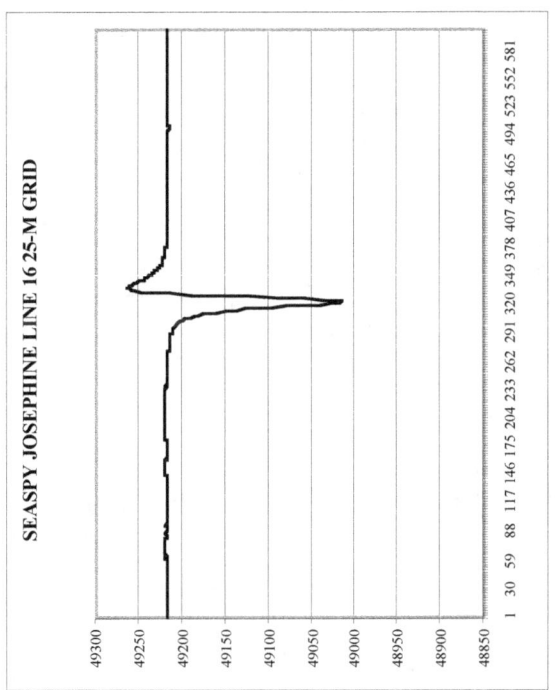

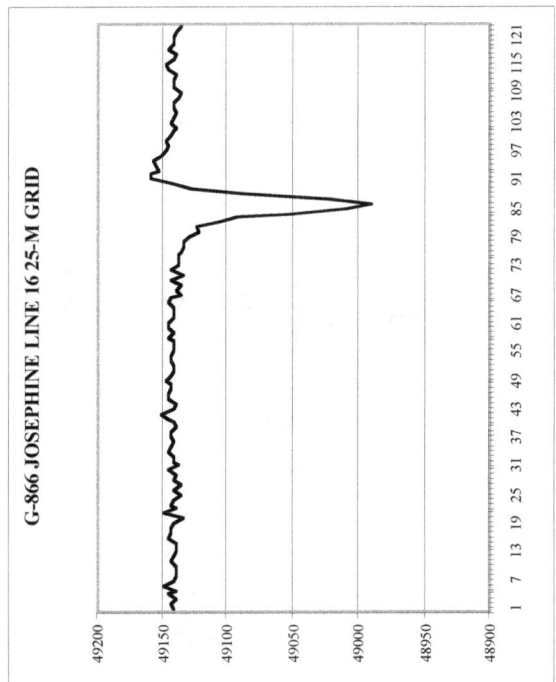

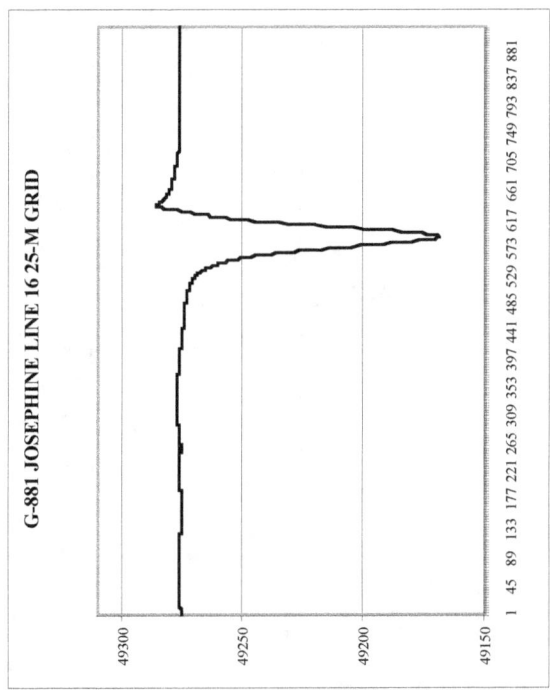

Josephine **25-Meter Survey Interval Grid Strip charts. Y-axis is the gamma scale, X-axis is the sampling rate.**

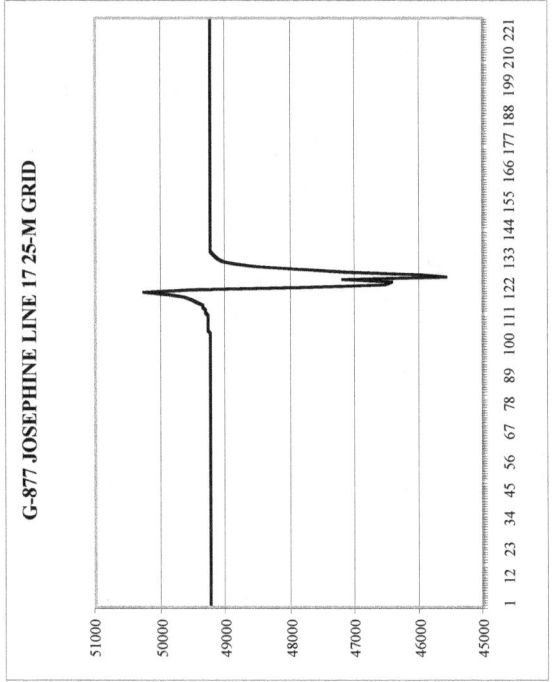

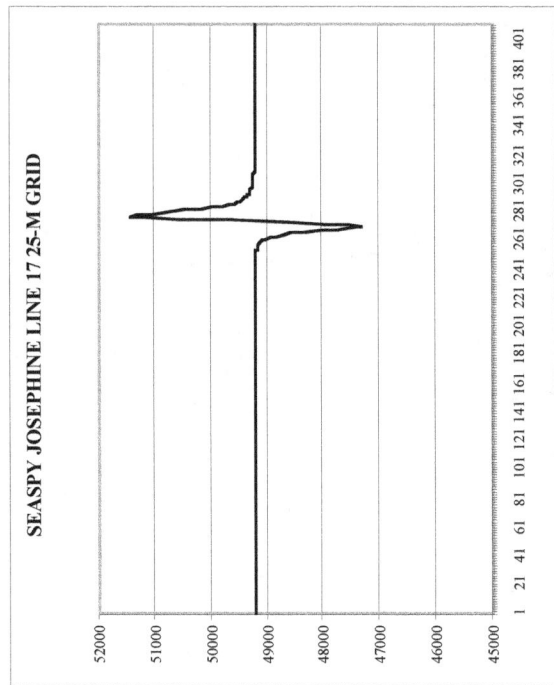

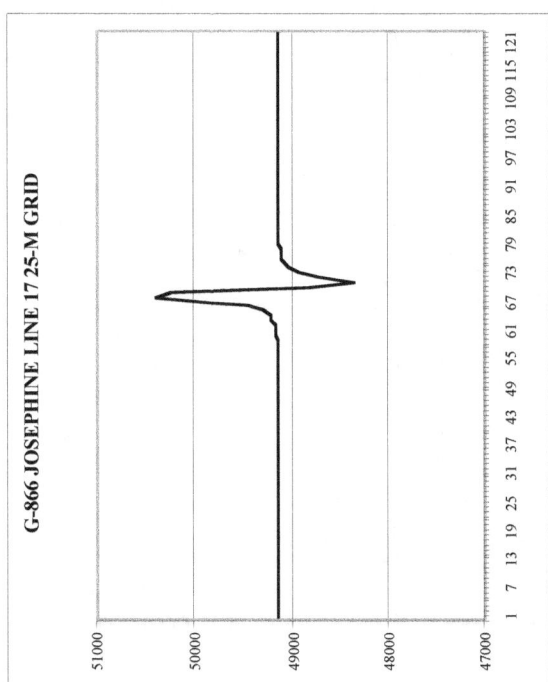

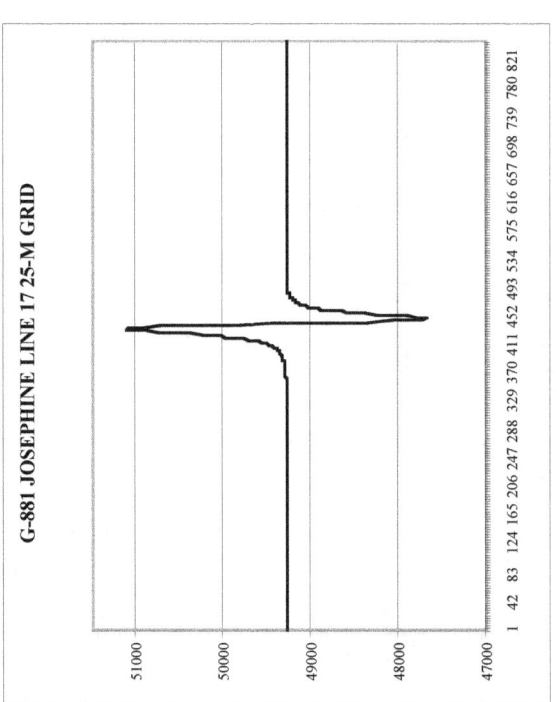

Josephine 25-Meter Survey Interval Grid Strip charts. Y-axis is the gamma scale, X-axis is the sampling rate.

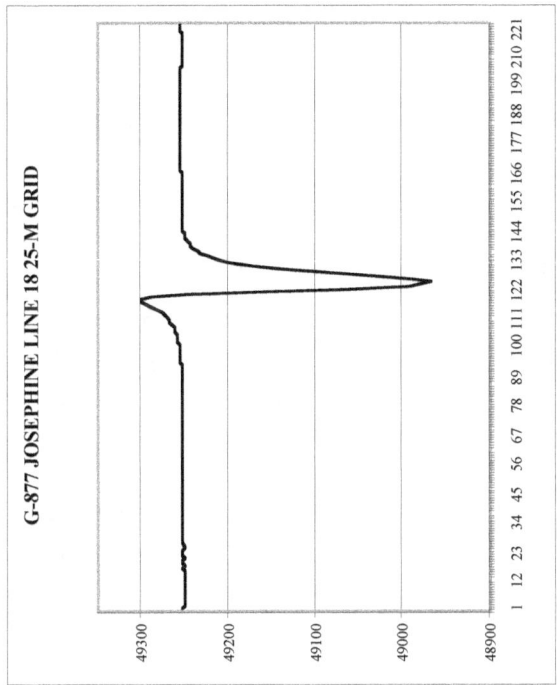

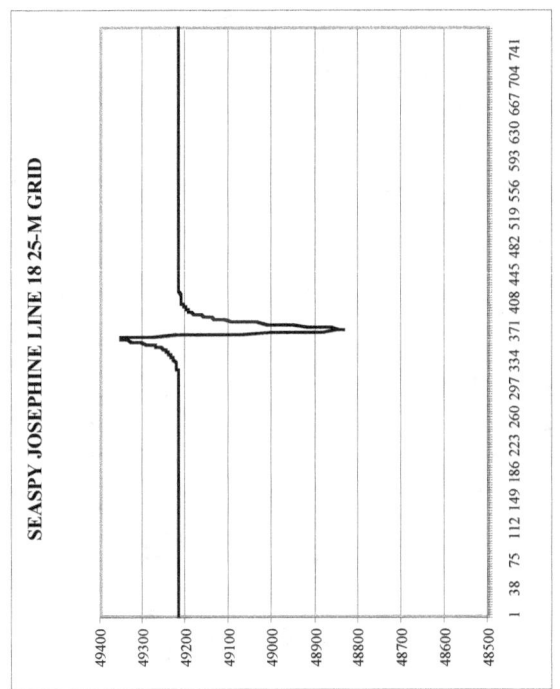

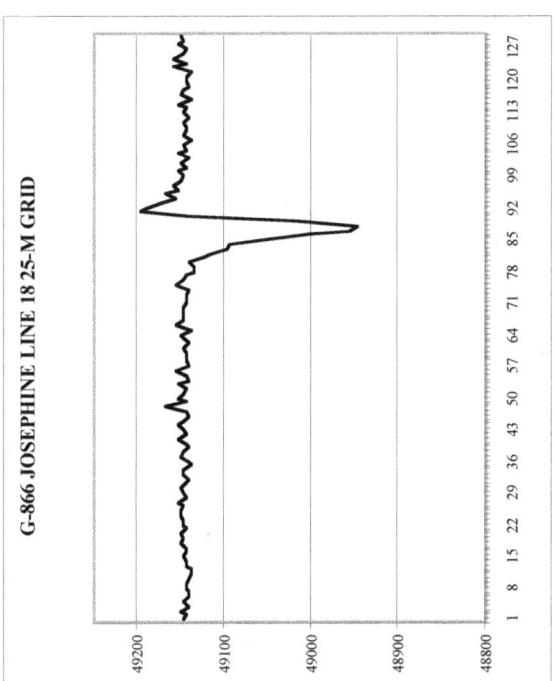

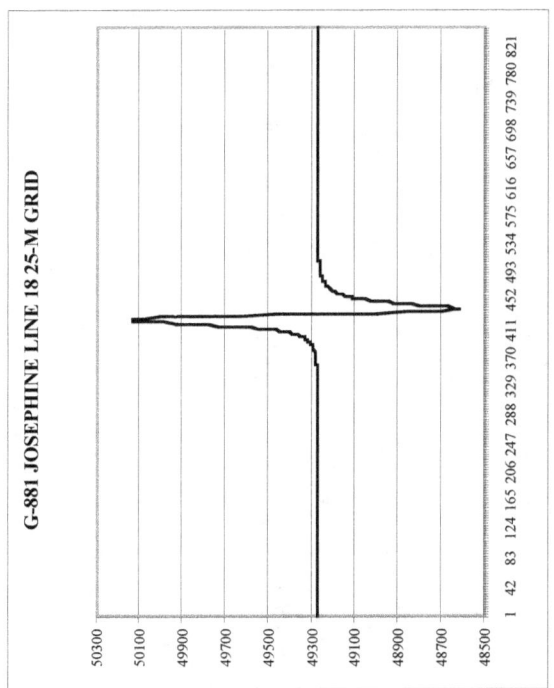

Josephine 25-Meter Survey Interval Grid Strip charts. Y-axis is the gamma scale, X-axis is the sampling rate.

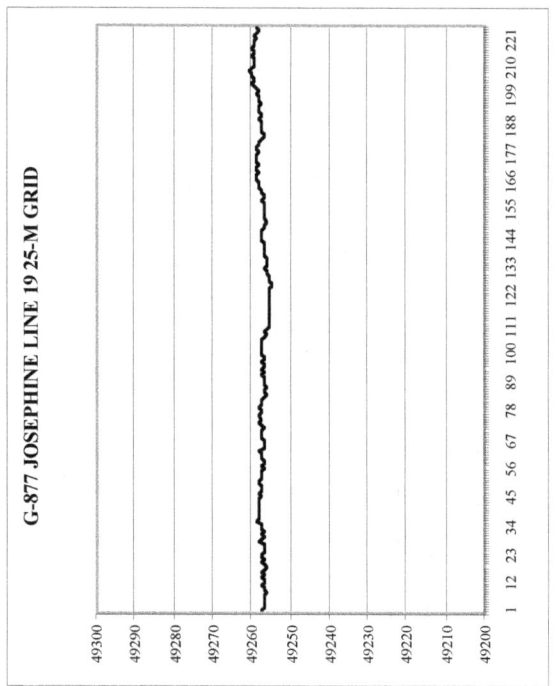

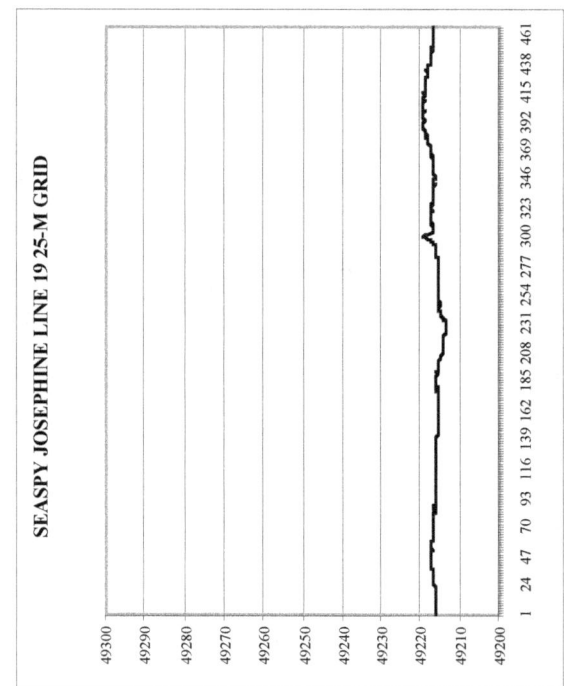

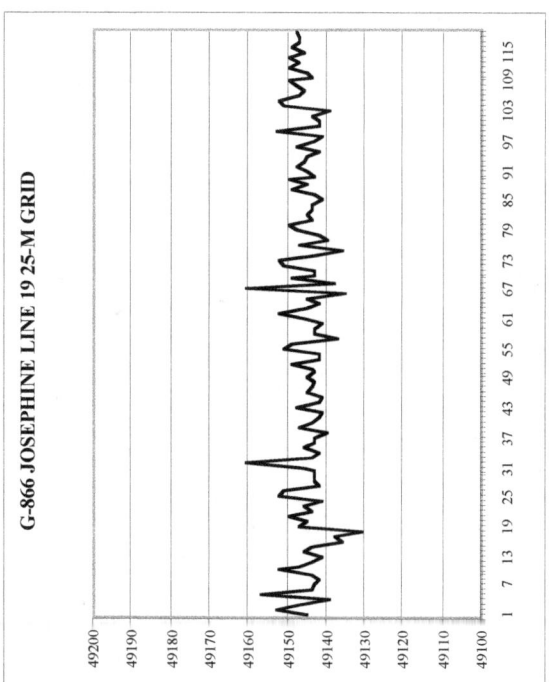

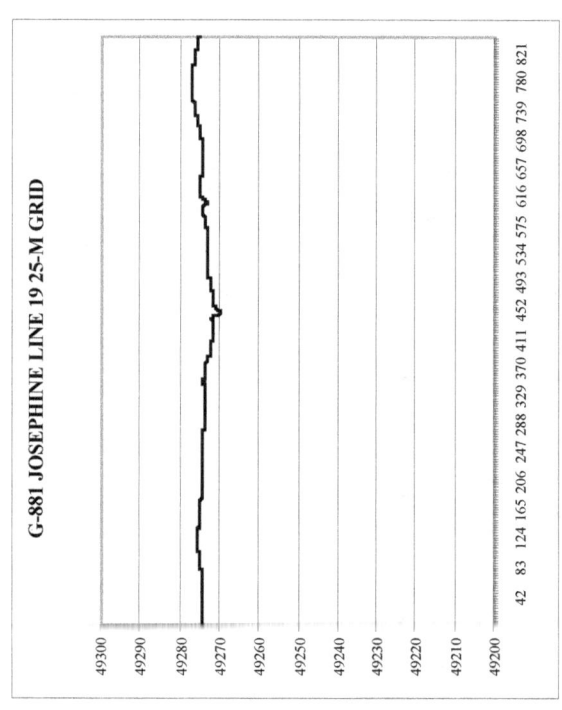

Josephine 25-Meter Survey Interval Grid Strip charts. Y-axis is the gamma scale, X-axis is the sampling rate.

APPENDIX J

STRIPCHARTS BY LINE FOR EACH INSTRUMENT
JOSEPHINE **30-METER SURVEY INTERVAL 4-KNOT GRID**

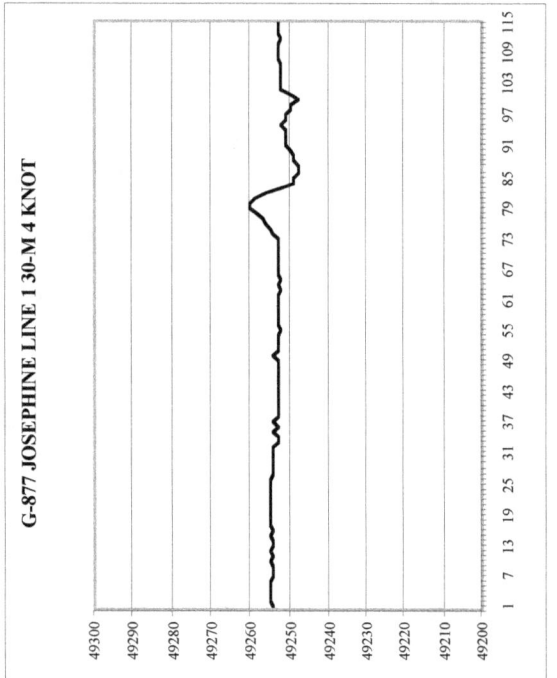

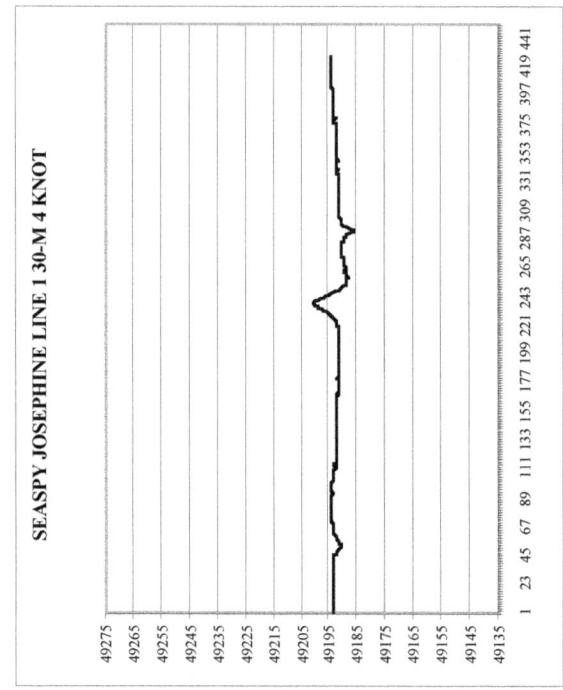

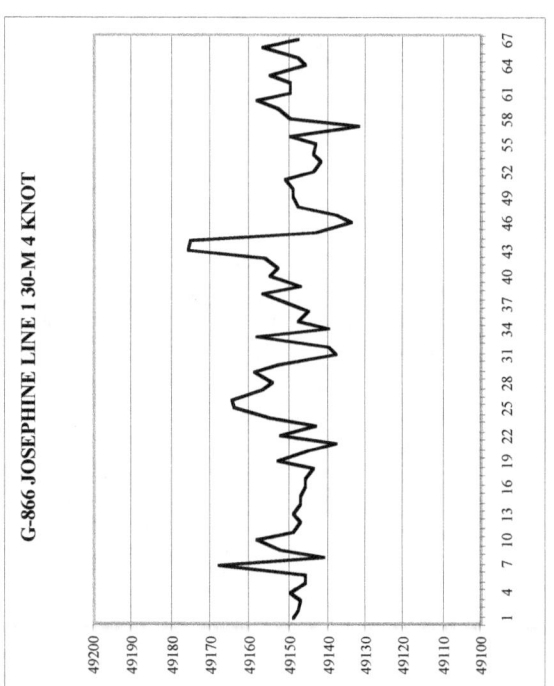

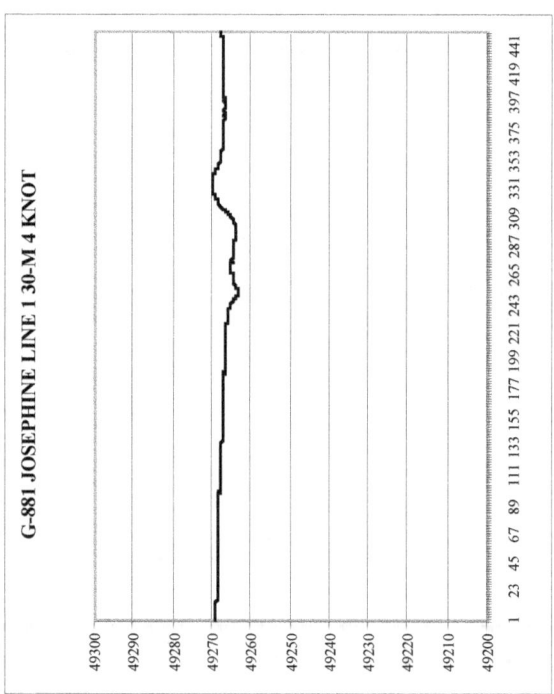

Josephine 30-Meter Survey Interval 4-Knot Grid Strip charts. Y-axis is the gamma scale, X-axis is the sampling rate.

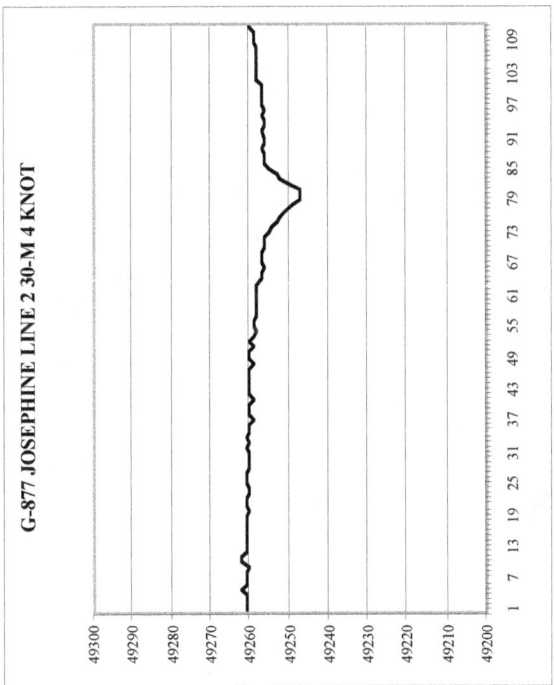

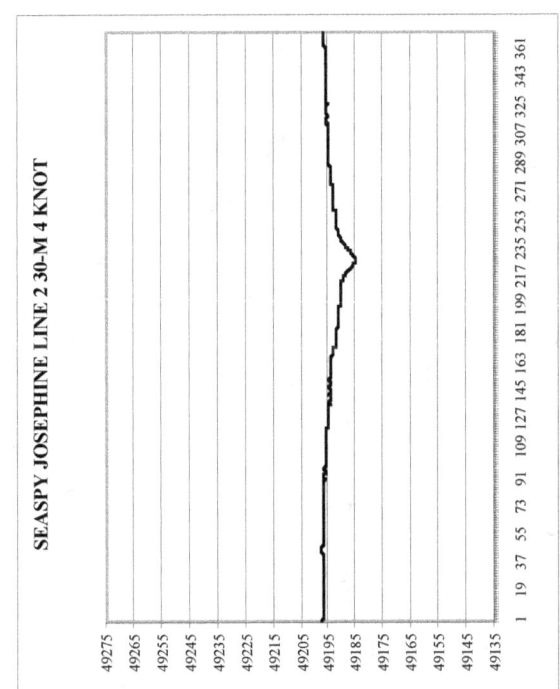

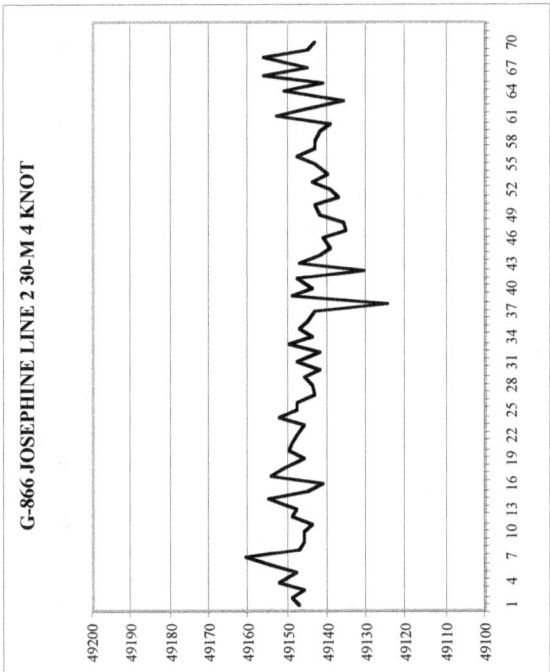

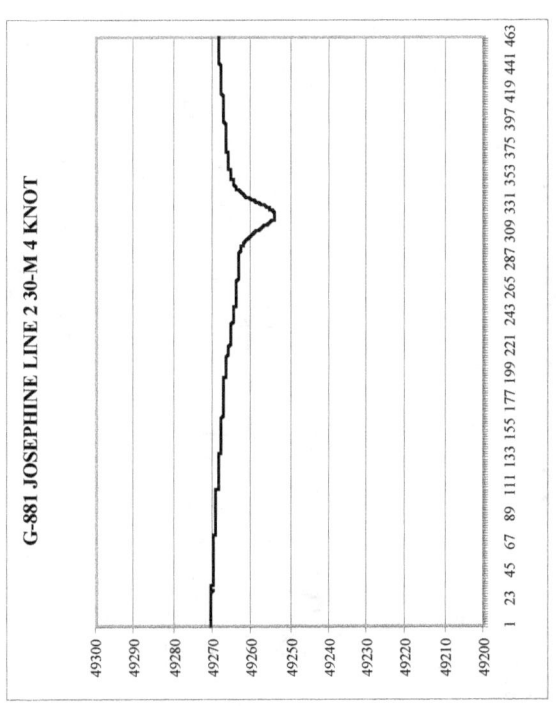

Josephine **30-Meter Survey Interval 4-Knot Grid Strip charts. Y-axis is the gamma scale, X-axis is the sampling rate.**

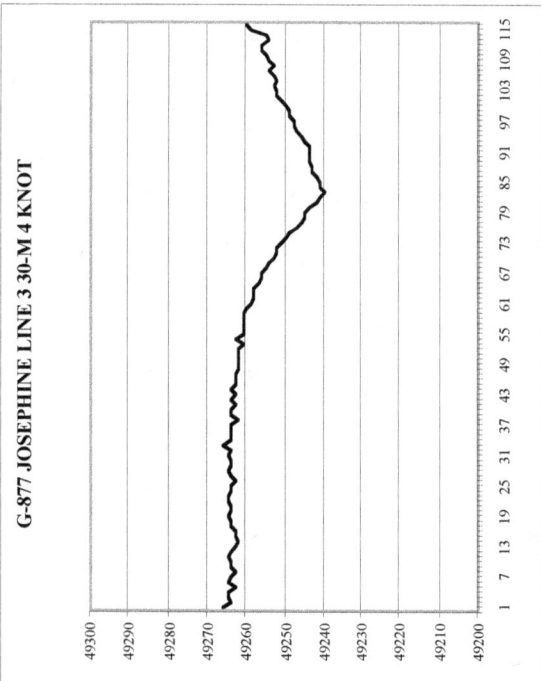

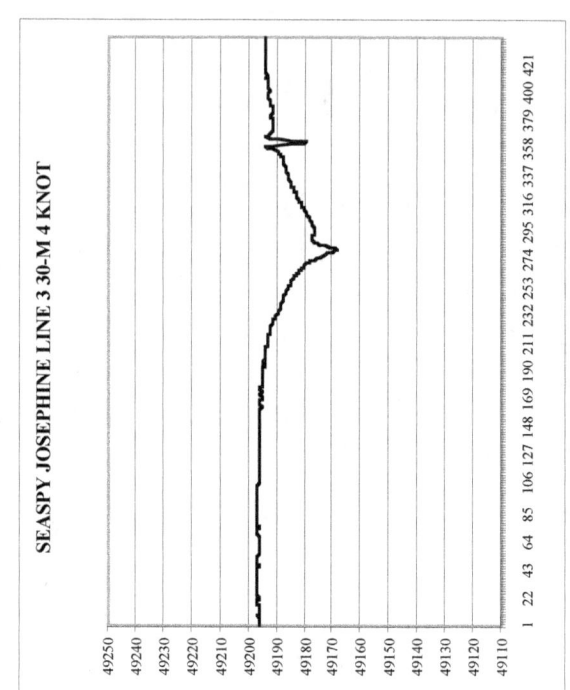

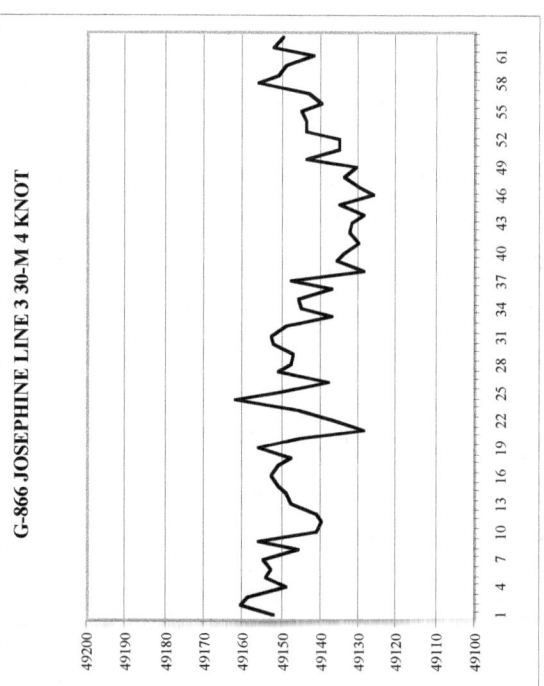

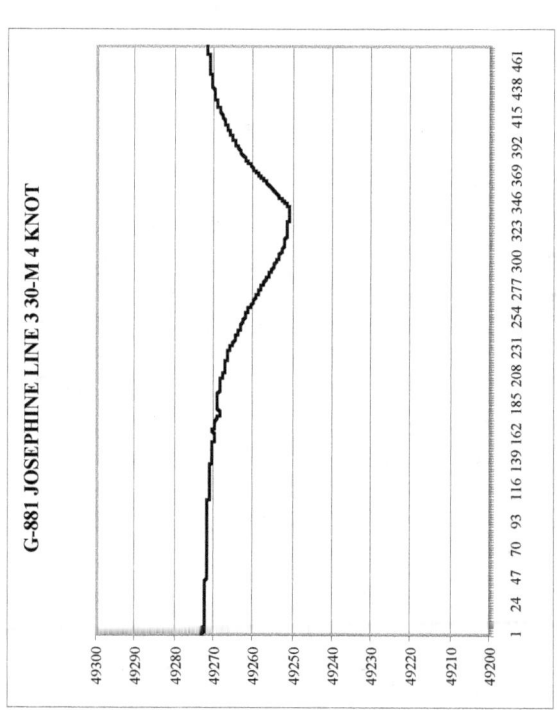

Josephine 30-Meter Survey Interval 4-Knot Grid Strip charts. Y-axis is the gamma scale, X-axis is the sampling rate.

J-5

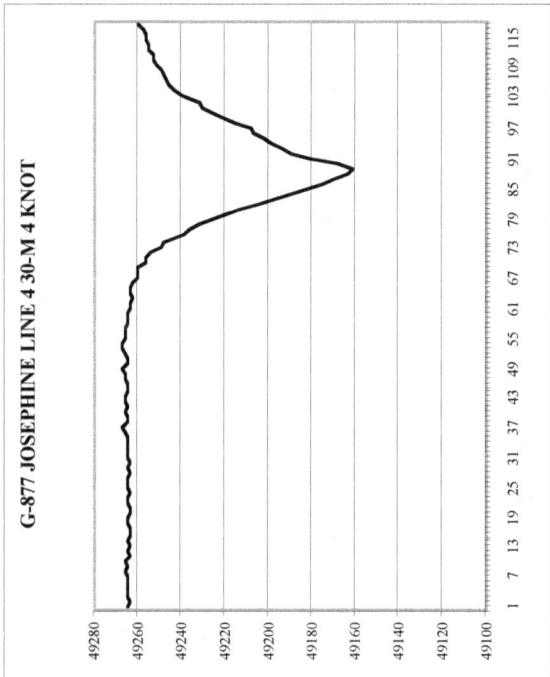

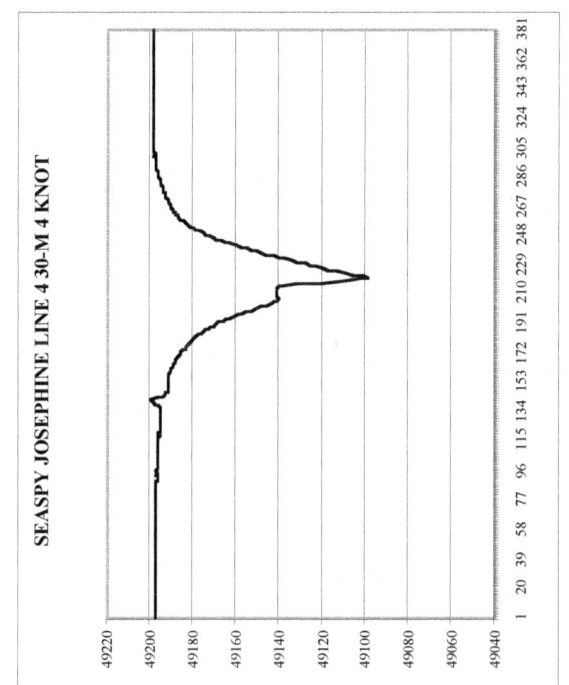

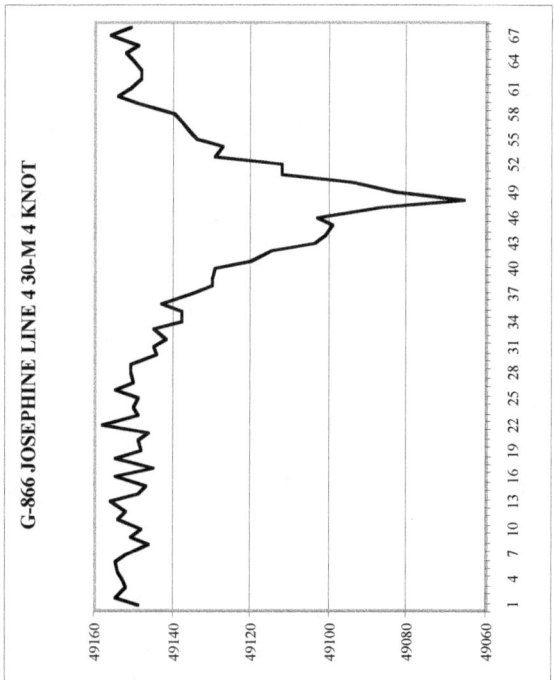

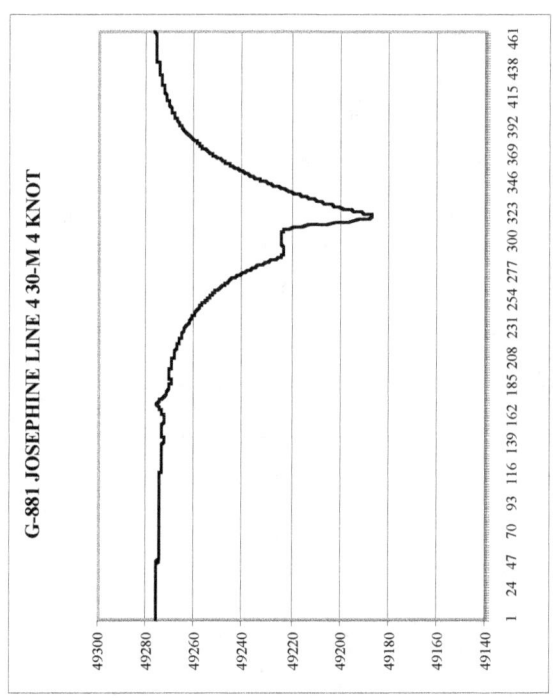

Josephine 30-Meter Survey Interval 4-Knot Grid Strip charts. Y-axis is the gamma scale, X-axis is the sampling rate.

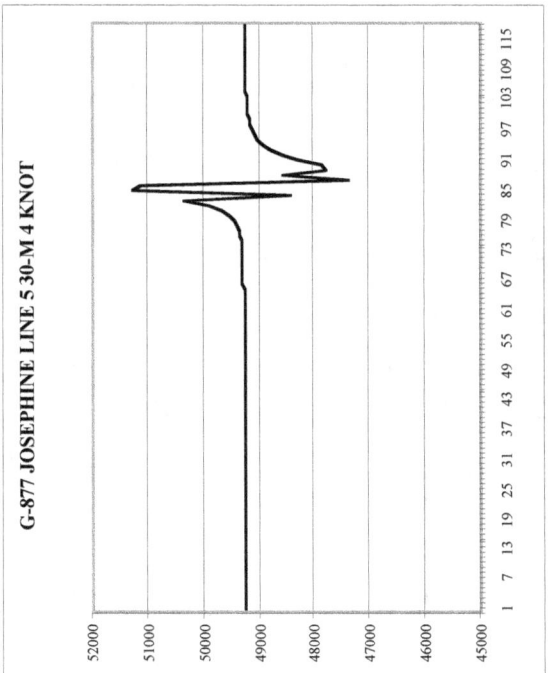

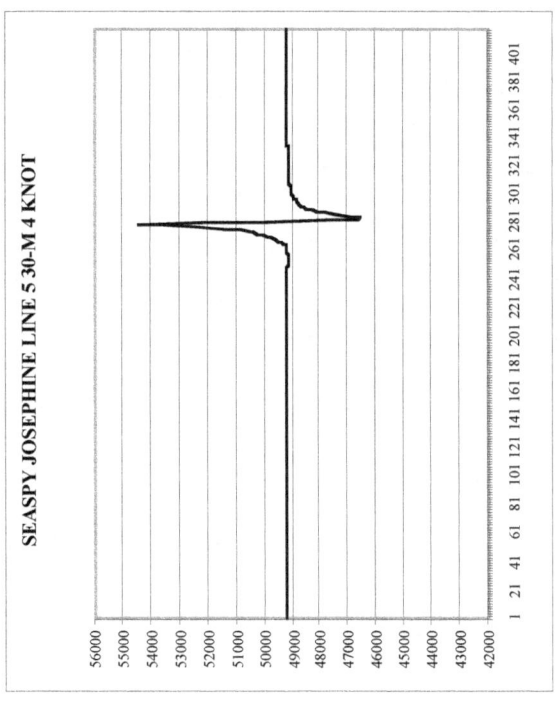

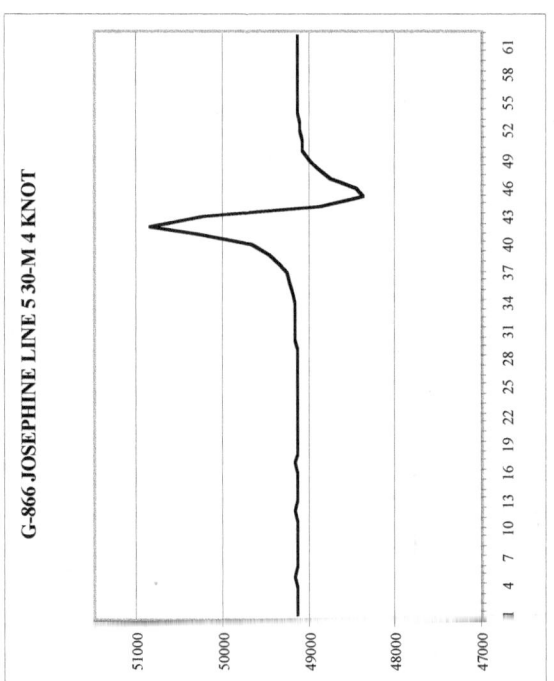

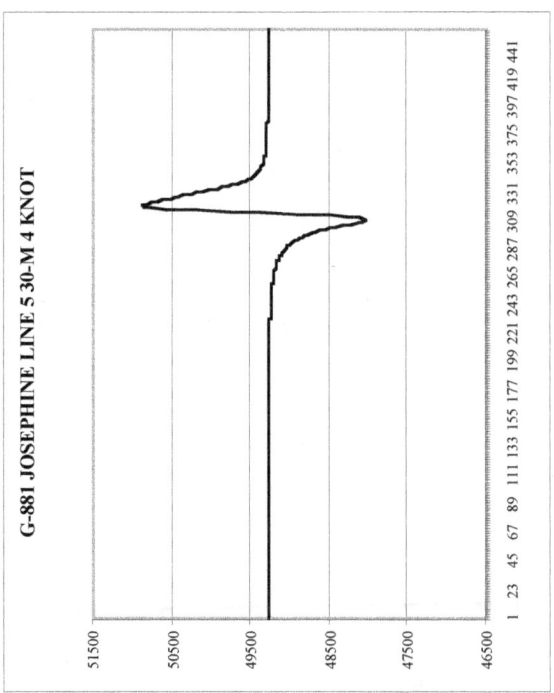

Josephine 30-Meter Survey Interval 4-Knot Grid Strip charts. Y-axis is the gamma scale, X-axis is the sampling rate.

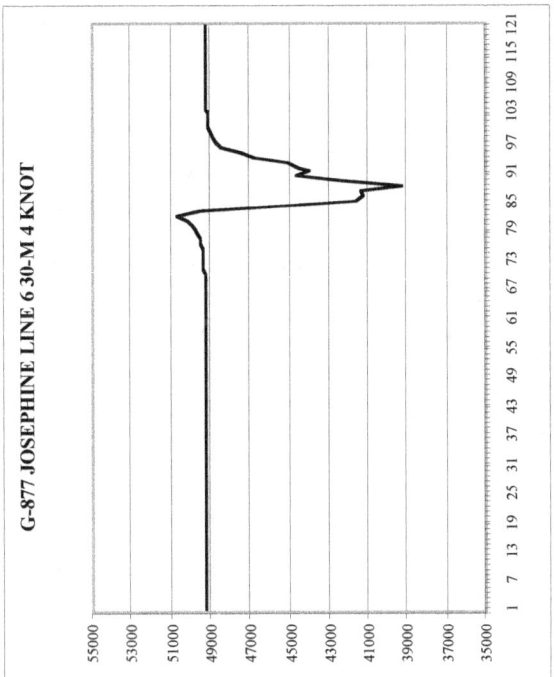

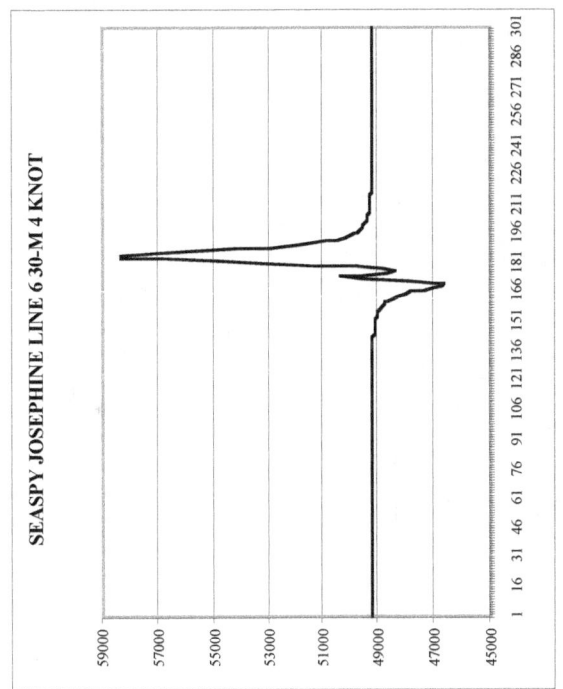

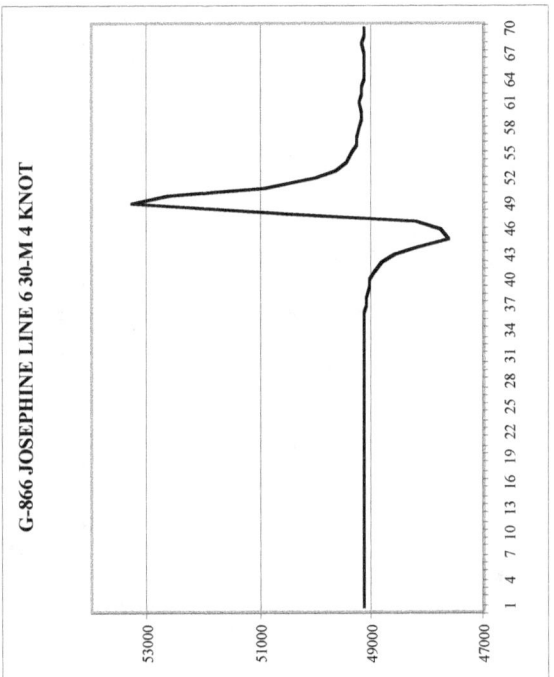

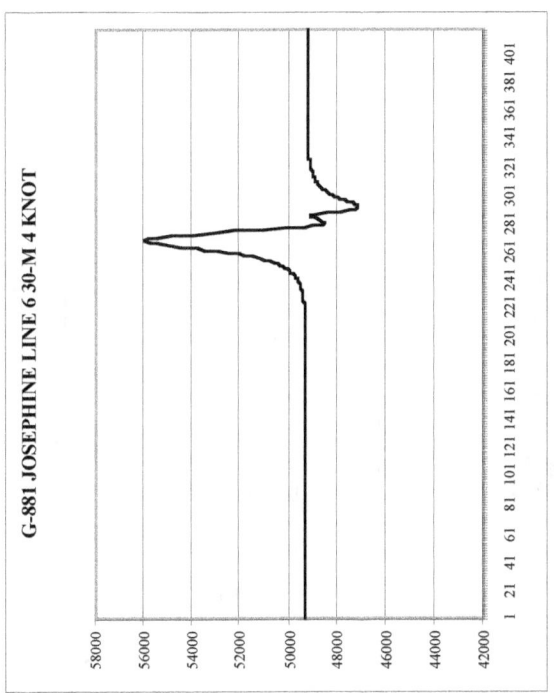

Josephine **30-Meter Survey Interval 4-Knot Grid Strip charts. Y-axis is the gamma scale, X-axis is the sampling rate.**

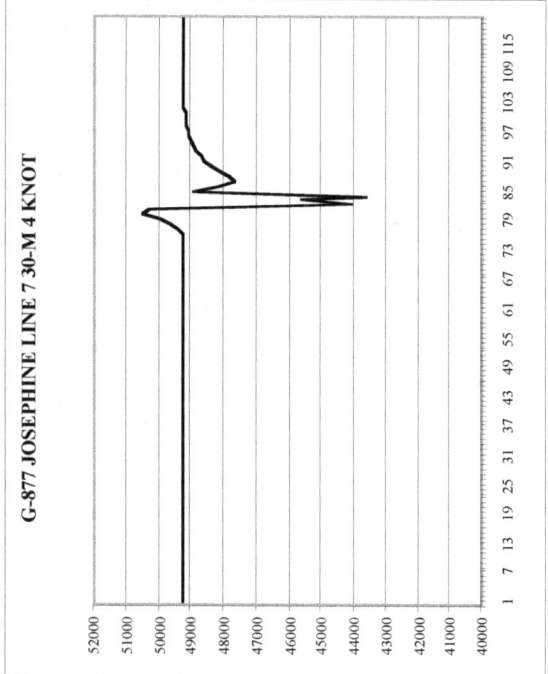

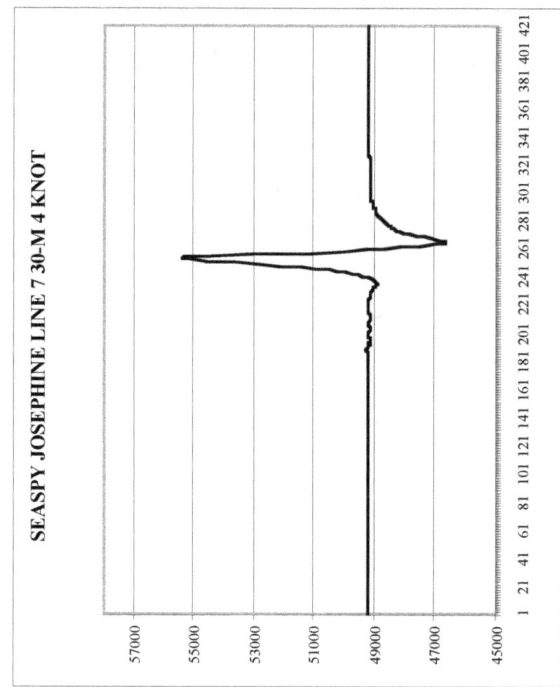

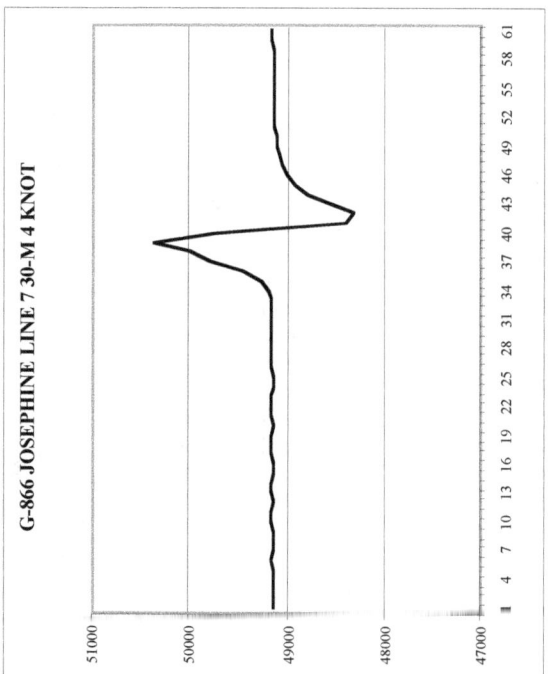

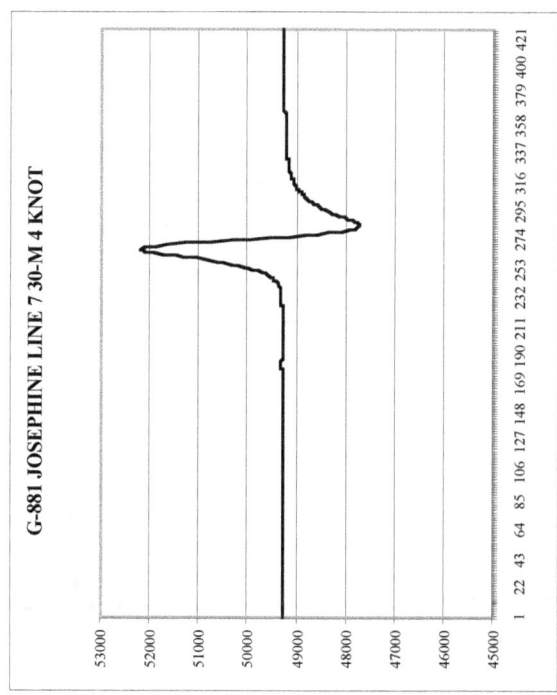

Josephine **30-Meter Survey Interval 4-Knot Grid Strip charts. Y-axis is the gamma scale, X-axis is the sampling rate.**

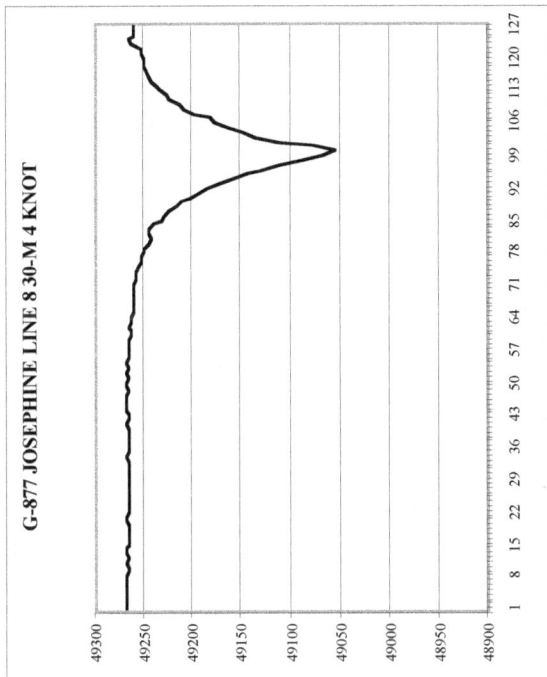

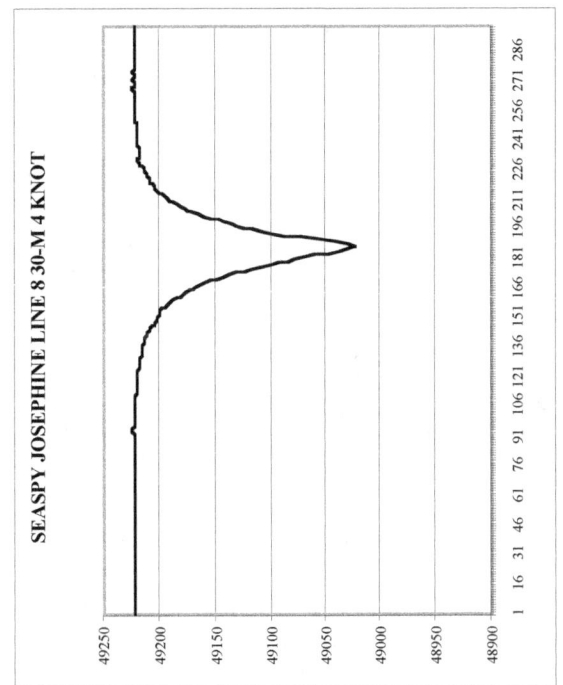

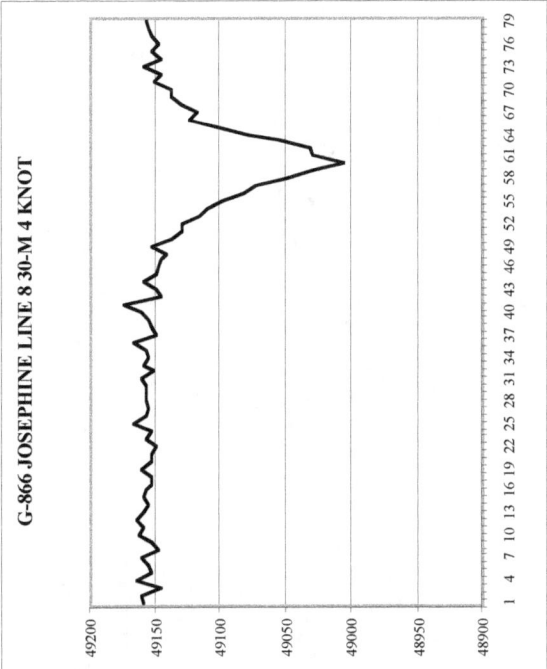

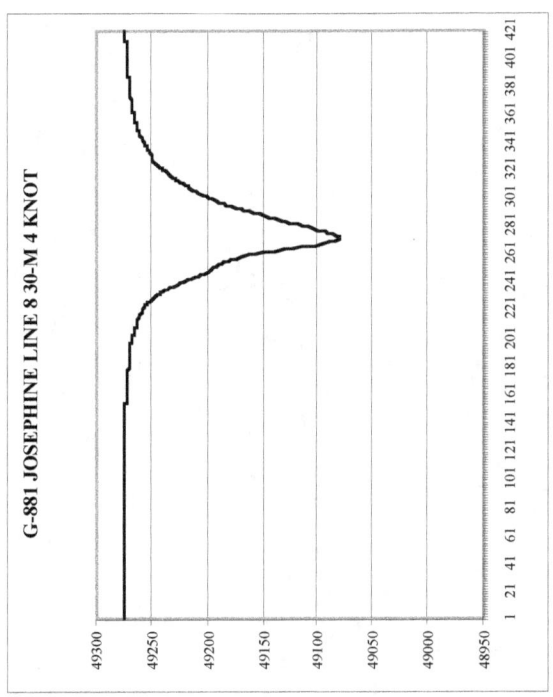

Josephine 30-Meter Survey Interval 4-Knot Grid Strip charts. Y-axis is the gamma scale, X-axis is the sampling rate.

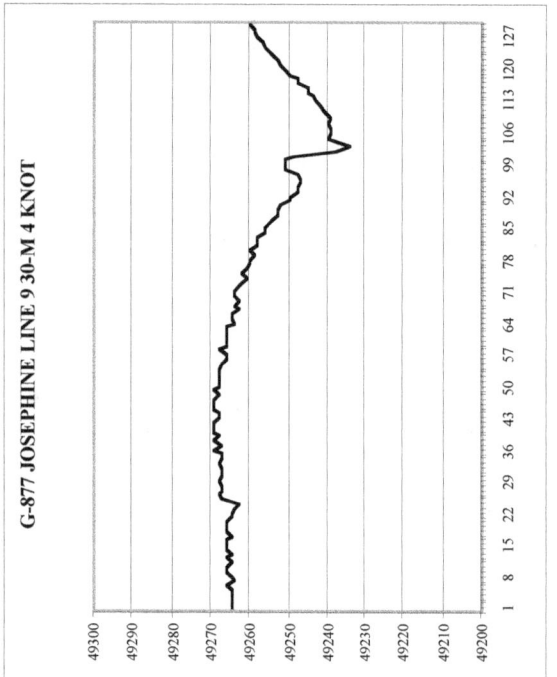

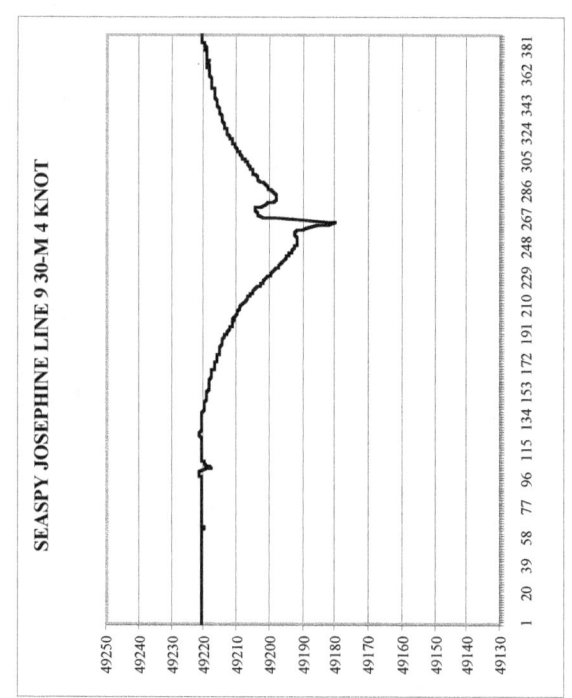

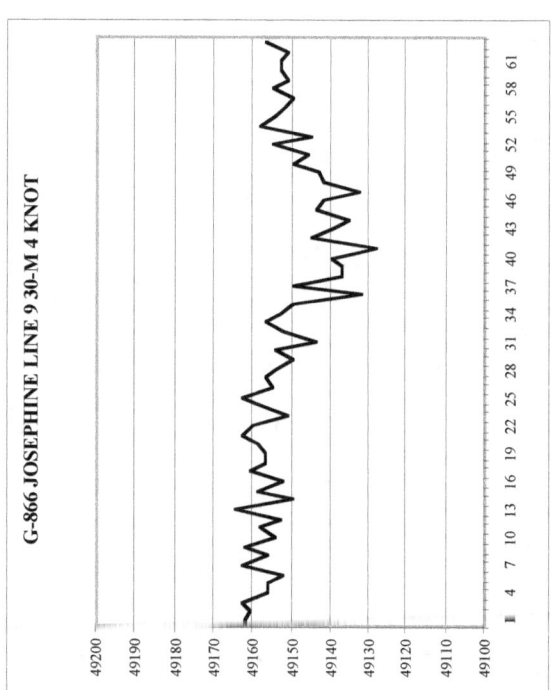

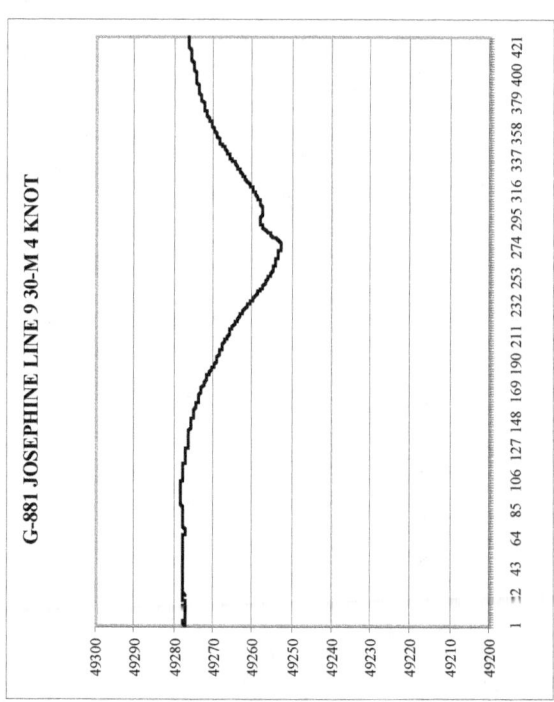

Josephine 30-Meter Survey Interval 4-Knot Grid Strip charts. Y-axis is the gamma scale, X-axis is the sampling rate.

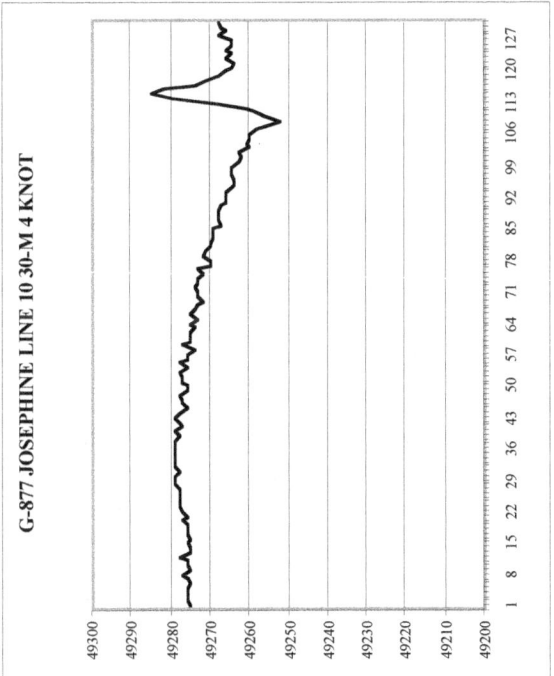

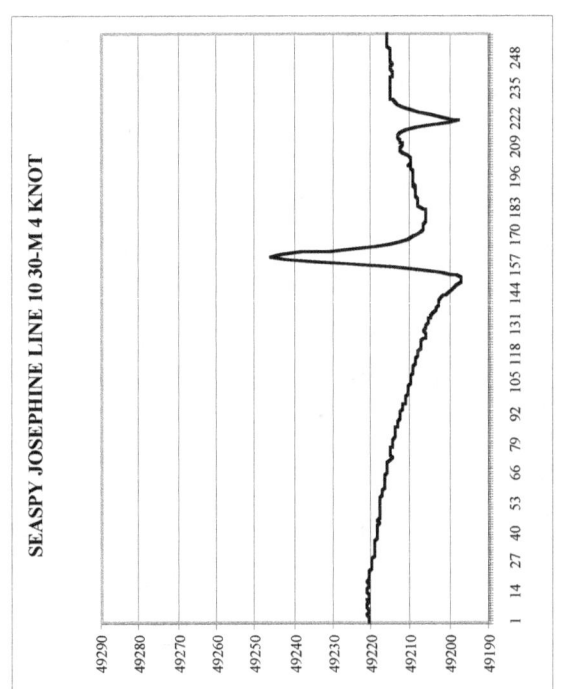

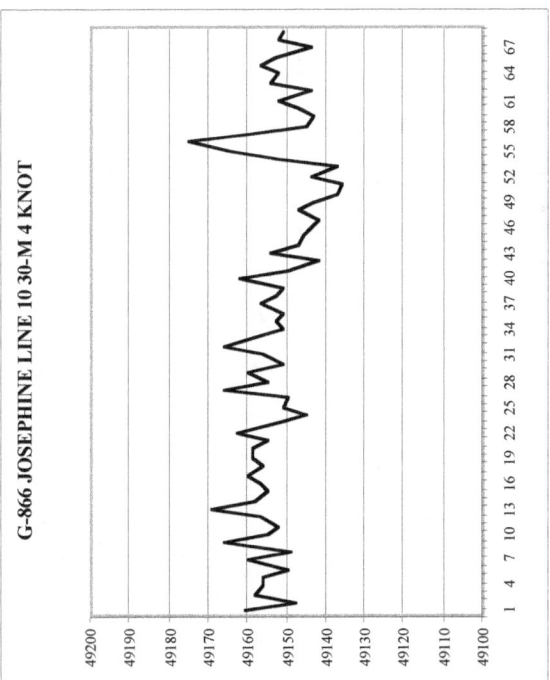

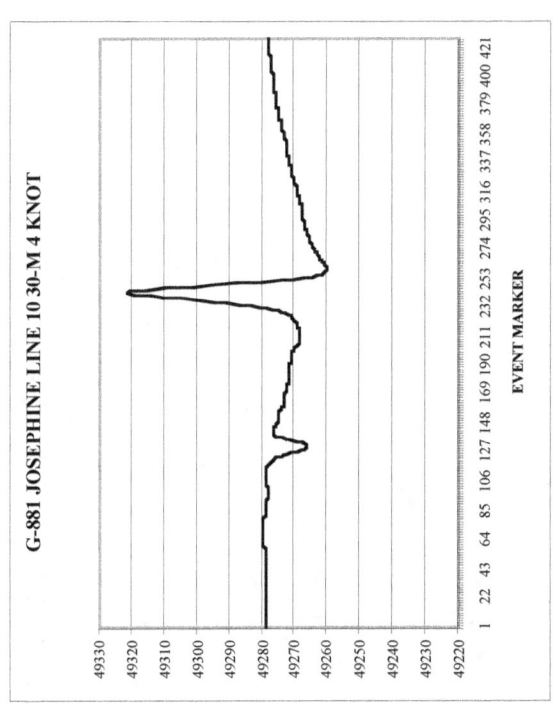

Josephine 30-Meter Survey Interval 4-Knot Grid Strip charts. Y-axis is the gamma scale, X-axis is the sampling rate.

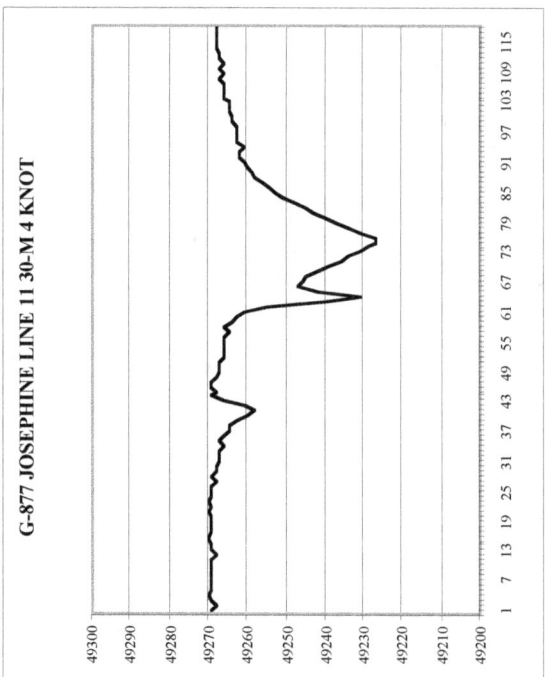

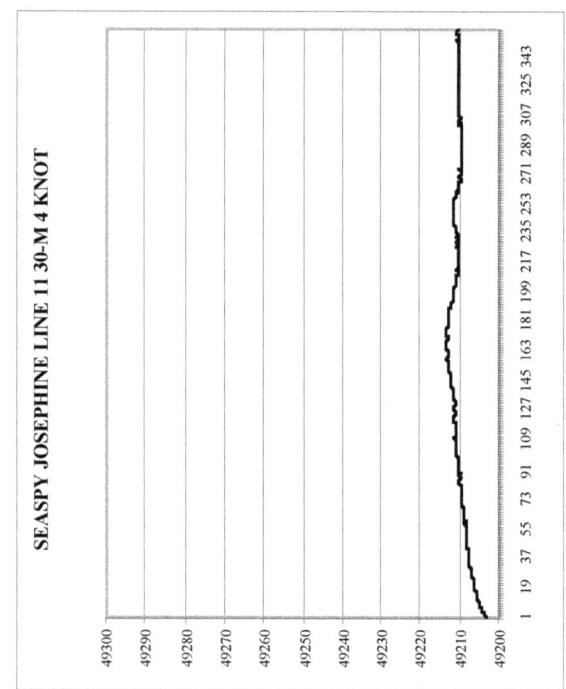

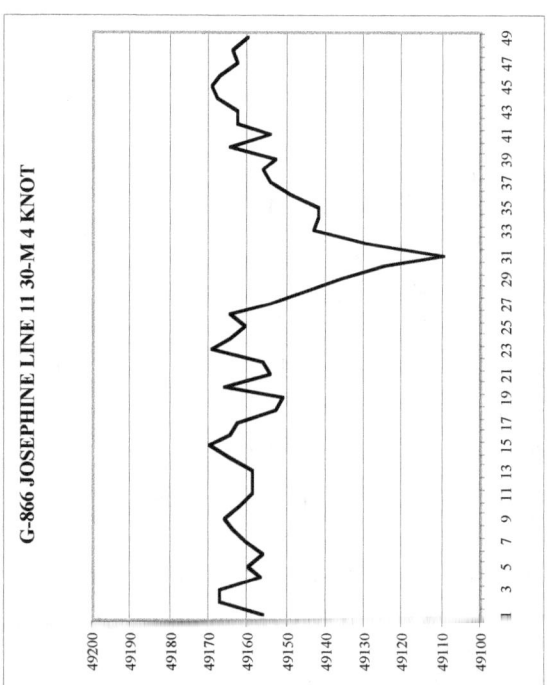

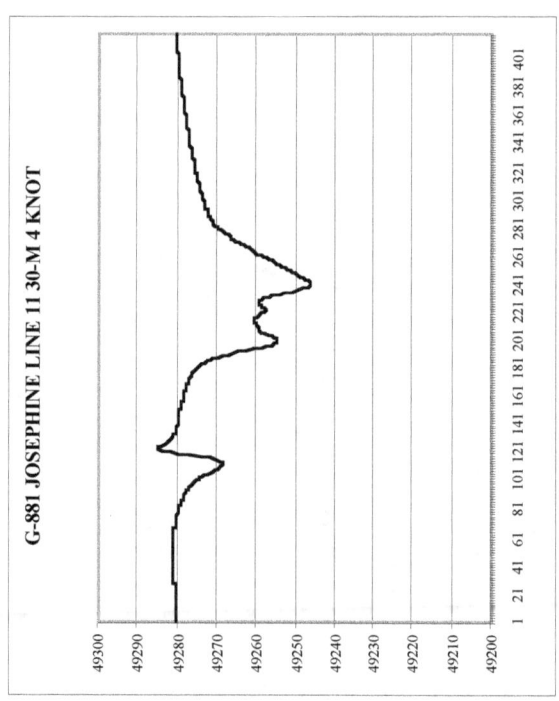

Josephine 30-Meter Survey Interval 4-Knot Grid Strip charts. Y-axis is the gamma scale, X-axis is the sampling rate.

APPENDIX K

STRIPCHARTS BY LINE FOR EACH INSTRUMENT
JOSEPHINE **30-METER SURVEY INTERVAL 7-KNOT GRID**

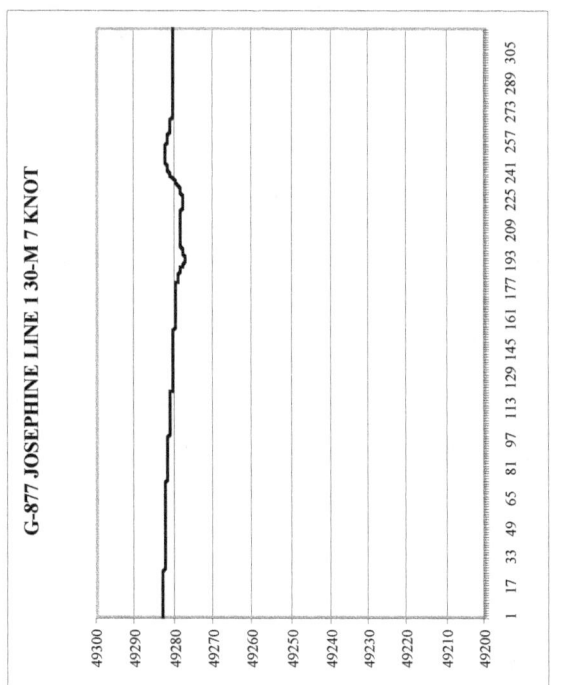

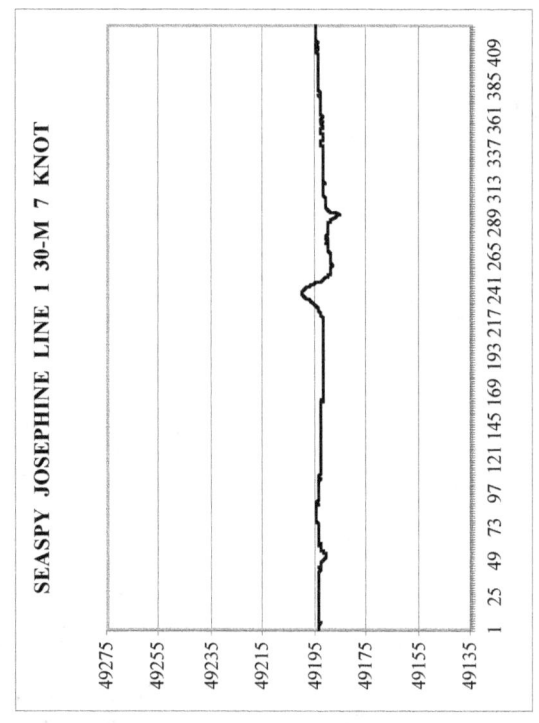

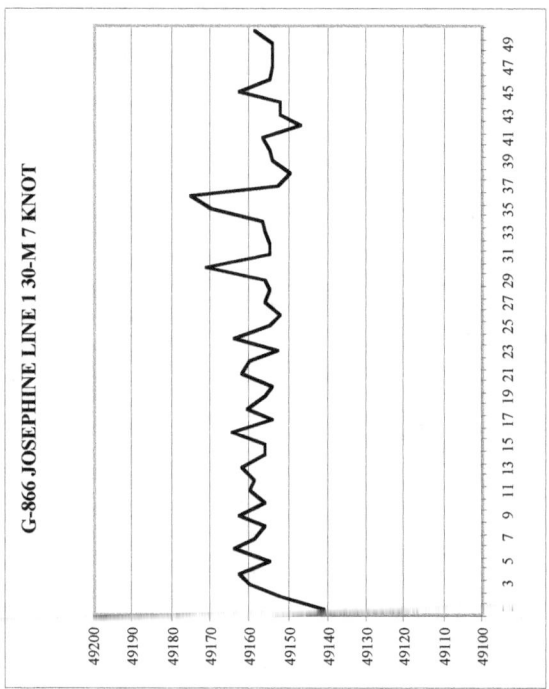

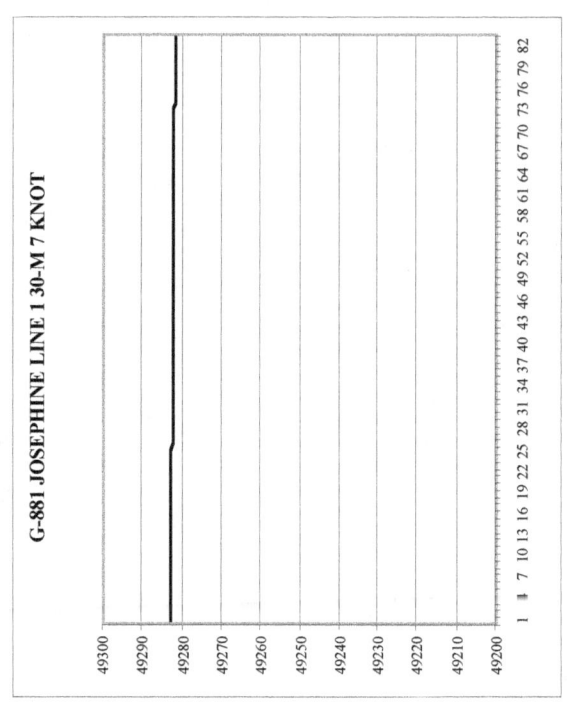

Josephine 30-Meter Survey Interval 7-Knot Grid Strip charts. Y-axis is the gamma scale, X-axis is the sampling rate.

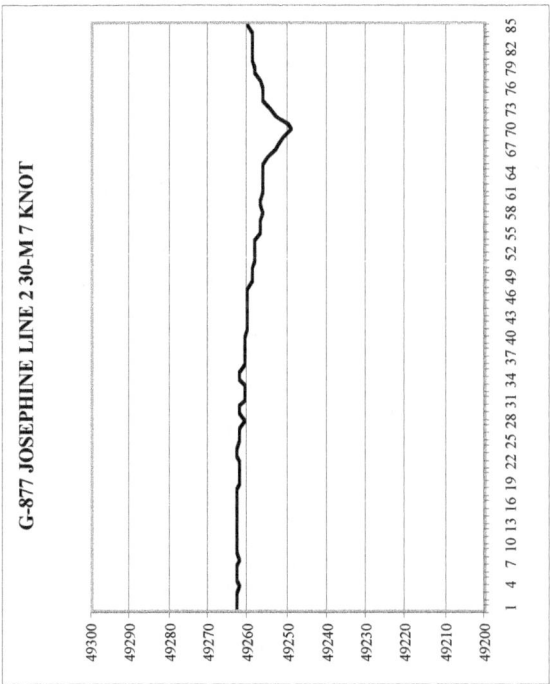

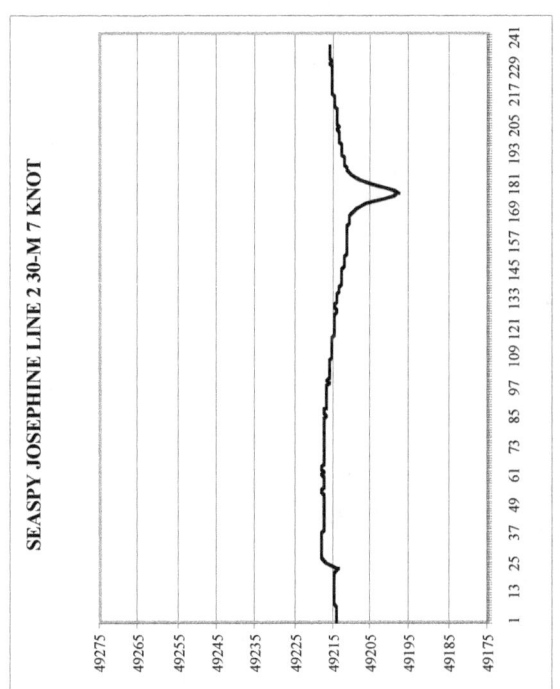

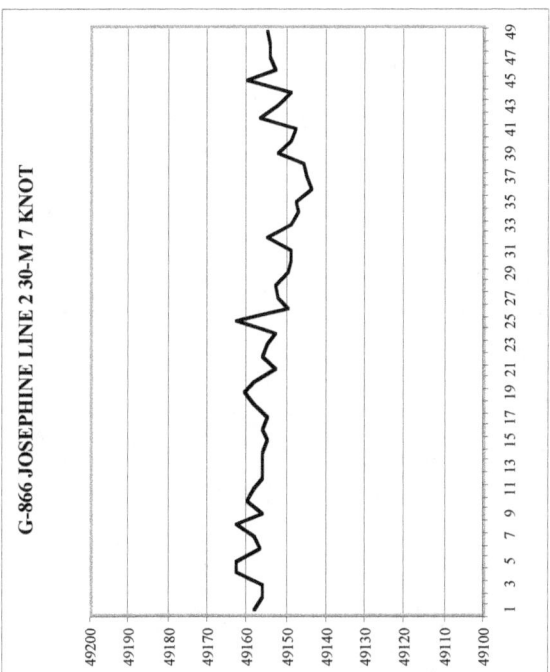

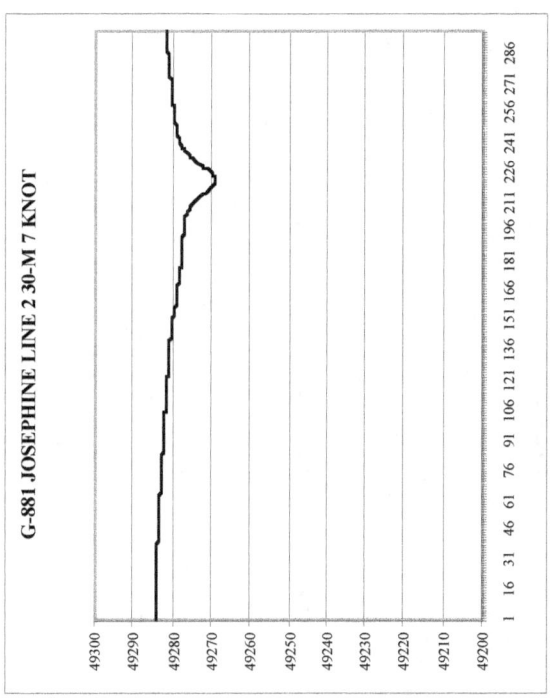

Josephine 30-Meter Survey Interval 7-Knot Grid Strip charts. Y-axis is the gamma scale, X-axis is the sampling rate.

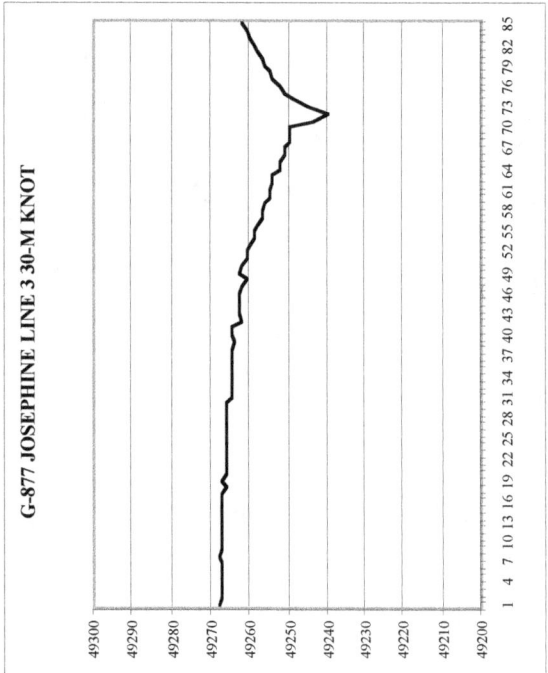

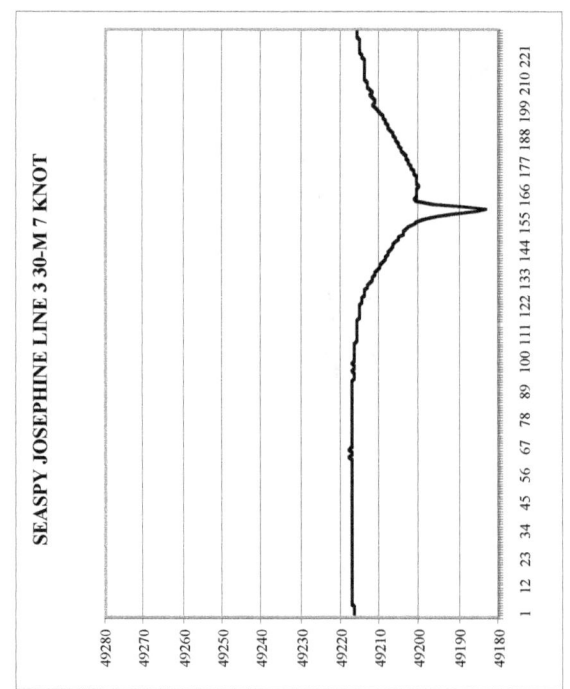

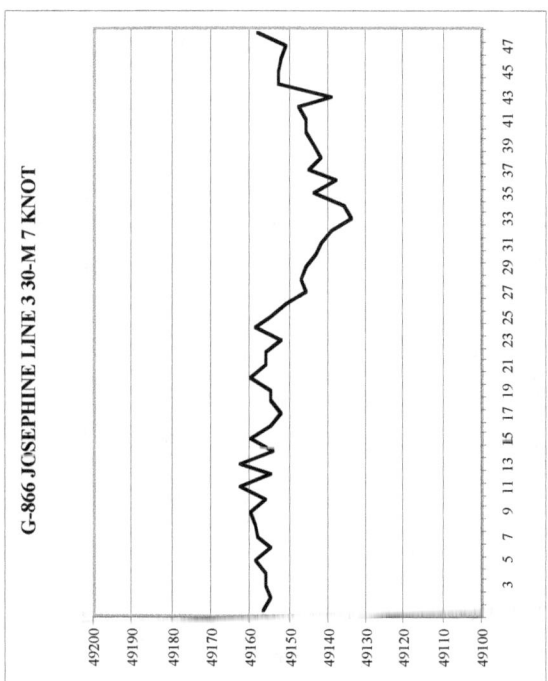

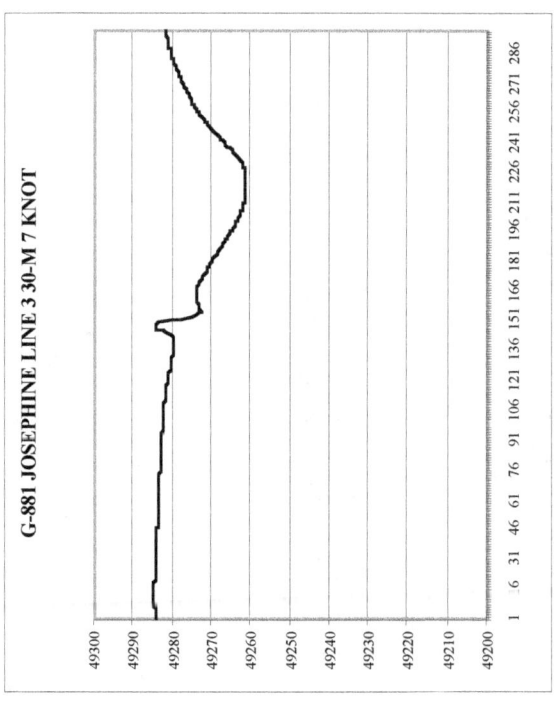

Josephine 30-Meter Survey Interval 7-Knot Grid Strip charts. Y-axis is the gamma scale, X-axis is the sampling rate.

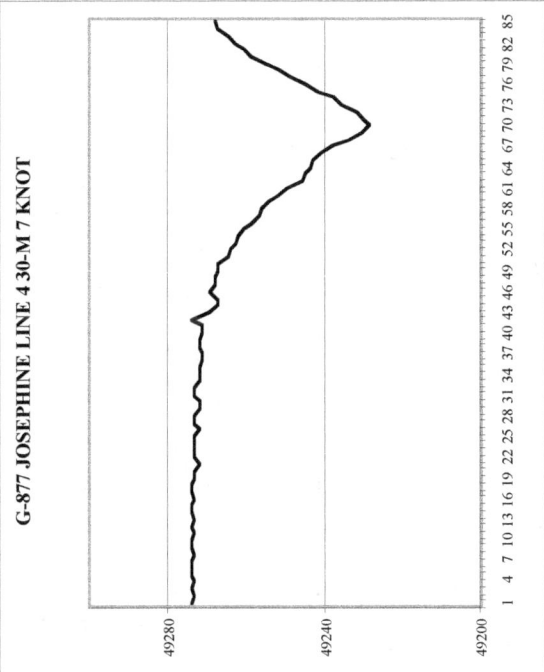

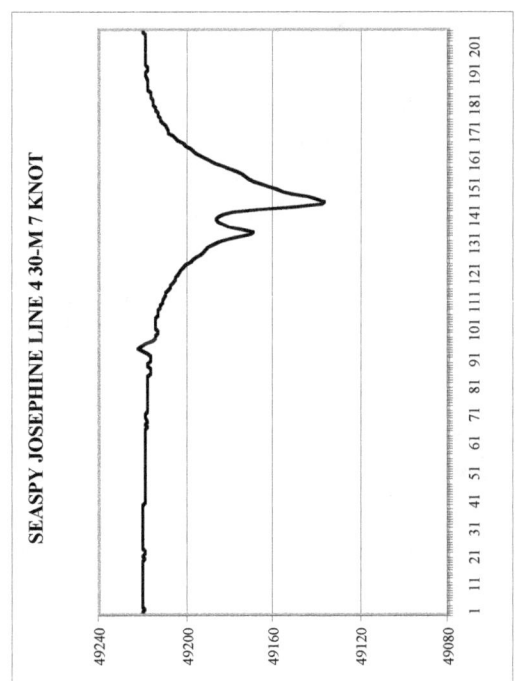

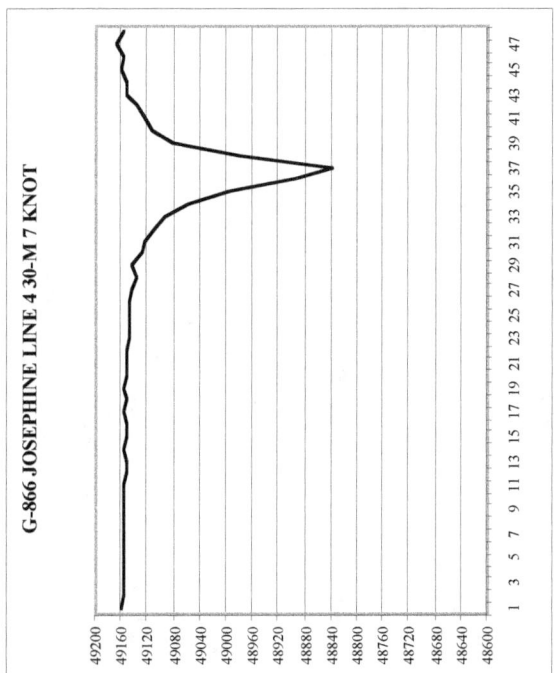

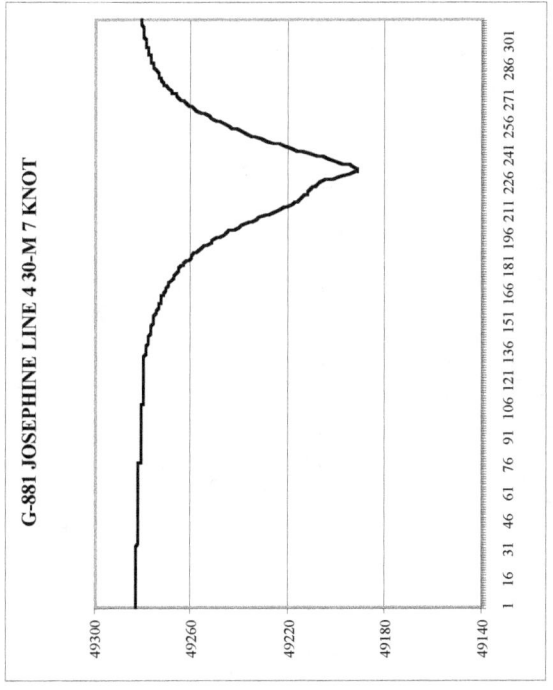

Josephine 30-Meter Survey Interval 7-Knot Grid Strip charts. Y-axis is the gamma scale, X-axis is the sampling rate.

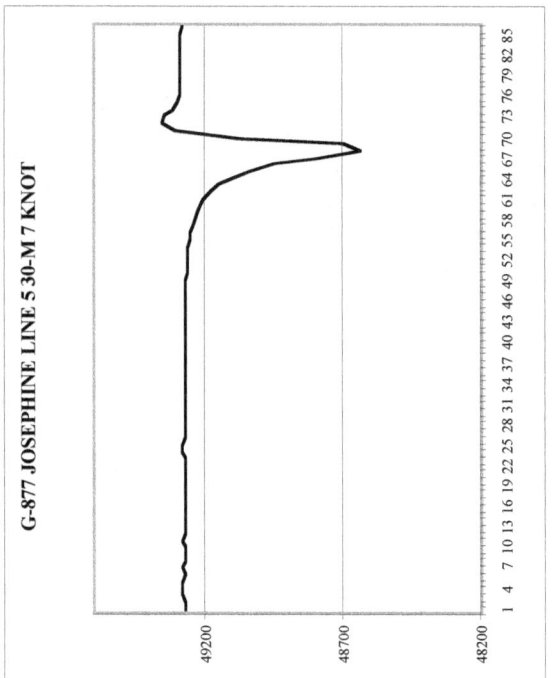

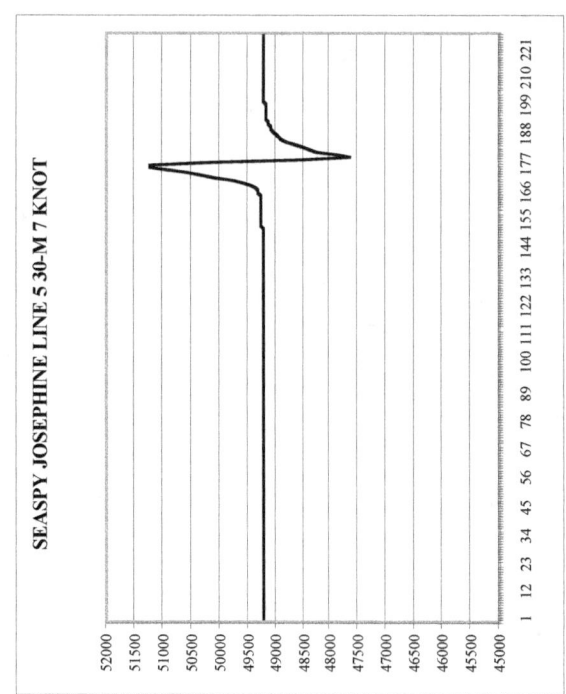

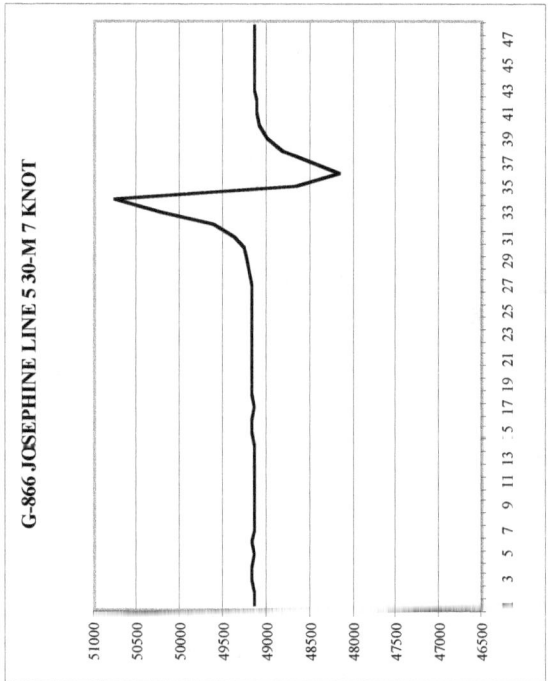

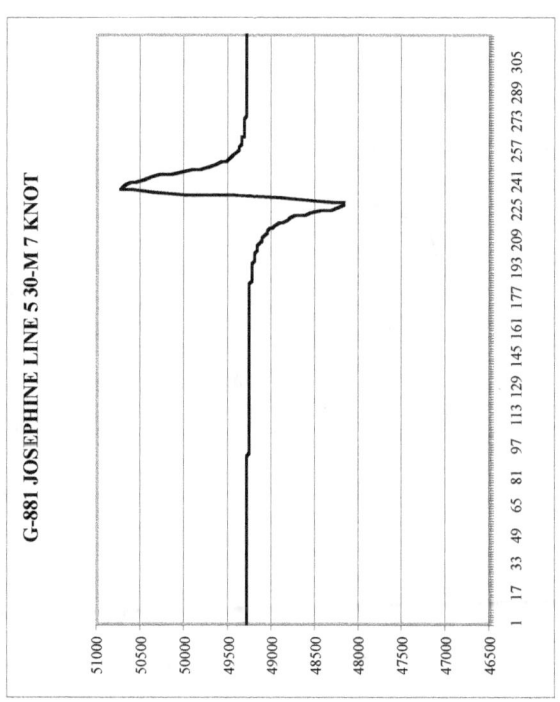

*Josephin*e 30-Meter Survey Interval 7-Knot Grid Strip charts. Y-axis is the gamma scale, X-axis is the sampling rate.

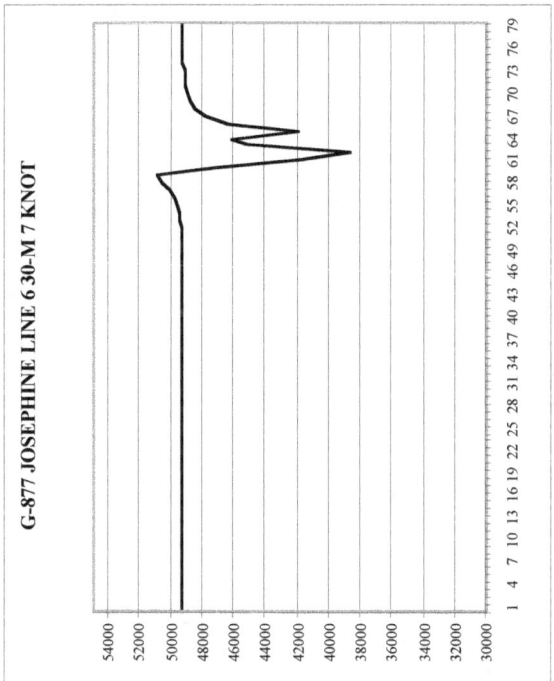

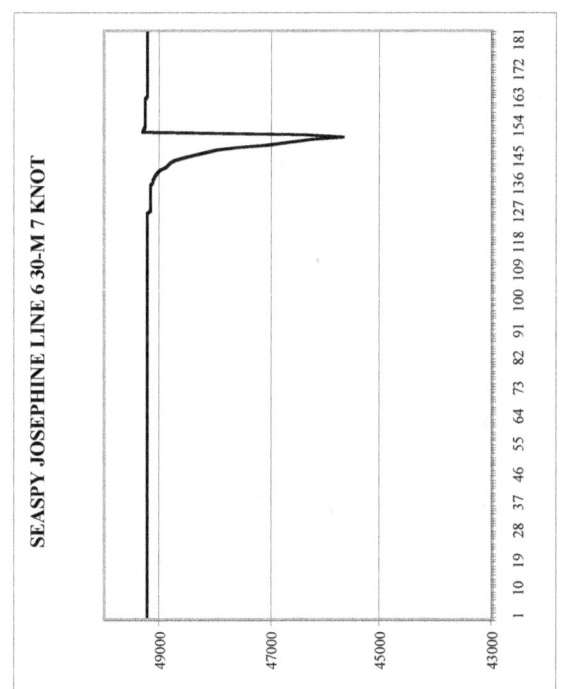

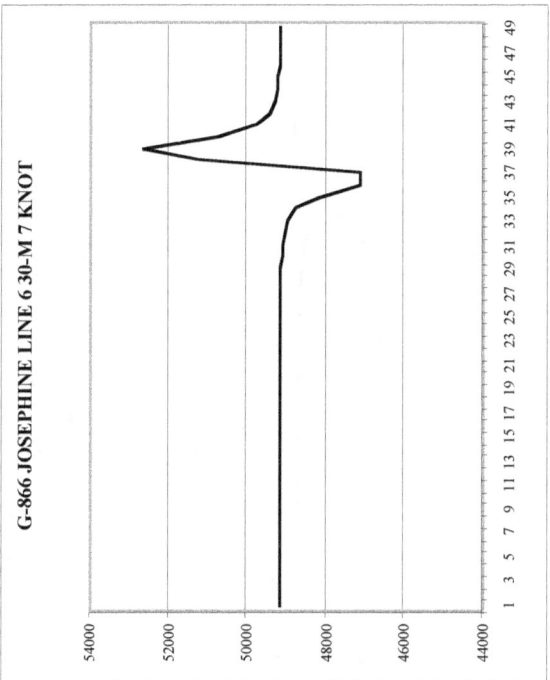

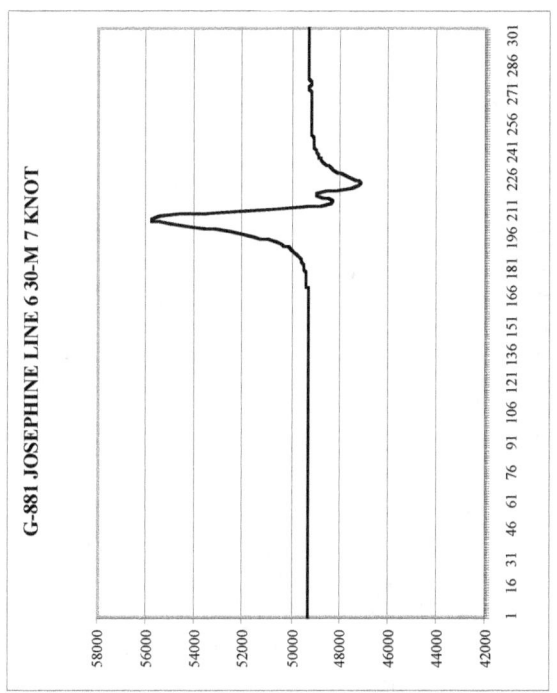

*Josephin*e 30-Meter Survey Interval 7-Knot Grid Strip charts. Y-axis is the gamma scale, X-axis is the sampling rate.

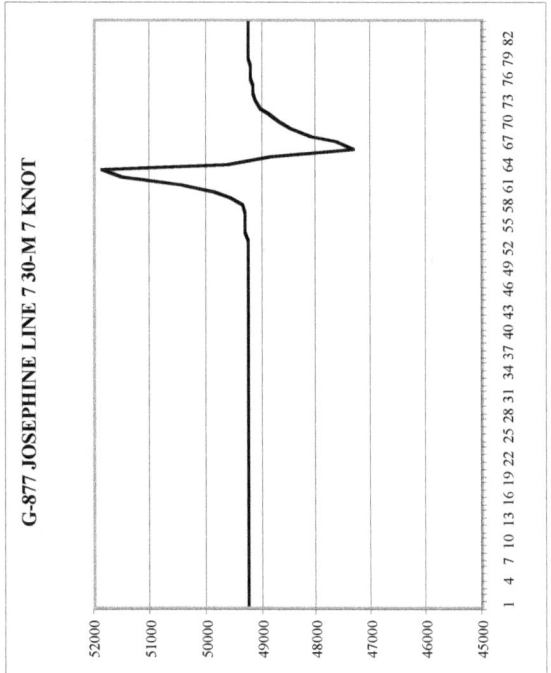

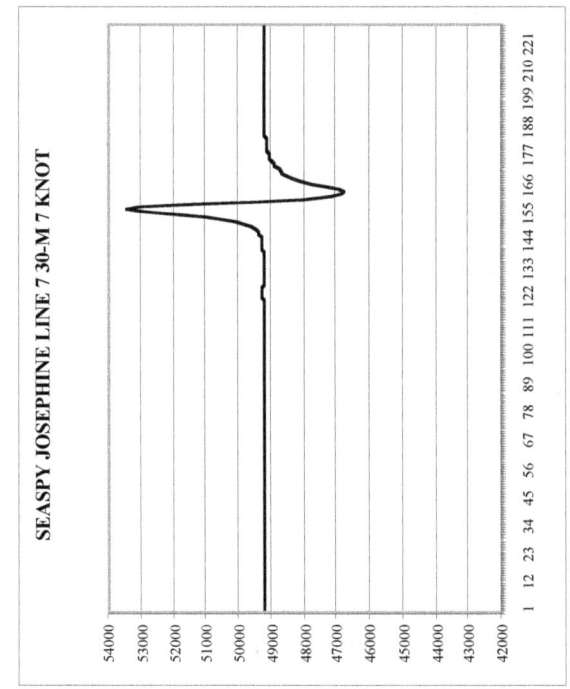

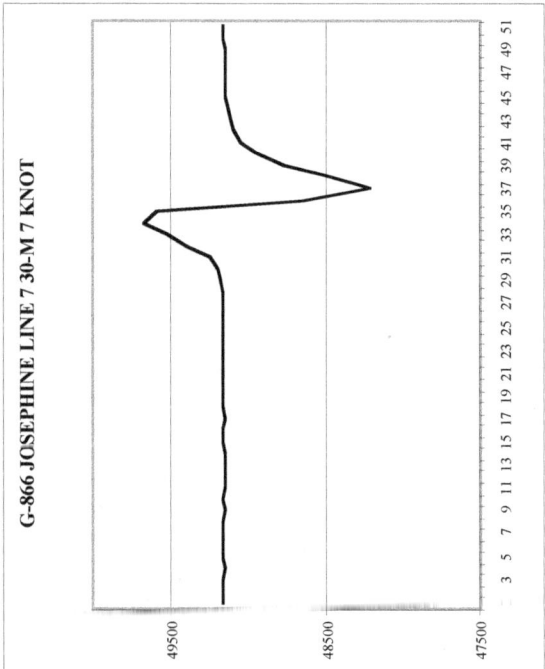

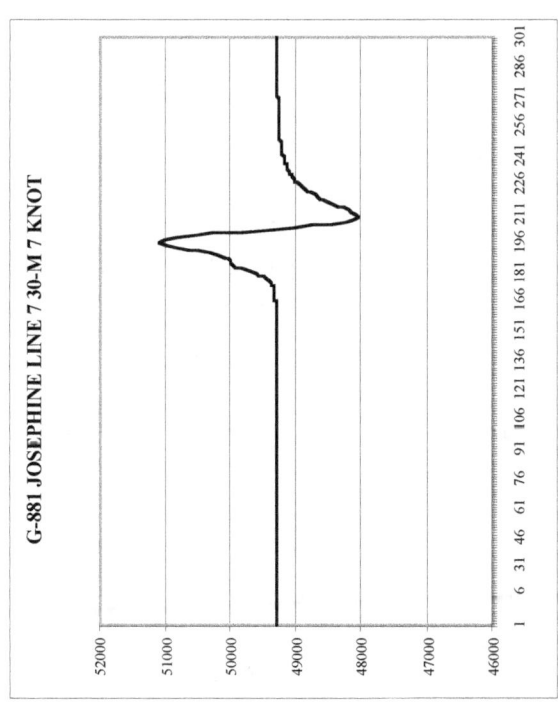

*Josephin*e **30-Meter Survey Interval 7-Knot Grid Strip charts. Y-axis is the gamma scale, X-axis is the sampling rate.**

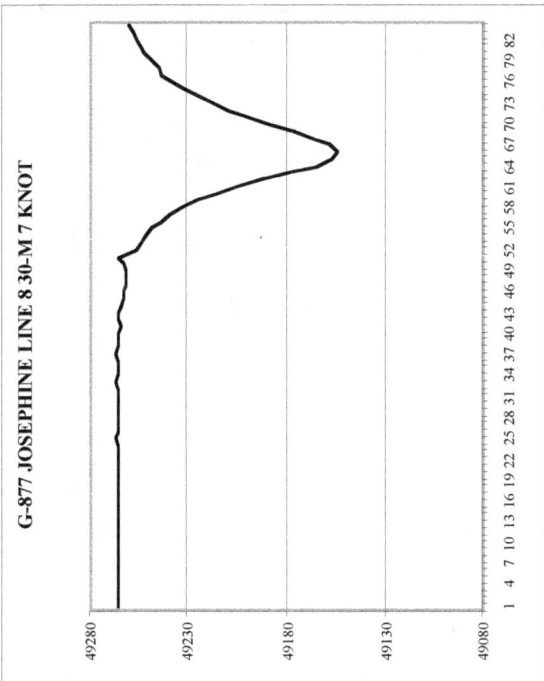

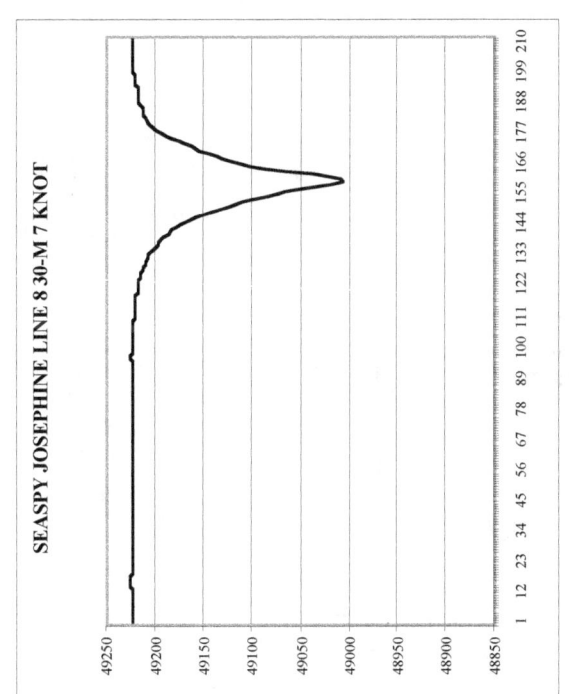

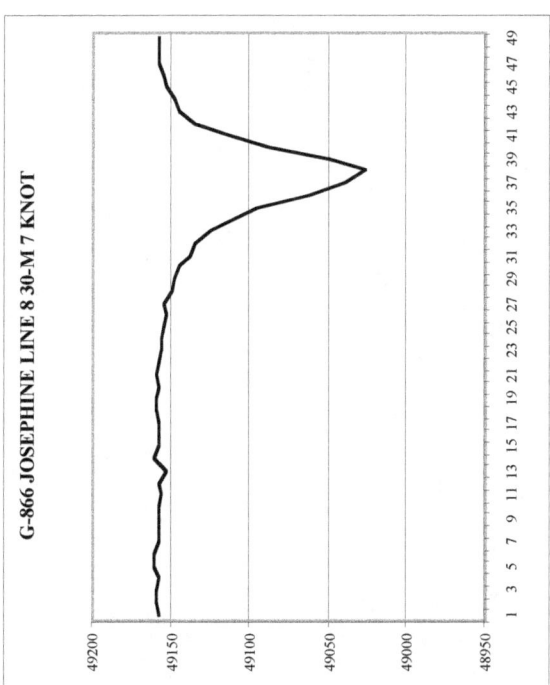

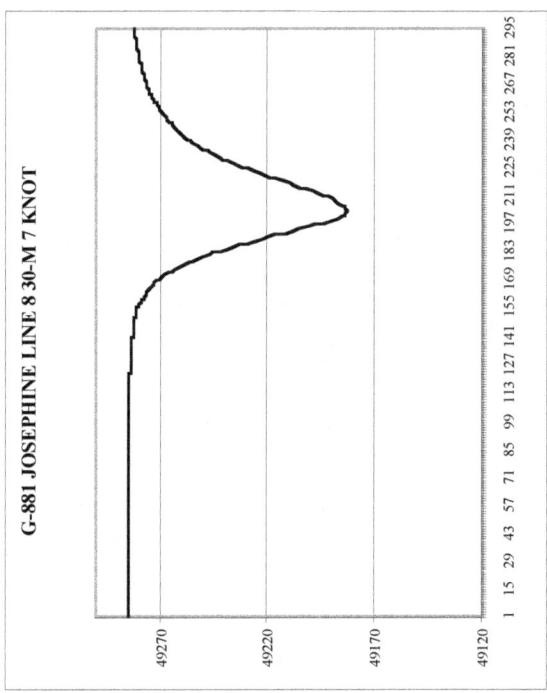

Josephine 30-Meter Survey Interval 7-Knot Grid Strip charts. Y-axis is the gamma scale, X-axis is the sampling rate.

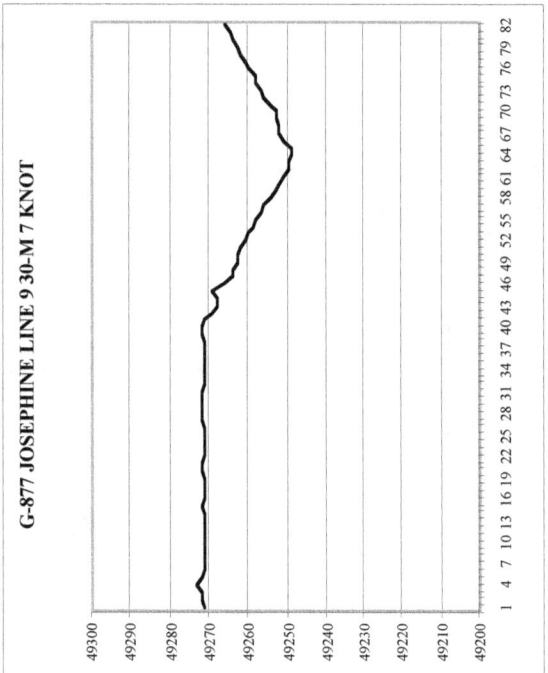

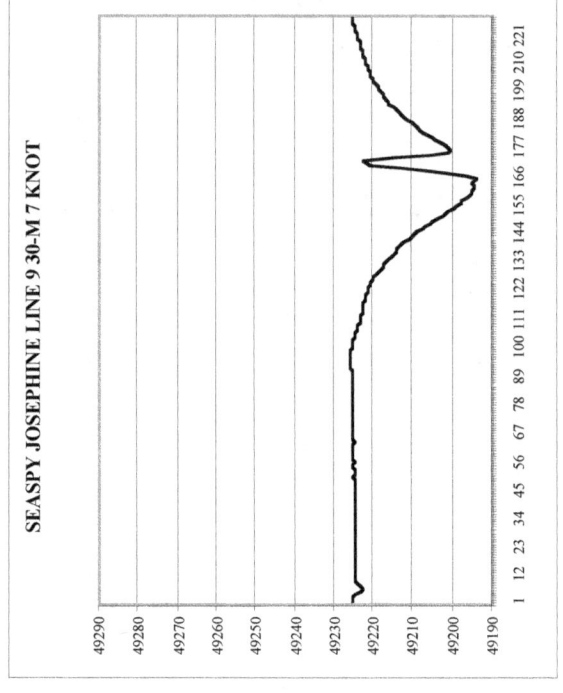

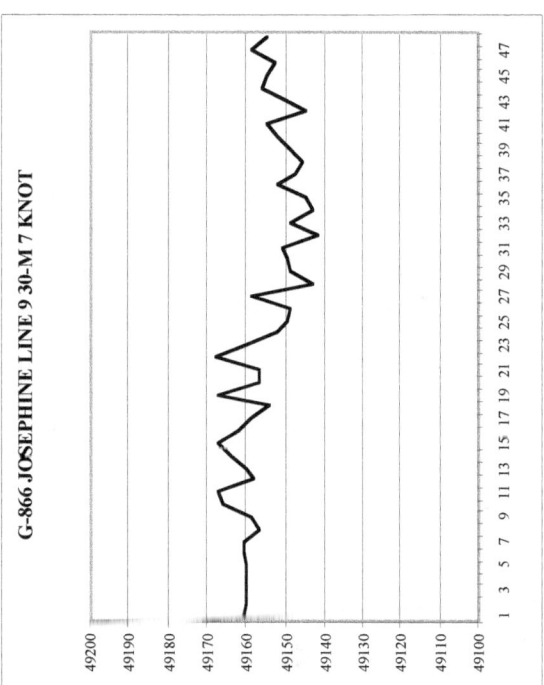

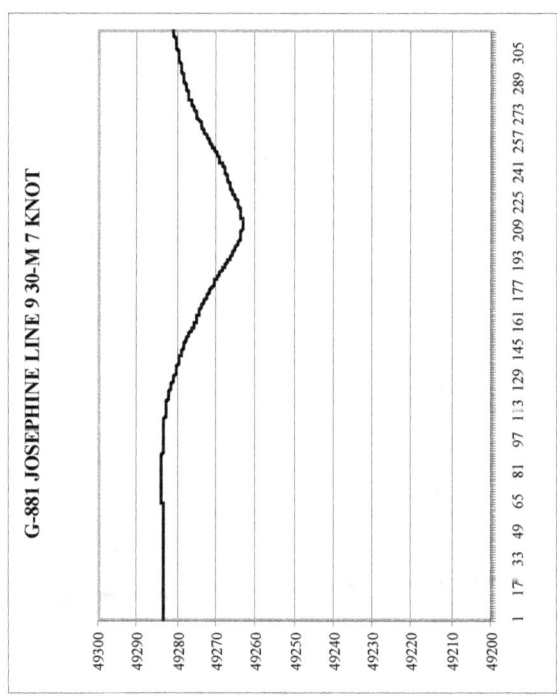

Josephine 30-Meter Survey Interval 7-Knot Grid Strip charts. Y-axis is the gamma scale, X-axis is the sampling rate.

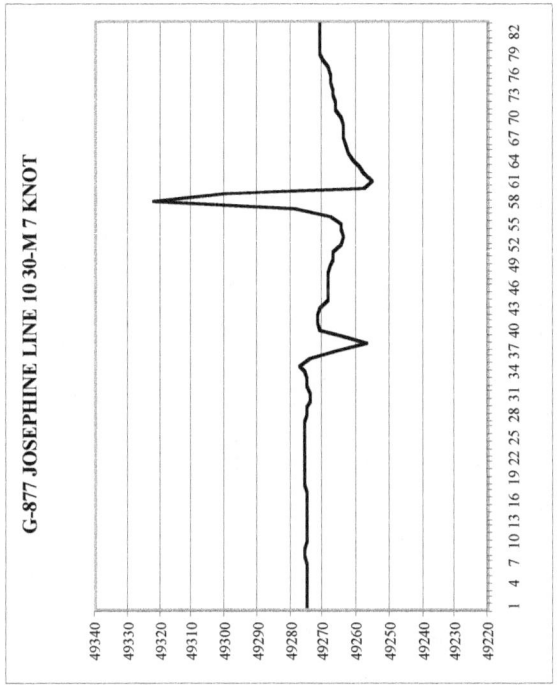

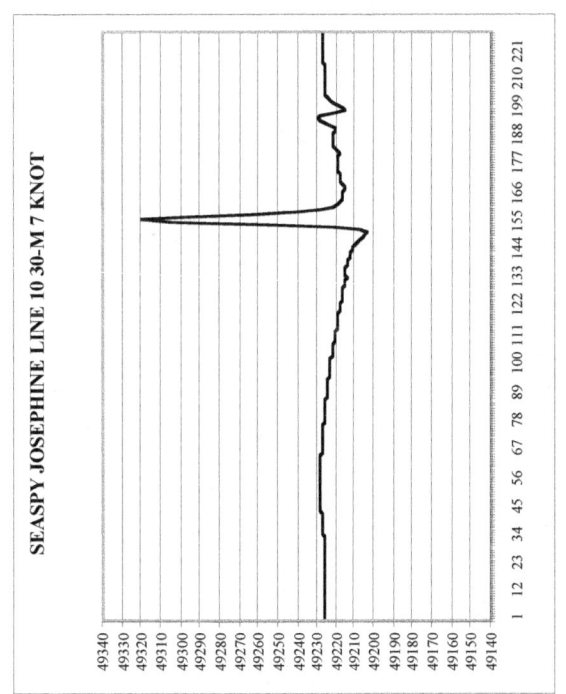

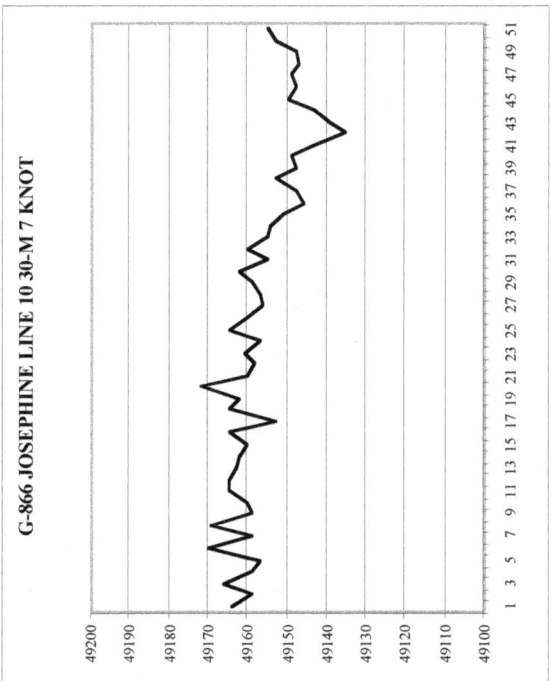

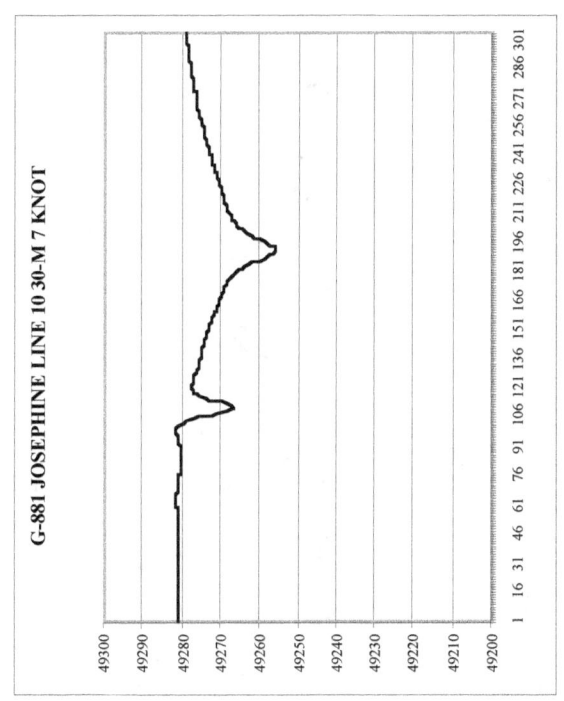

Josephine **30-Meter Survey Interval 7-Knot Grid Strip charts. Y-axis is the gamma scale, X-axis is the sampling rate.**

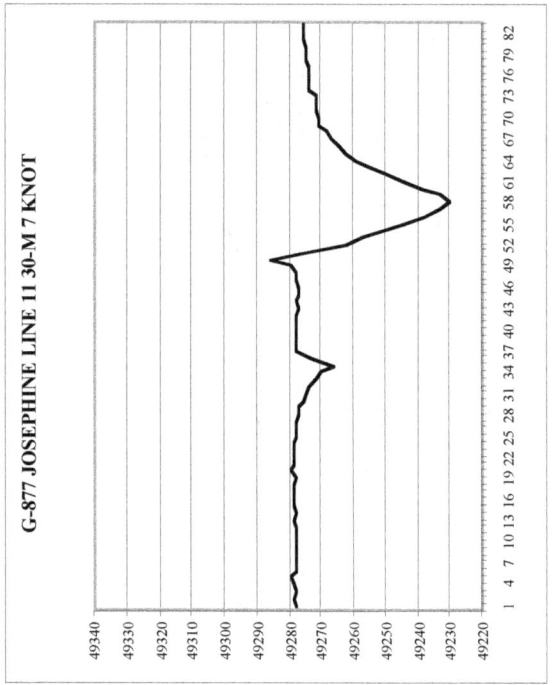

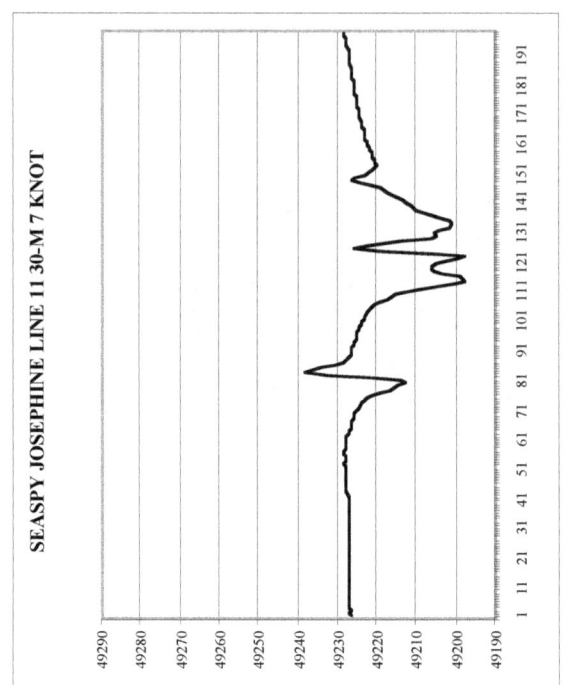

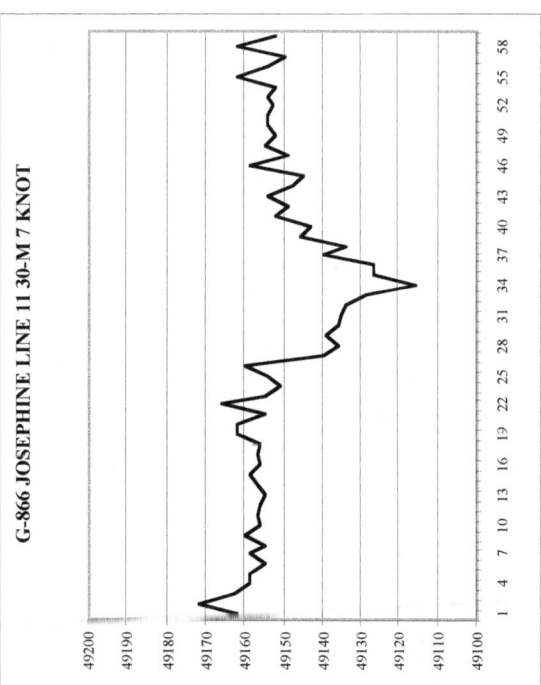

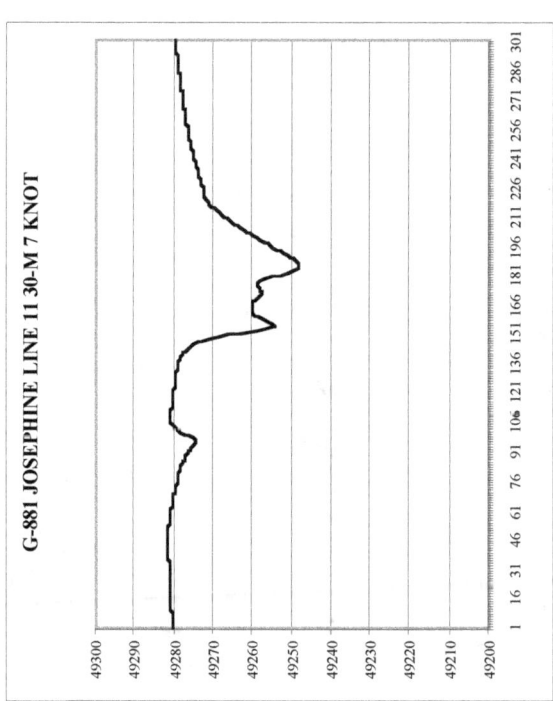

Josephine 30-Meter Survey Interval 7-Knot Grid Strip charts. Y-axis is the gamma scale, X-axis is the sampling rate.

APPENDIX L

STRIPCHARTS BY LINE FOR EACH INSTRUMENT
RHODA **25-METER SURVEY INTERVAL GRID**

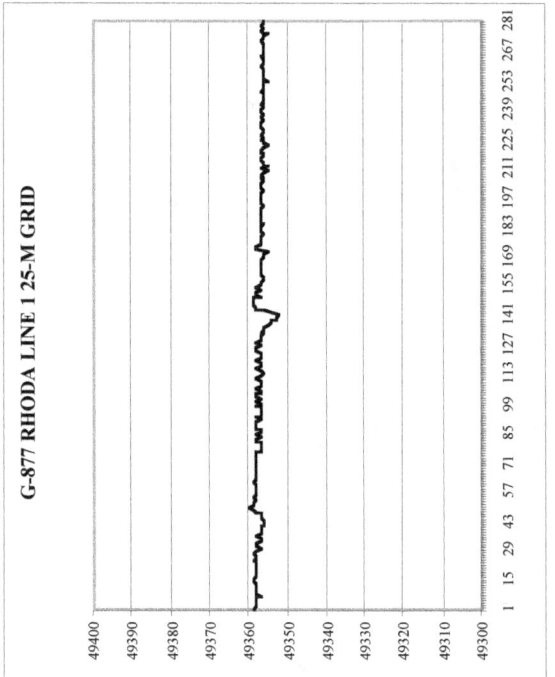

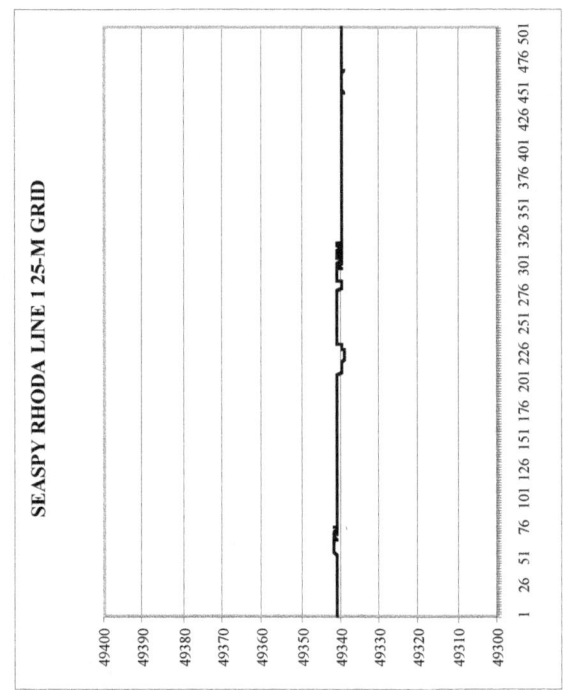

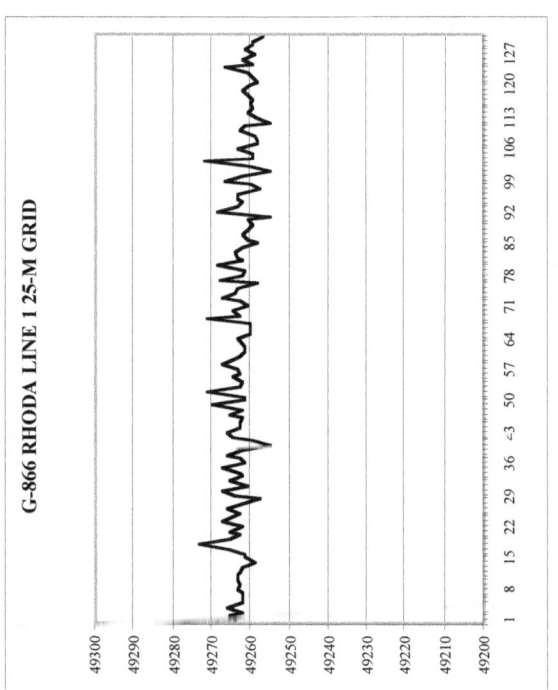

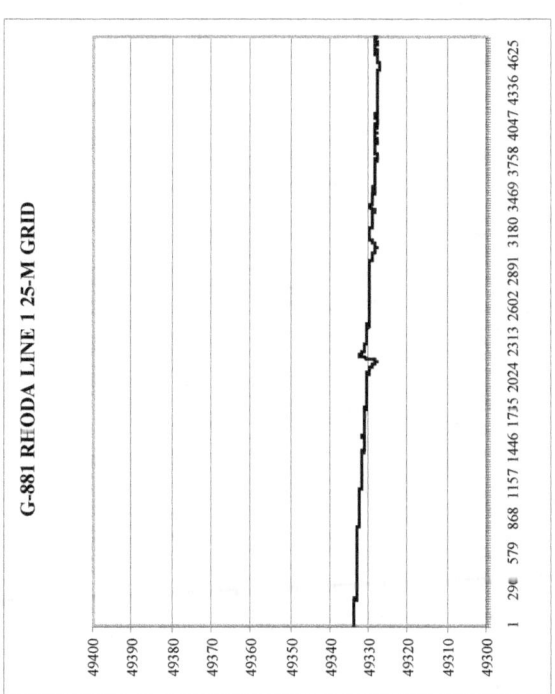

Rhoda **25-Meter Survey Interval Grid Strip charts. Y-axis is the gamma scale, X-axis is the sampling rate.**

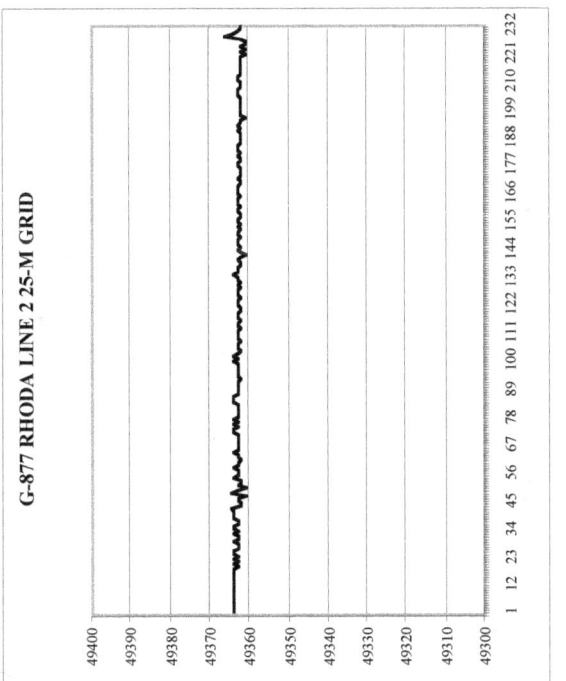

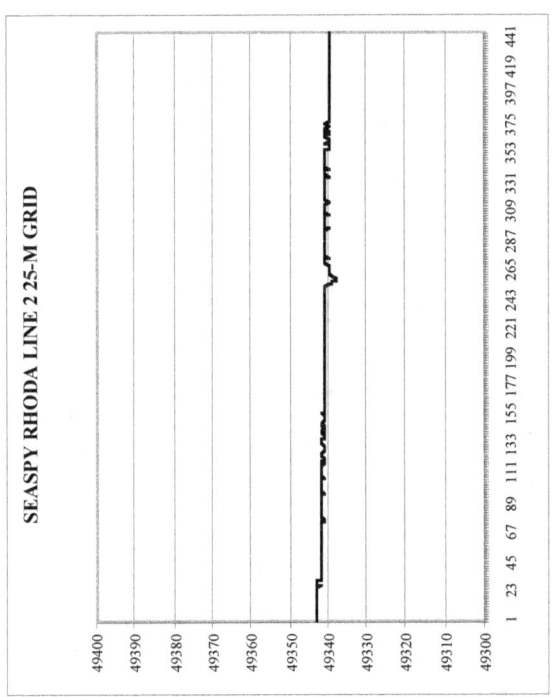

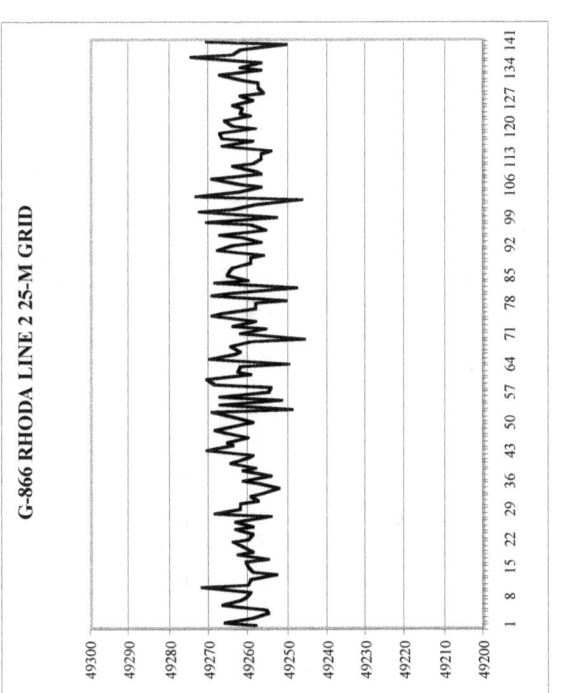

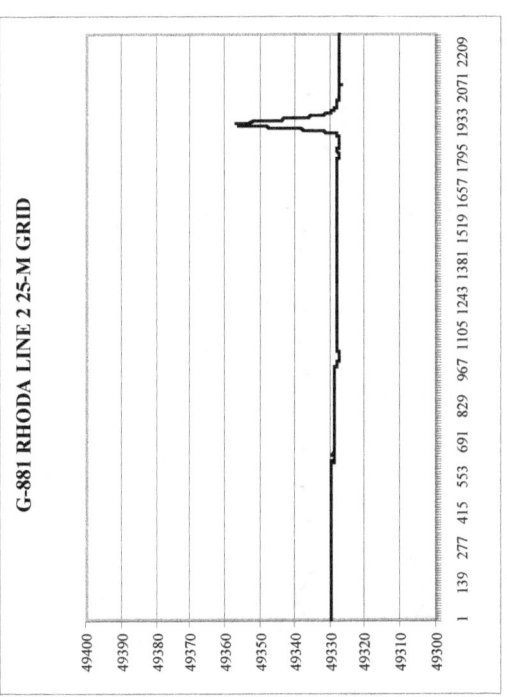

Rhoda **25-Meter Survey Interval Grid Strip charts. Y-axis is the gamma scale, X-axis is the sampling rate.**

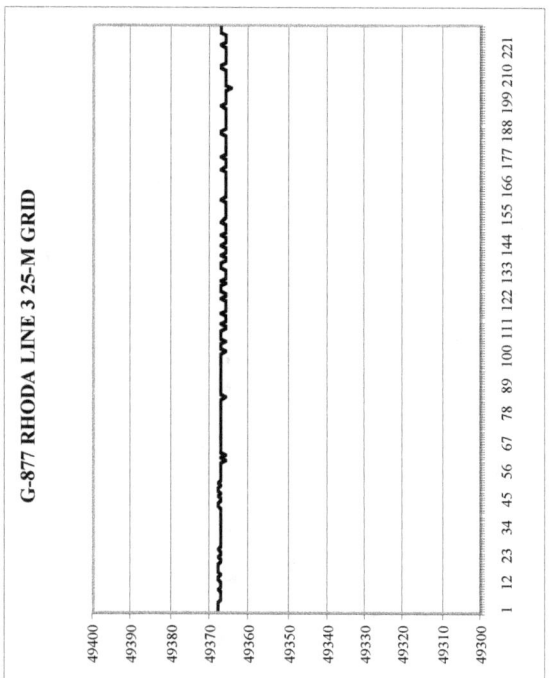

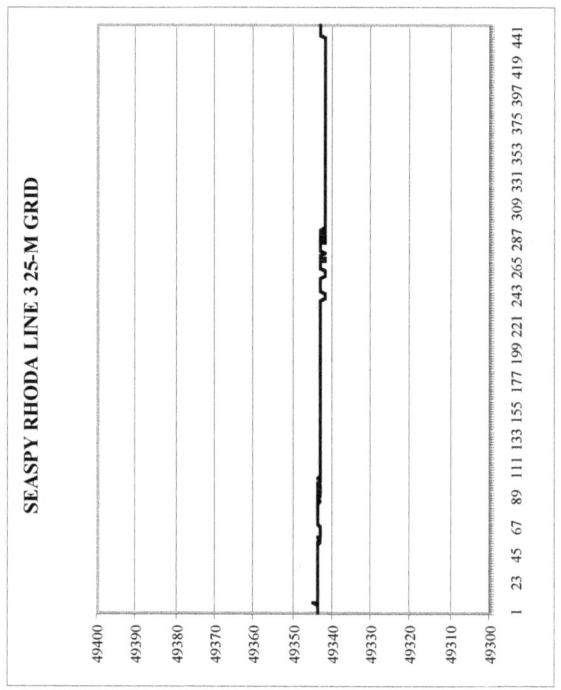

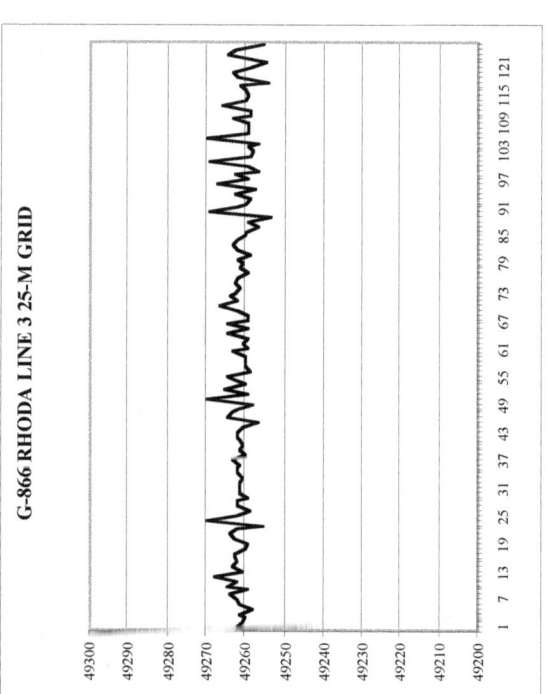

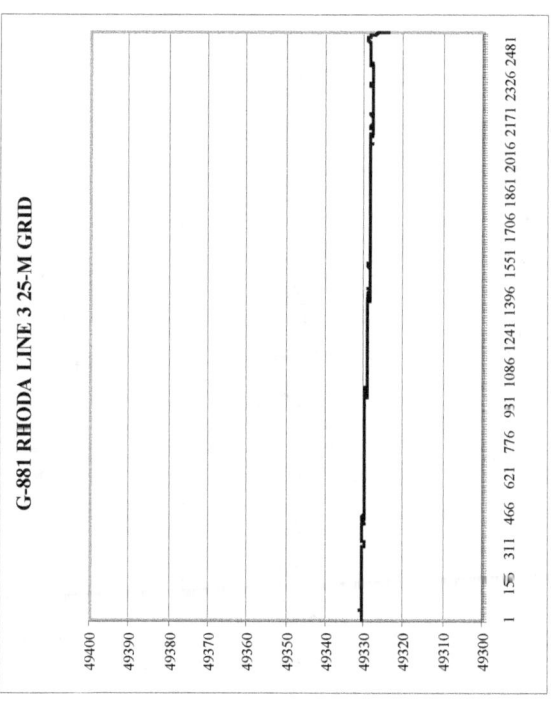

Rhoda 25-Meter Survey Interval Grid Strip charts. Y-axis is the gamma scale, X-axis is the sampling rate.

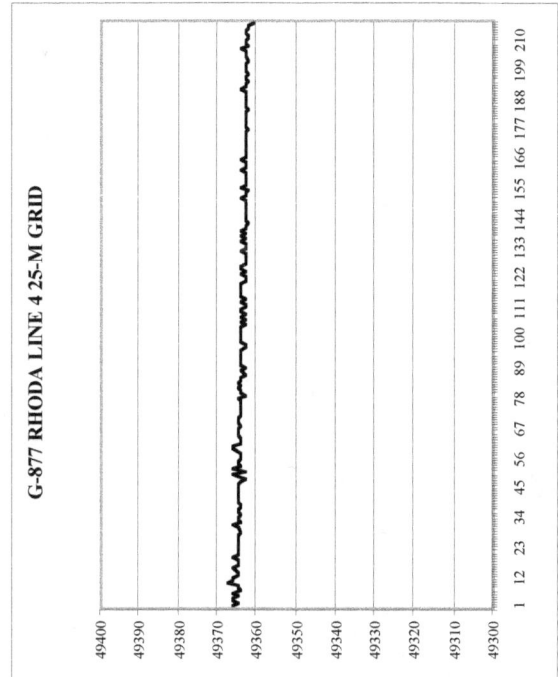

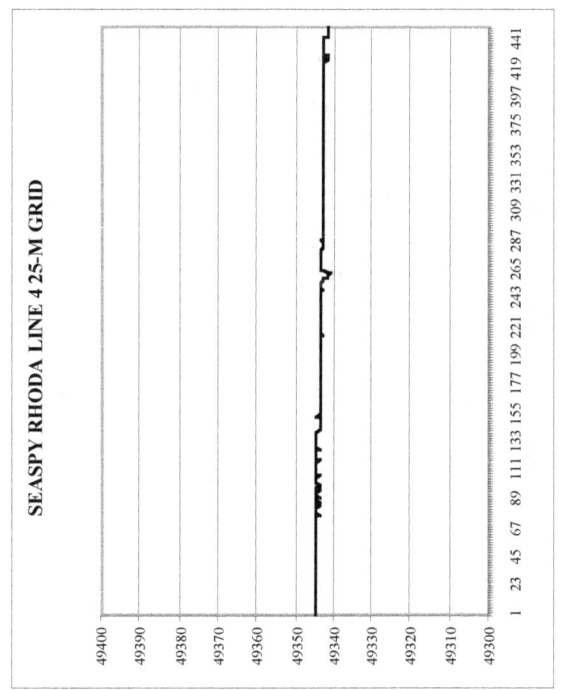

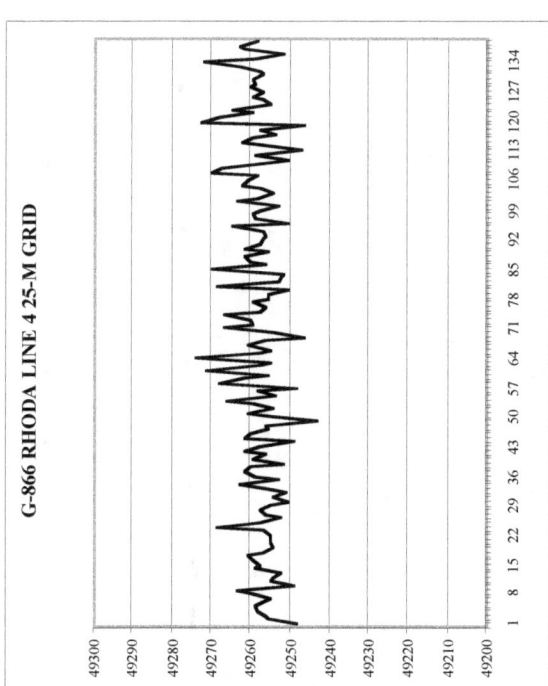

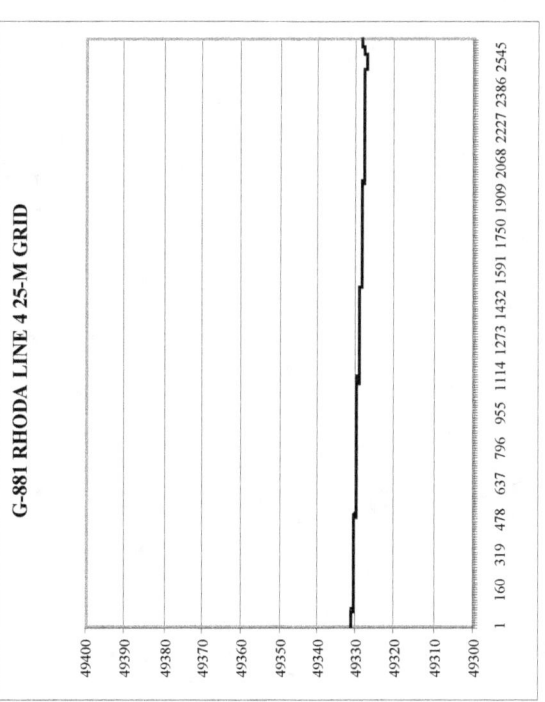

Rhoda **25-Meter Survey Interval Grid Strip charts. Y-axis is the gamma scale, X-axis is the sampling rate.**

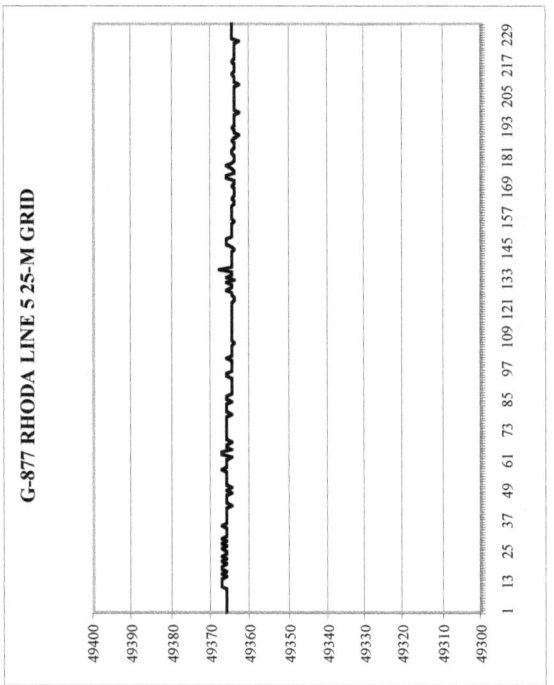

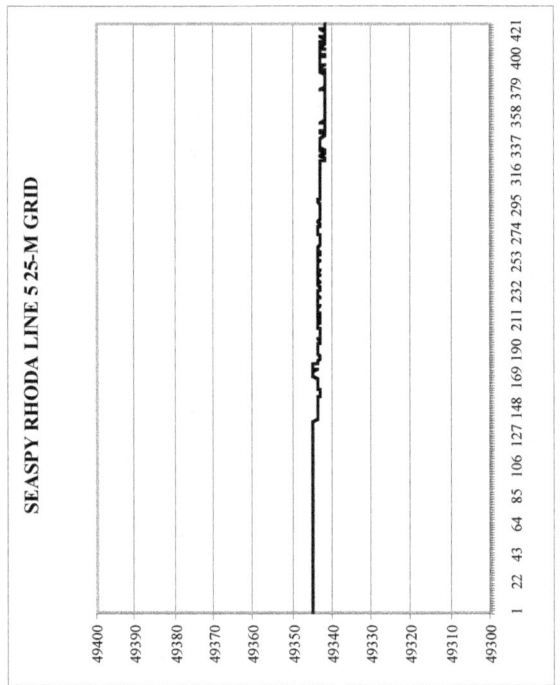

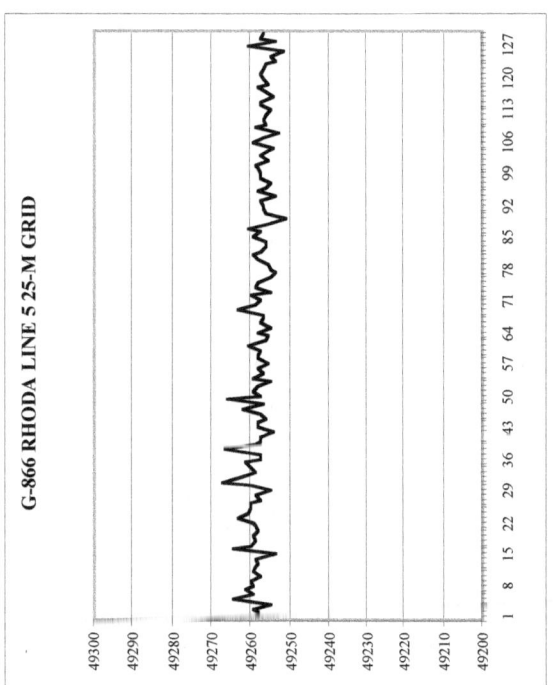

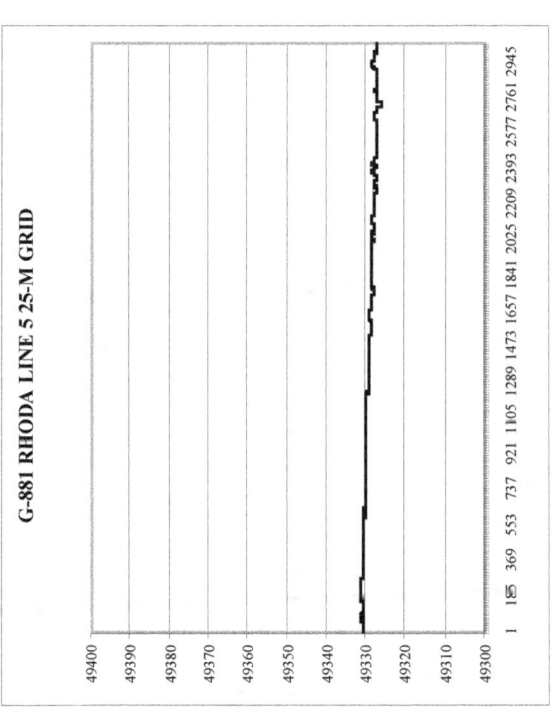

Rhoda 25-Meter Survey Interval Grid Strip charts. Y-axis is the gamma scale, X-axis is the sampling rate.

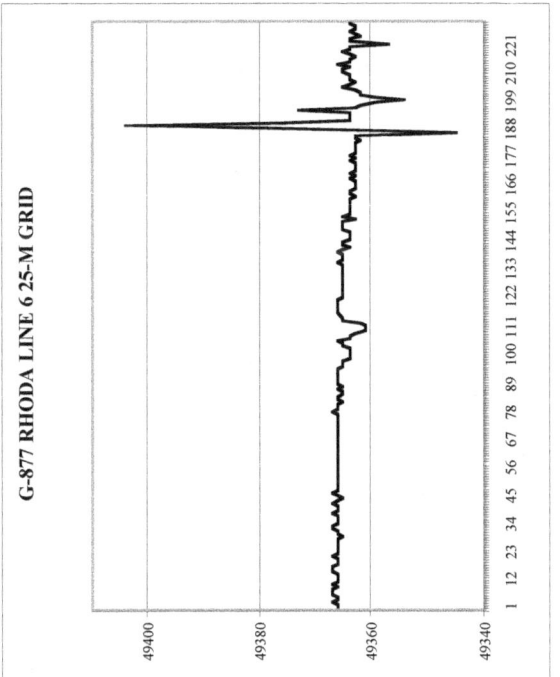

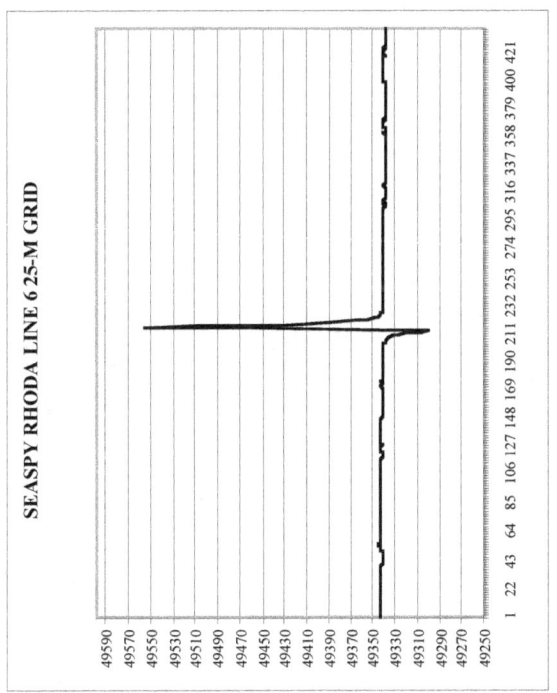

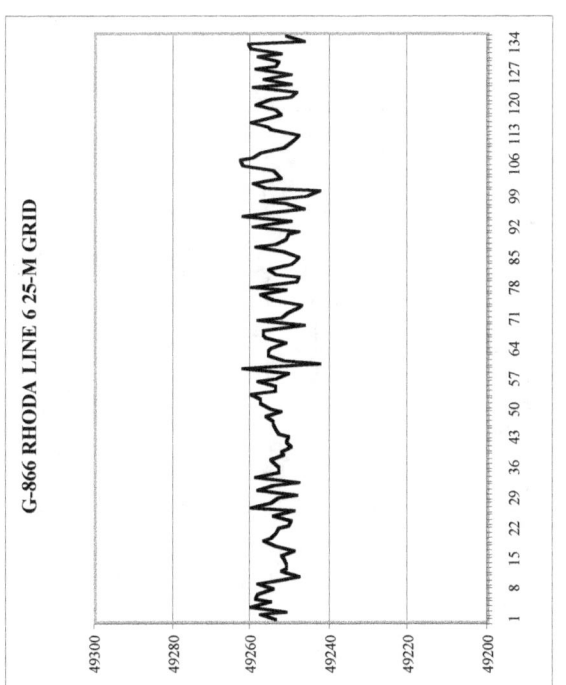

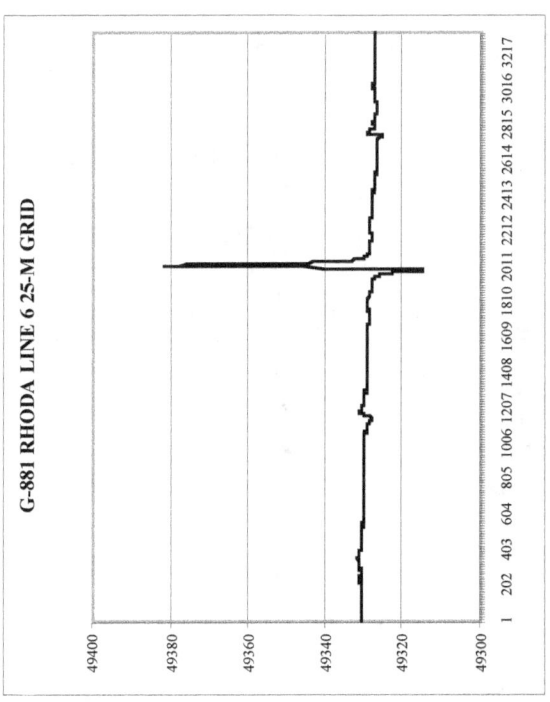

Rhoda 25-Meter Survey Interval Grid Strip charts. Y-axis is the gamma scale, X-axis is the sampling rate.

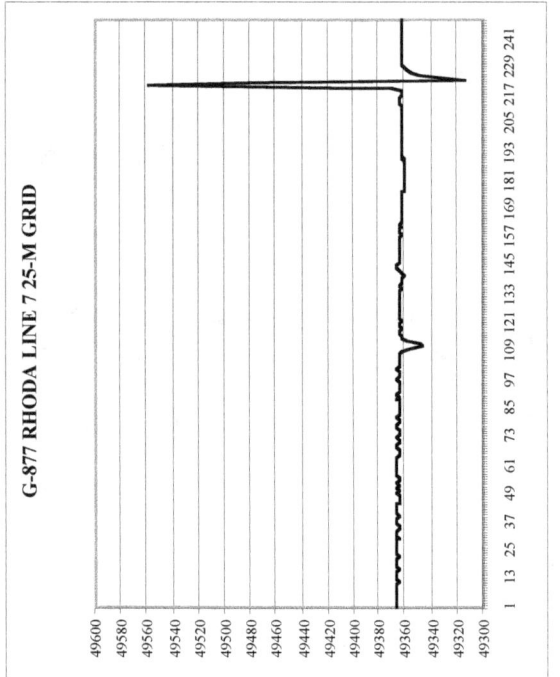

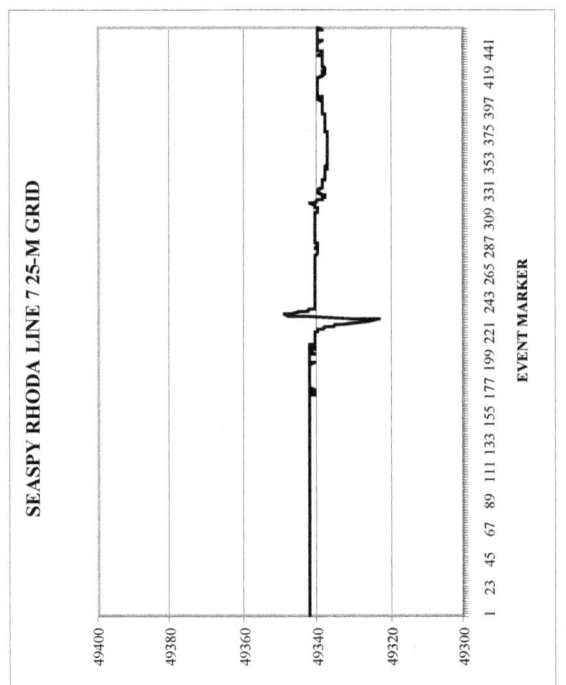

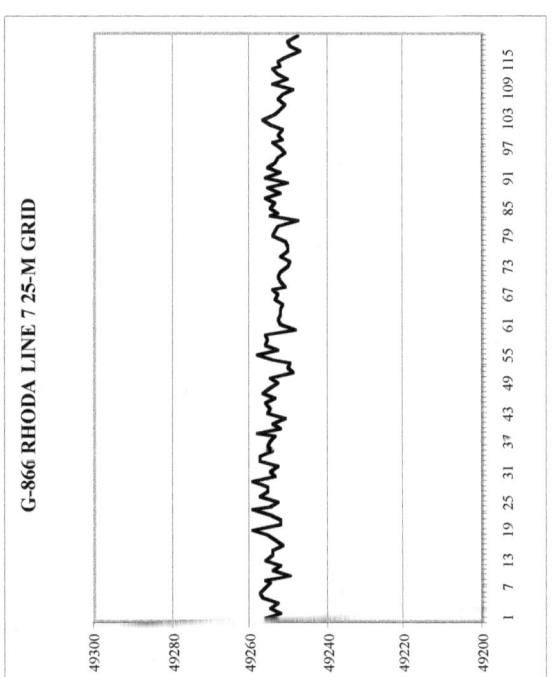

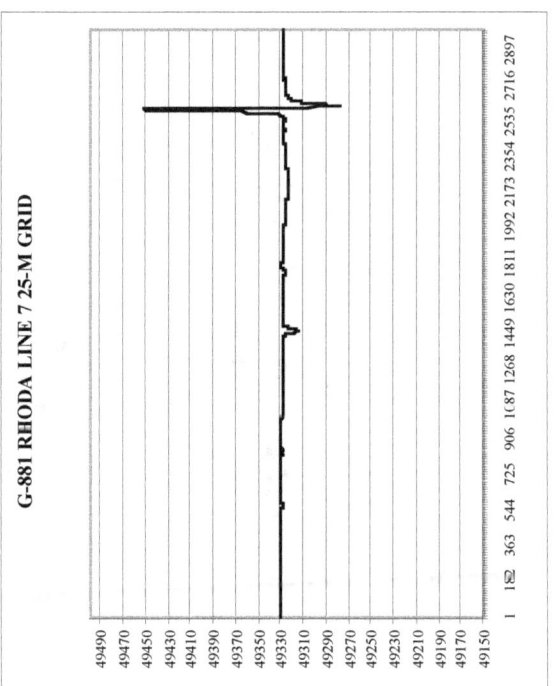

Rhoda **25-Meter Survey Interval Grid Strip charts. Y-axis is the gamma scale, X-axis is the sampling rate.**

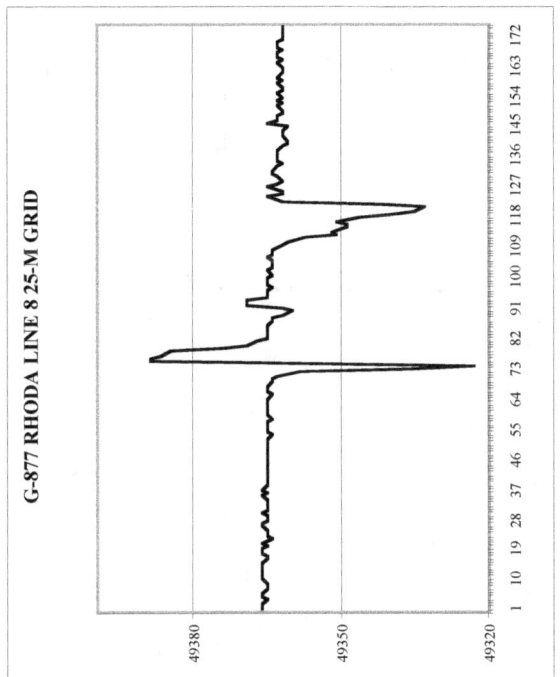

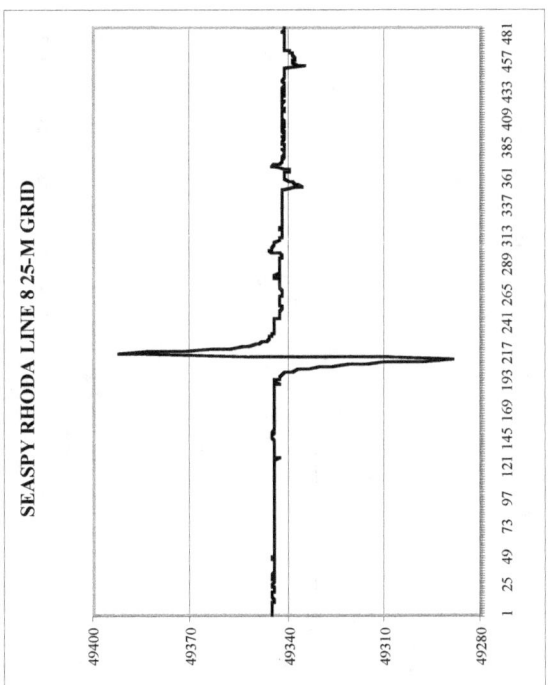

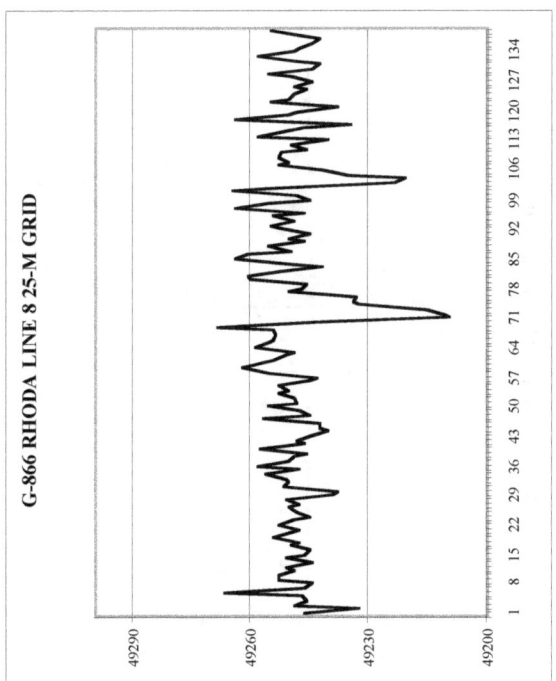

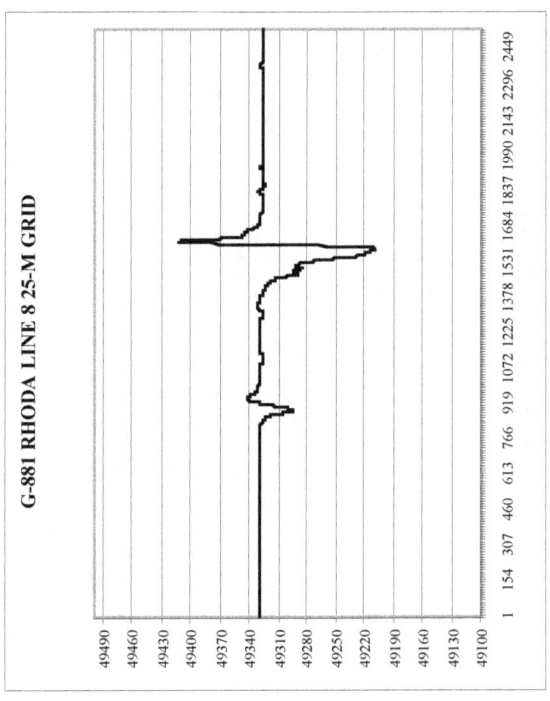

Rhoda **25-Meter Survey Interval Grid Strip charts. Y-axis is the gamma scale, X-axis is the sampling rate.**

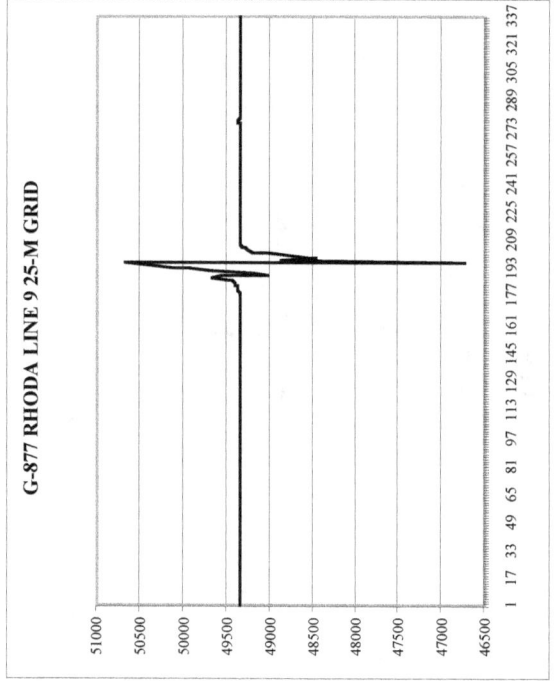

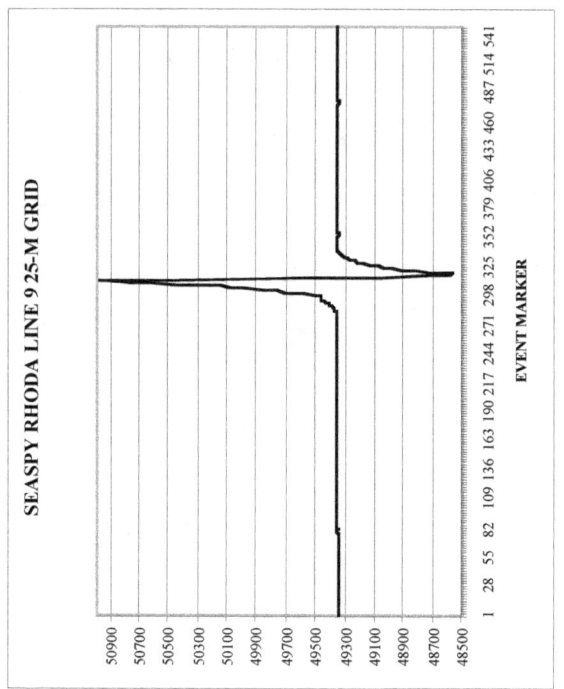

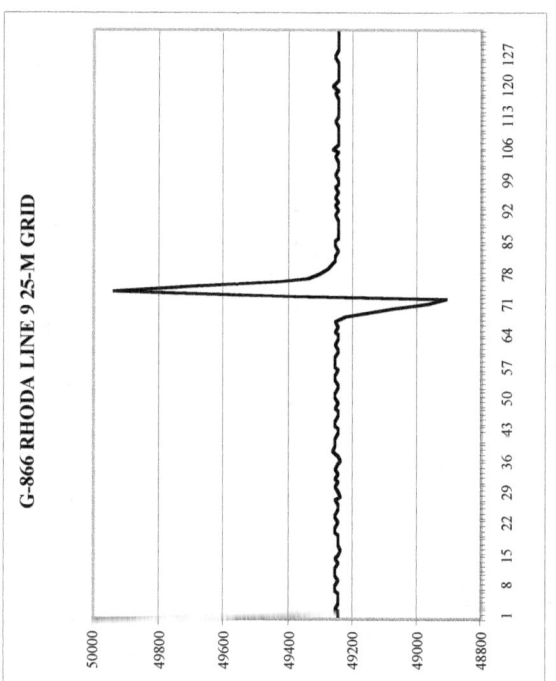

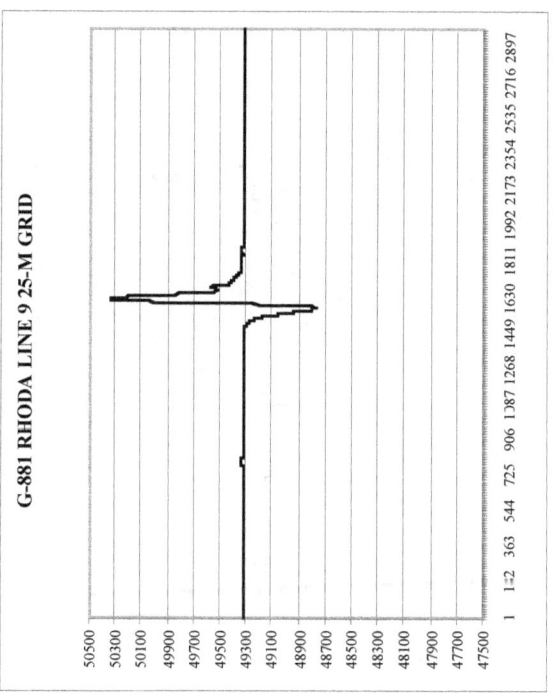

Rhoda 25-Meter Survey Interval Grid Strip charts. Y-axis is the gamma scale, X-axis is the sampling rate.

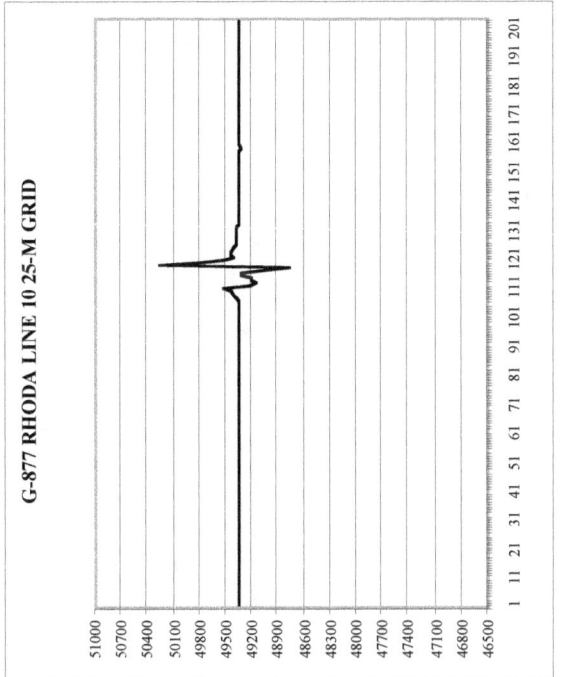

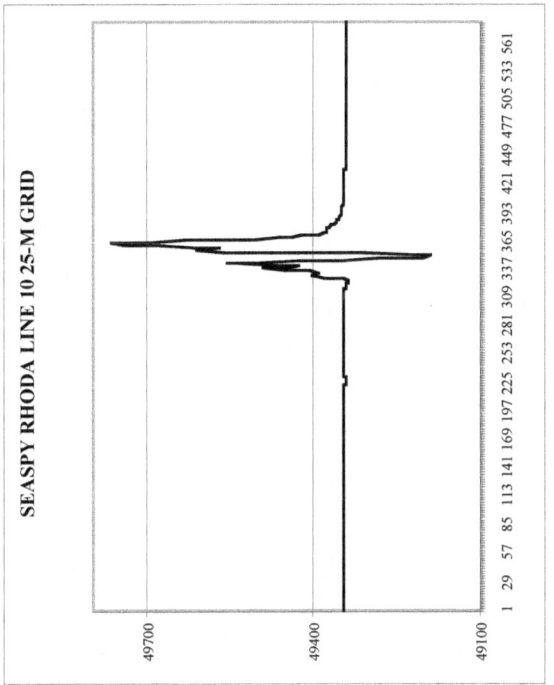

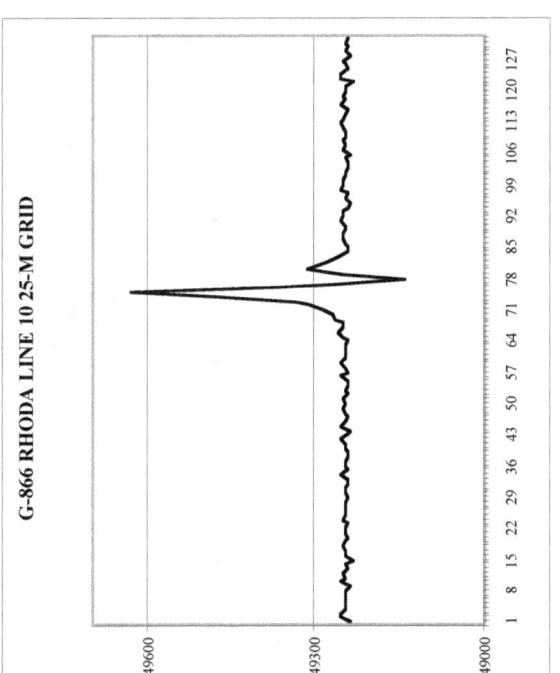

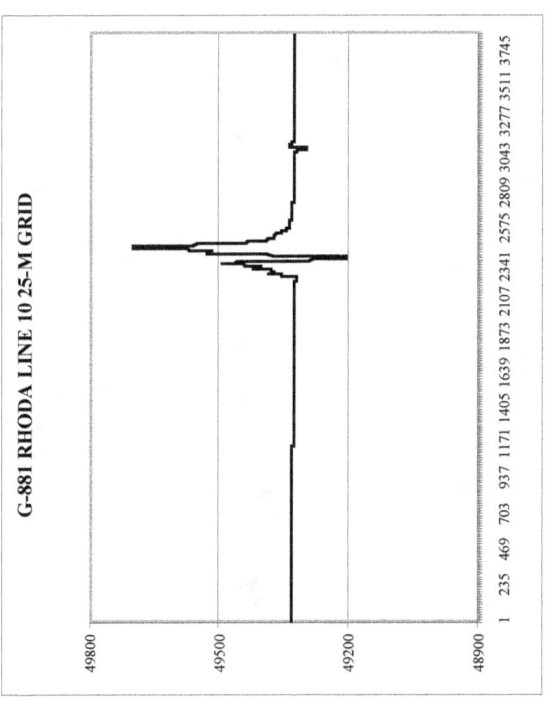

Rhoda **25-Meter Survey Interval Grid Strip charts. Y-axis is the gamma scale, X-axis is the sampling rate.**

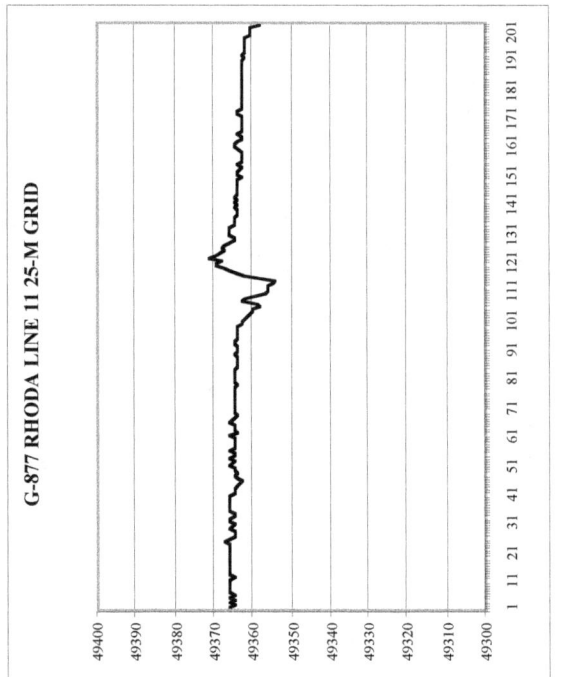

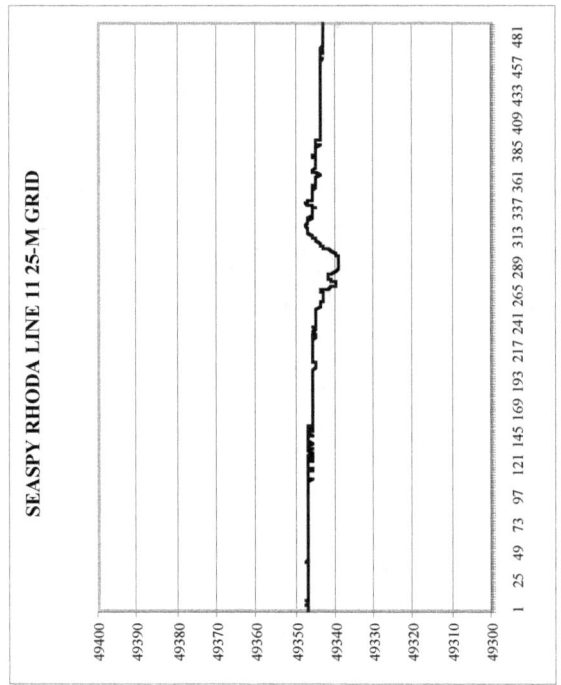

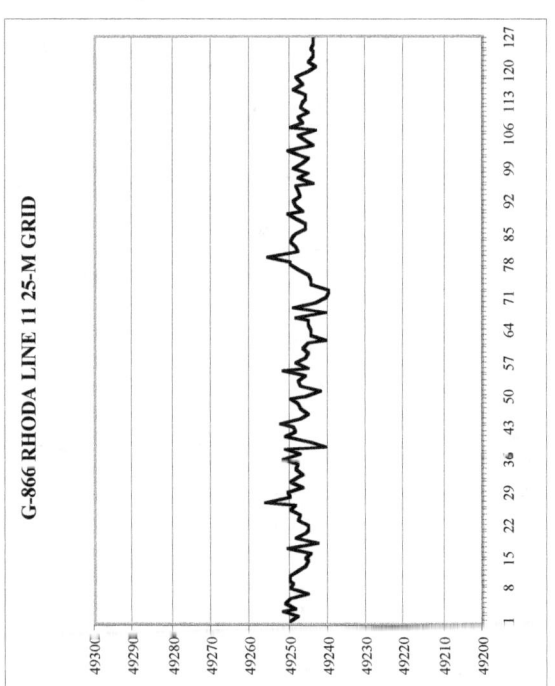

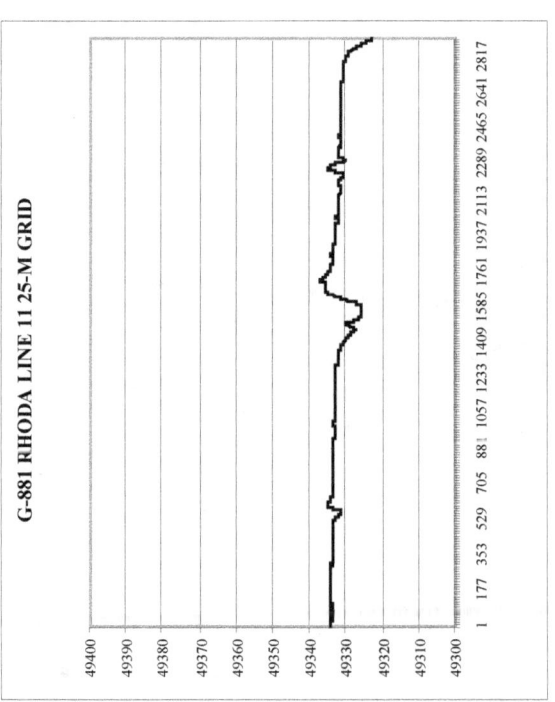

Rhoda 25-Meter Survey Interval Grid Strip charts. Y-axis is the gamma scale, X-axis is the sampling rate.

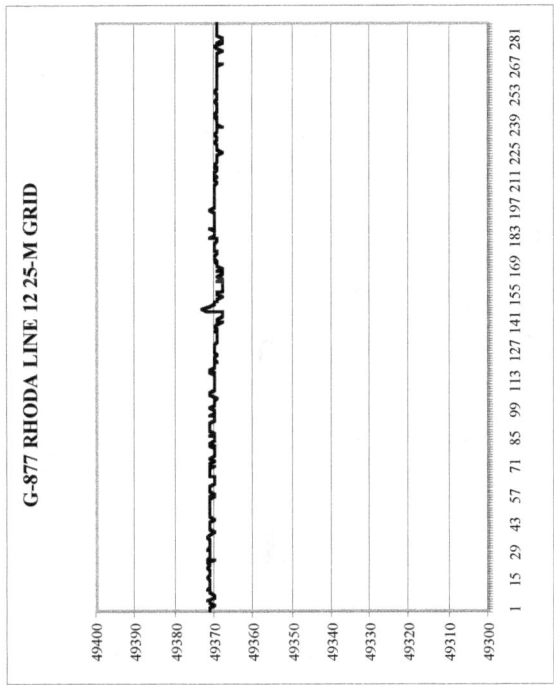

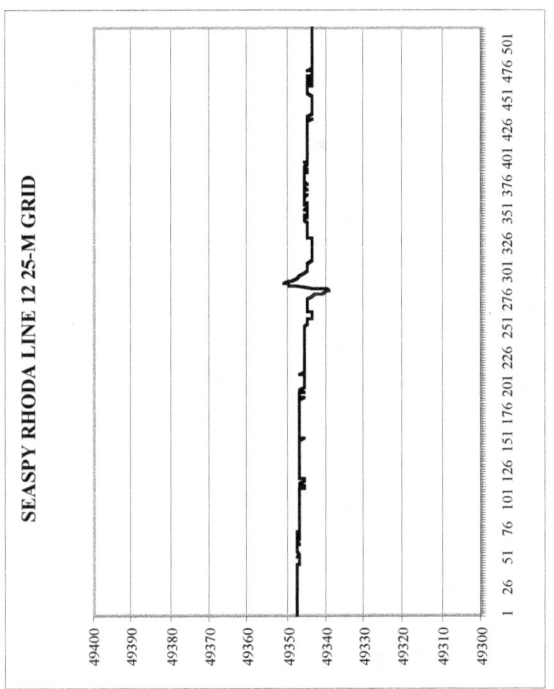

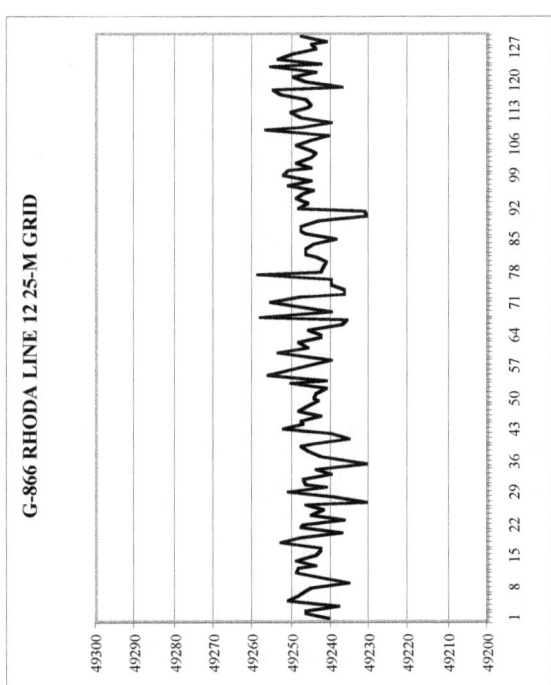

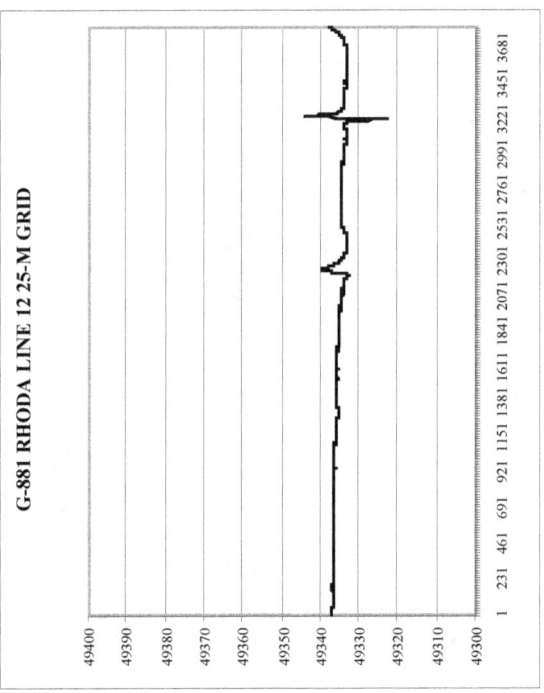

Rhoda **25-Meter Survey Interval Grid Strip charts. Y-axis is the gamma scale, X-axis is the sampling rate.**

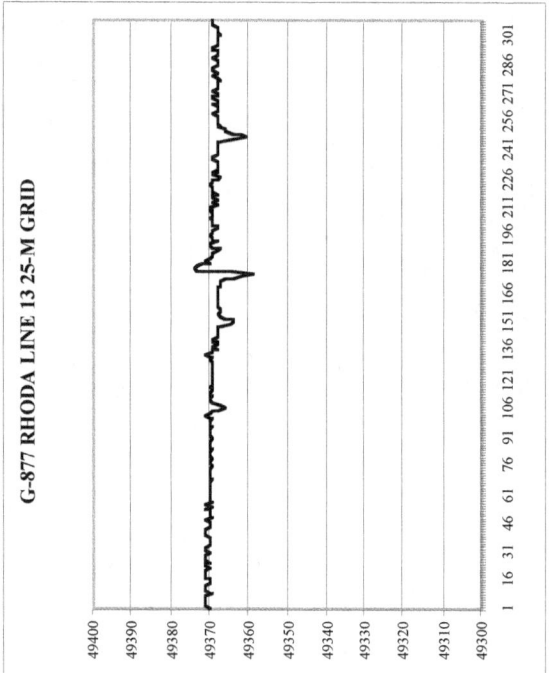

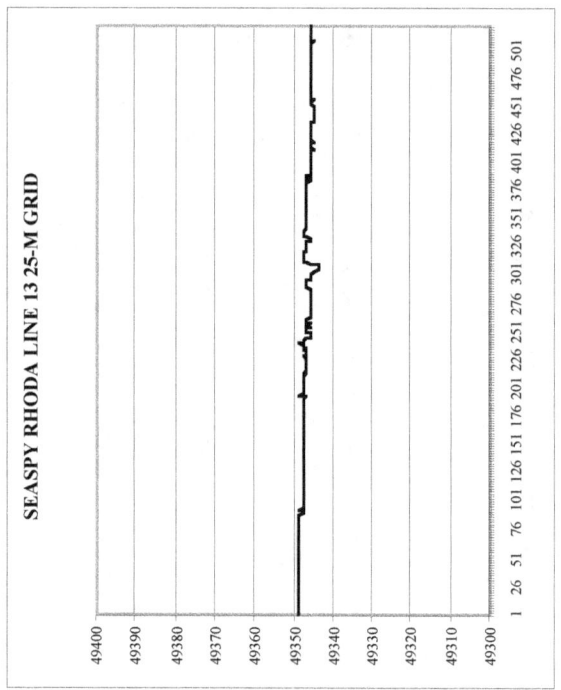

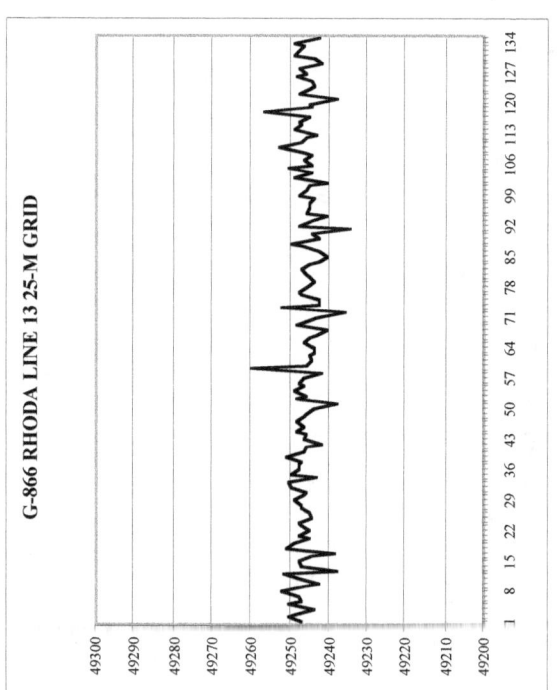

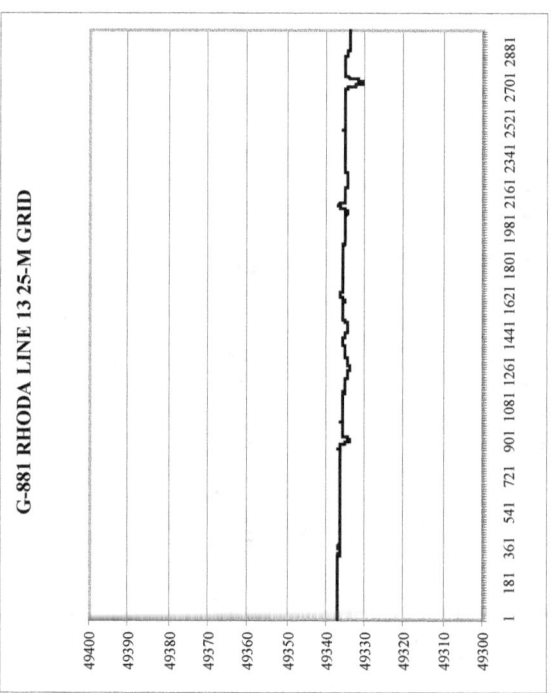

Rhoda **25-Meter Survey Interval Grid Strip charts. Y-axis is the gamma scale, X-axis is the sampling rate.**

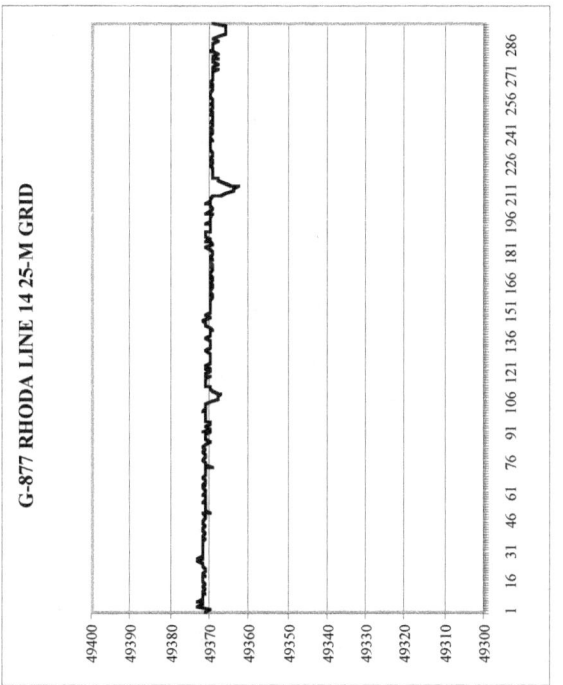

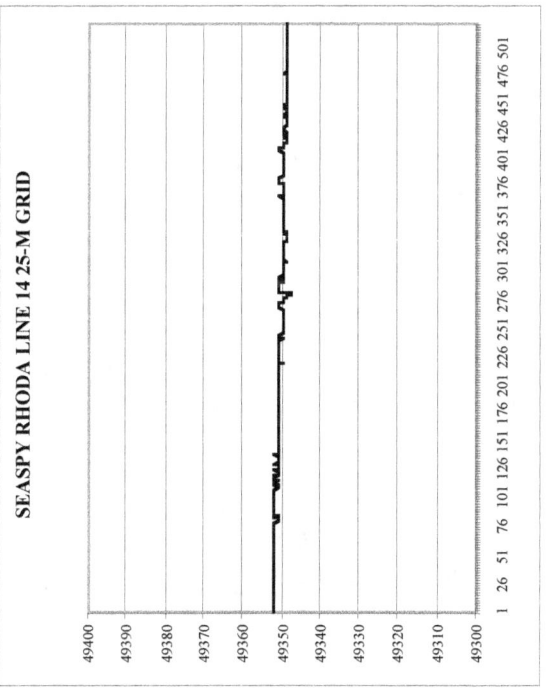

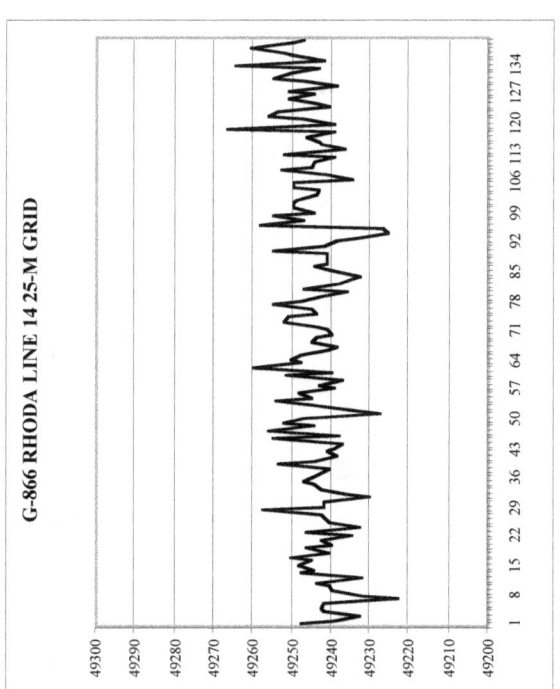

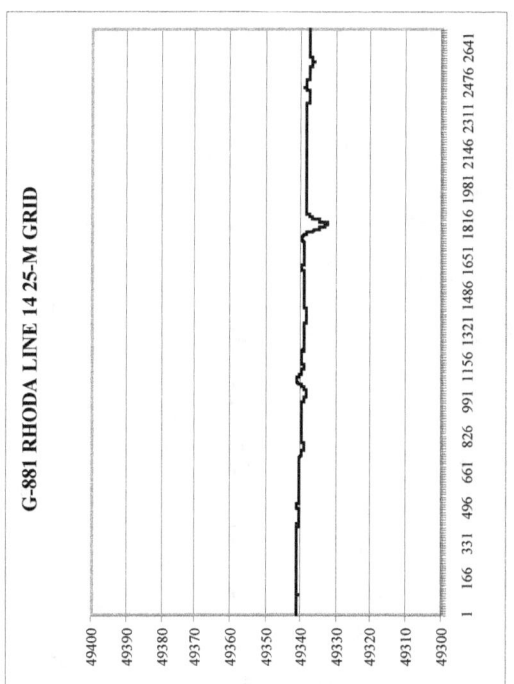

Rhoda **25-Meter Survey Interval Grid Strip charts. Y-axis is the gamma scale, X-axis is the sampling rate.**

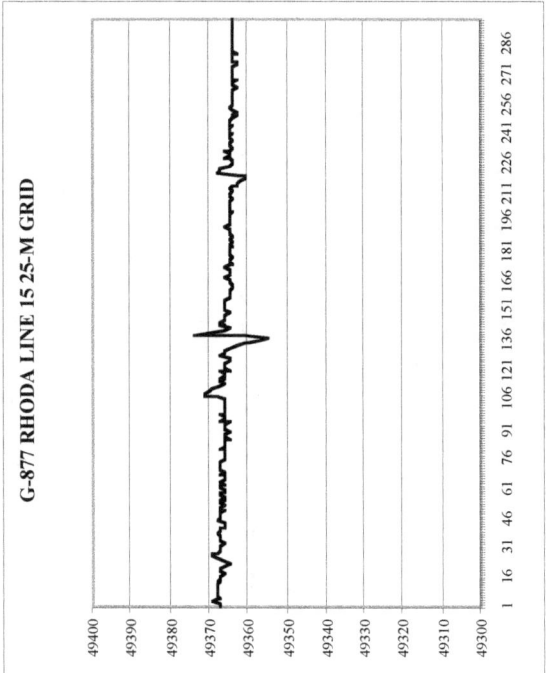

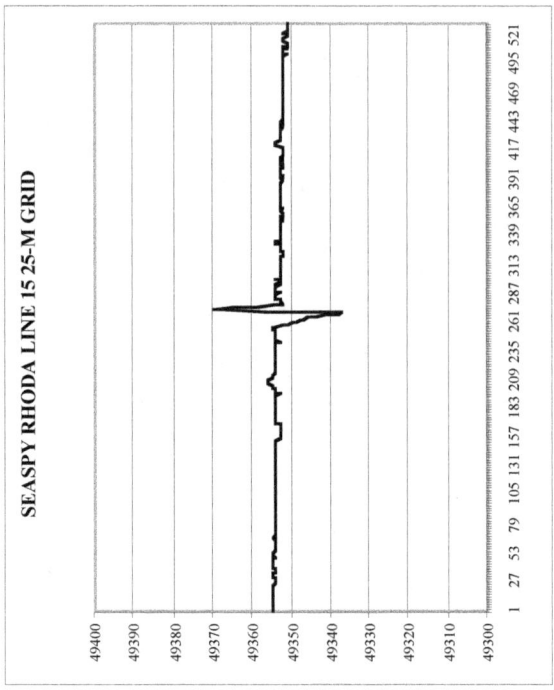

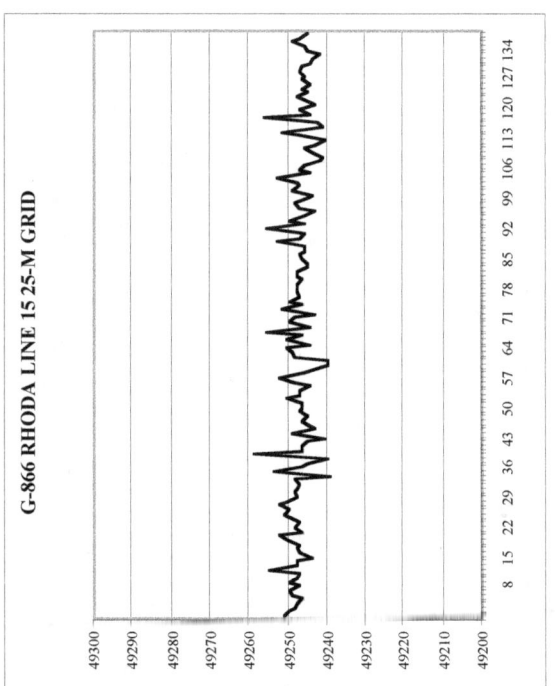

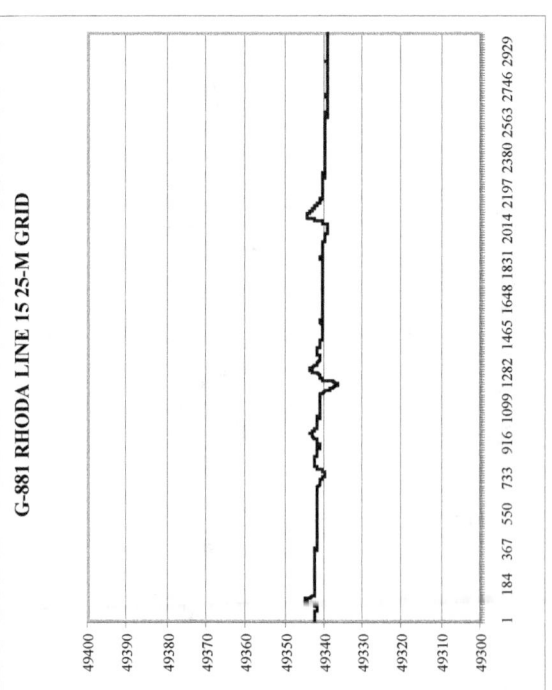

Rhoda **25-Meter Survey Interval Grid Strip charts. Y-axis is the gamma scale, X-axis is the sampling rate.**

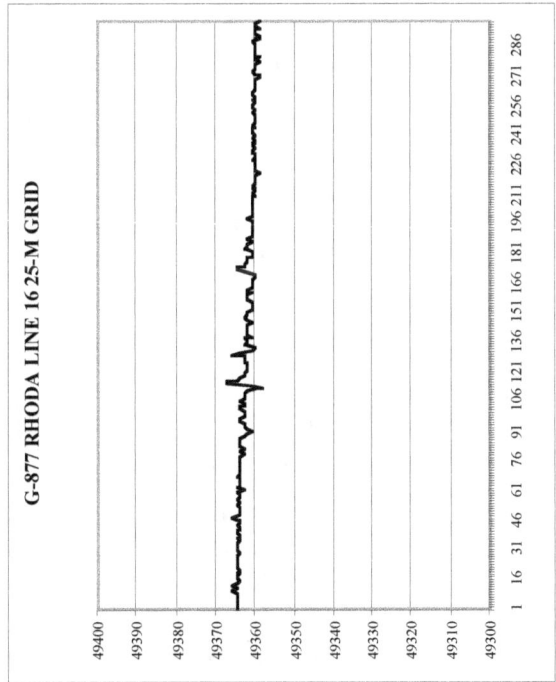

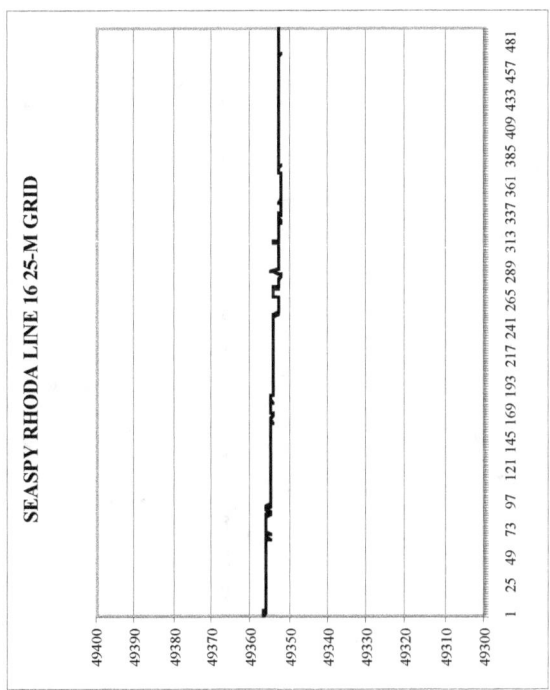

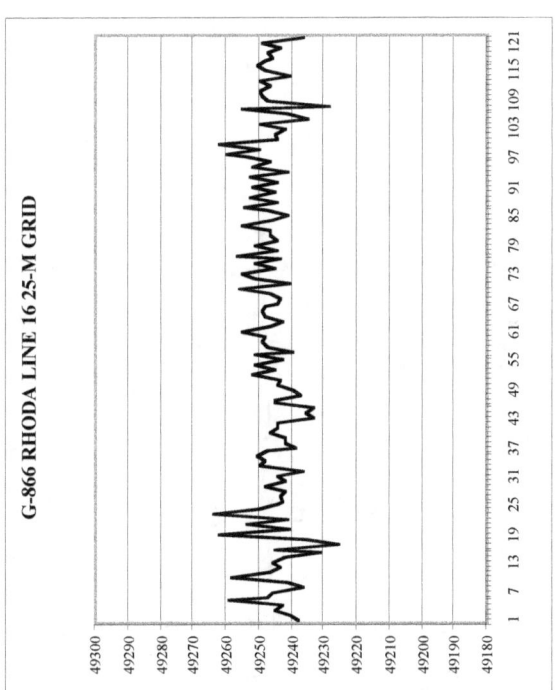

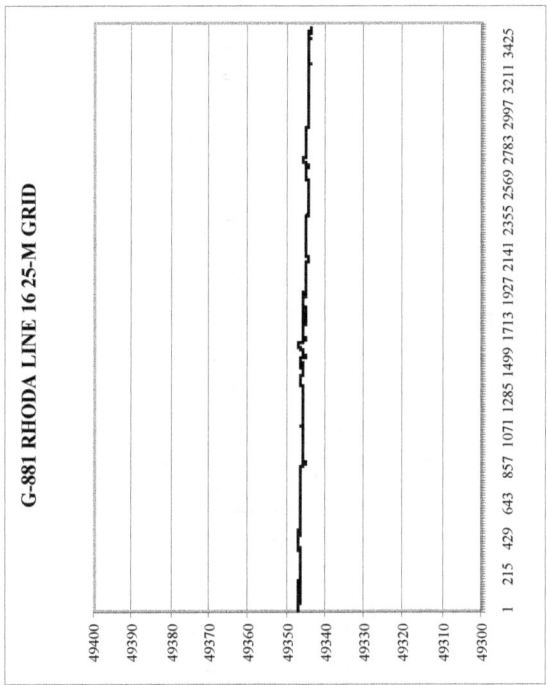

Rhoda **25-Meter Survey Interval Grid Strip charts. Y-axis is the gamma scale, X-axis is the sampling rate.**

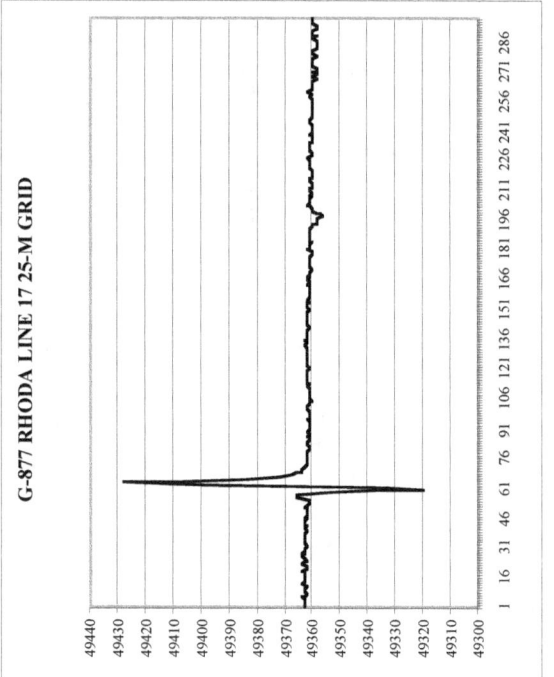

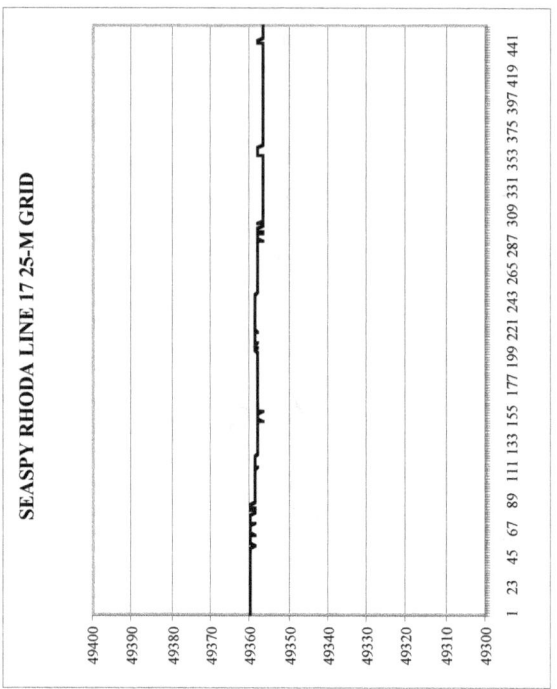

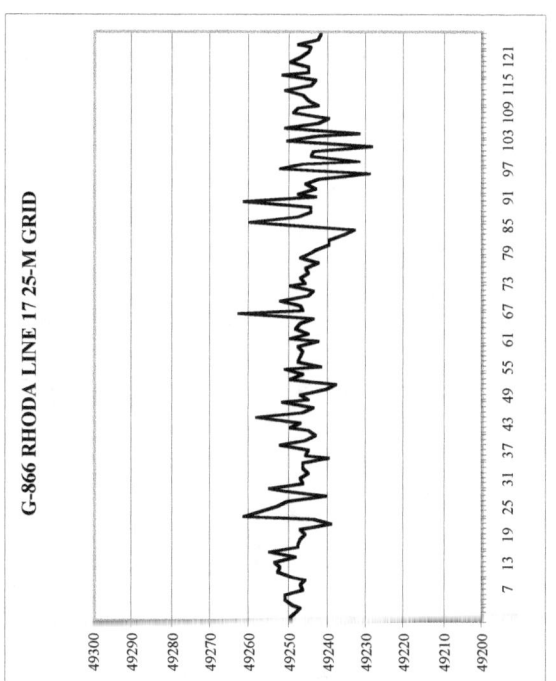

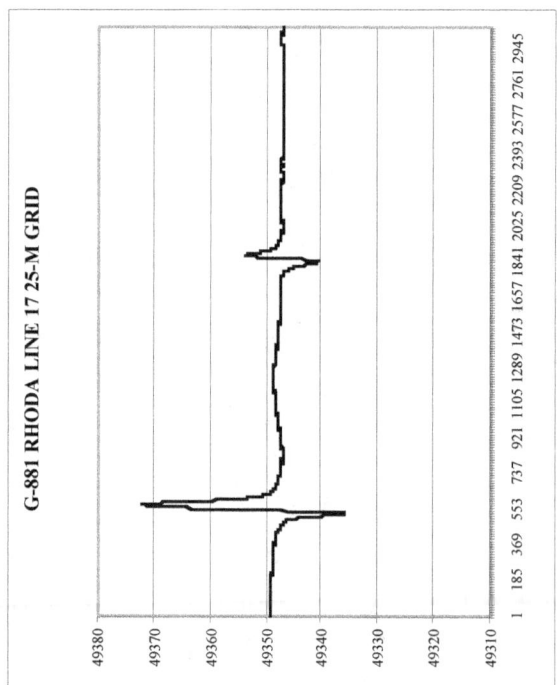

Rhoda **25-Meter Survey Interval Grid Strip charts. Y-axis is the gamma scale, X-axis is the sampling rate.**

APPENDIX M

STRIPCHARTS BY LINE FOR EACH INSTRUMENT
RHODA **30-METER SURVEY INTERVAL 4-KNOT GRID**

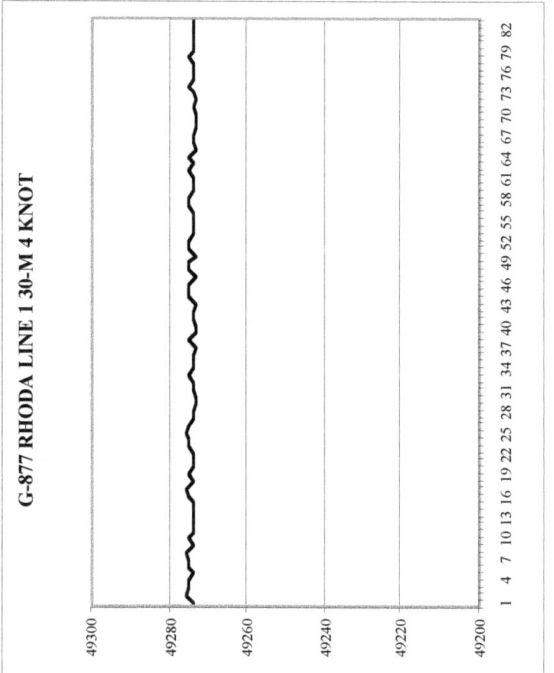

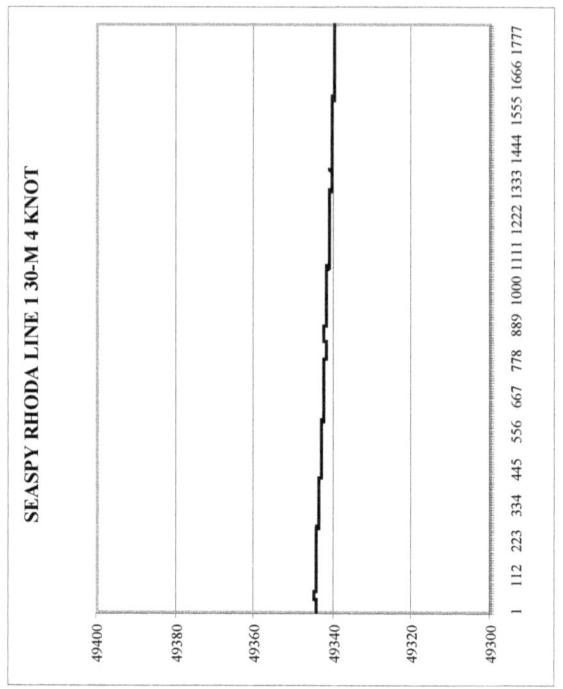

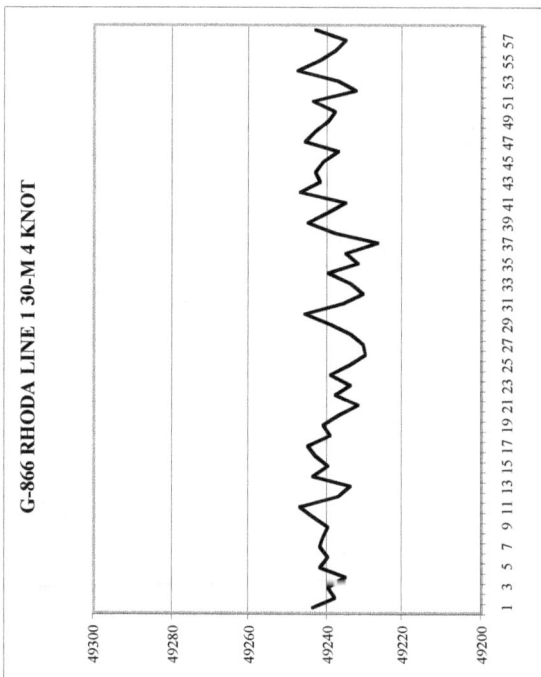

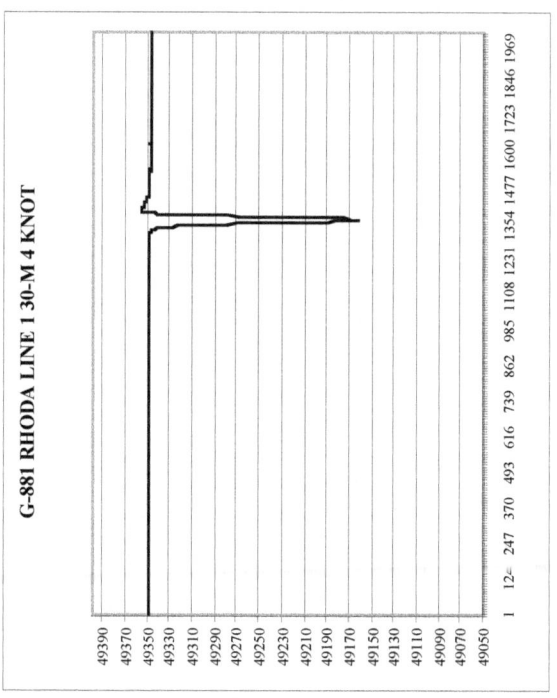

Rhoda **30-Meter Survey Interval 4-Knot Grid Strip charts. Y-axis is the gamma scale, X-axis is the sampling rate.**

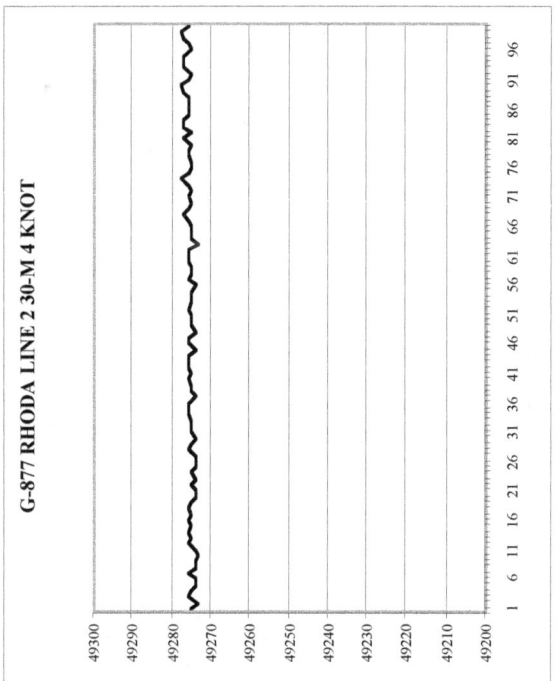

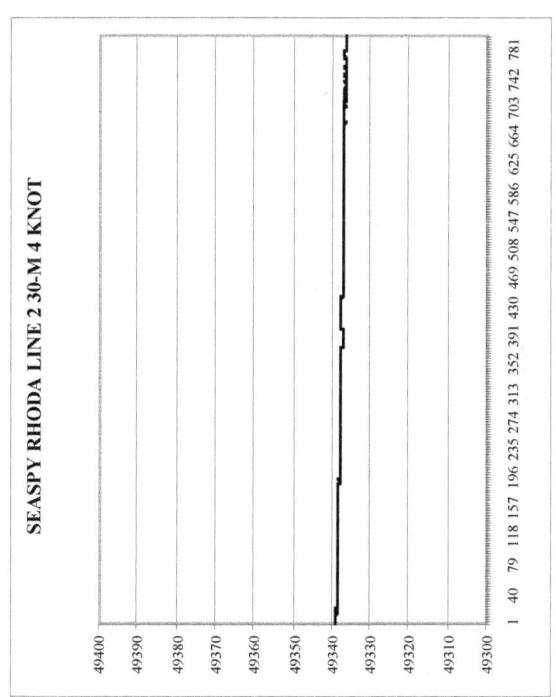

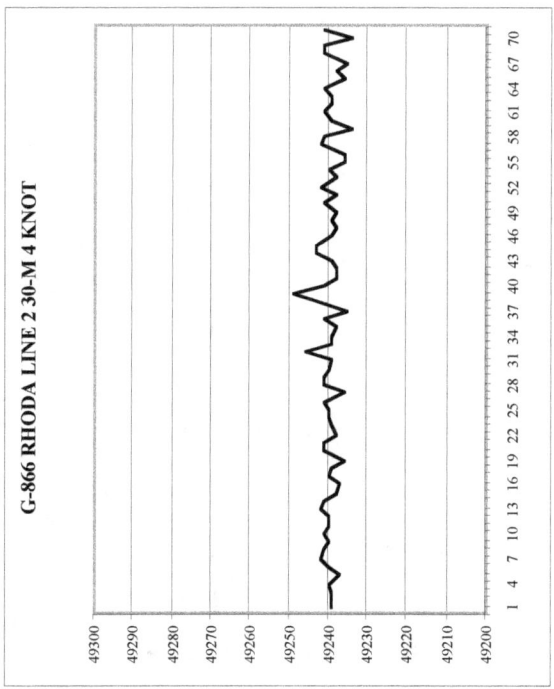

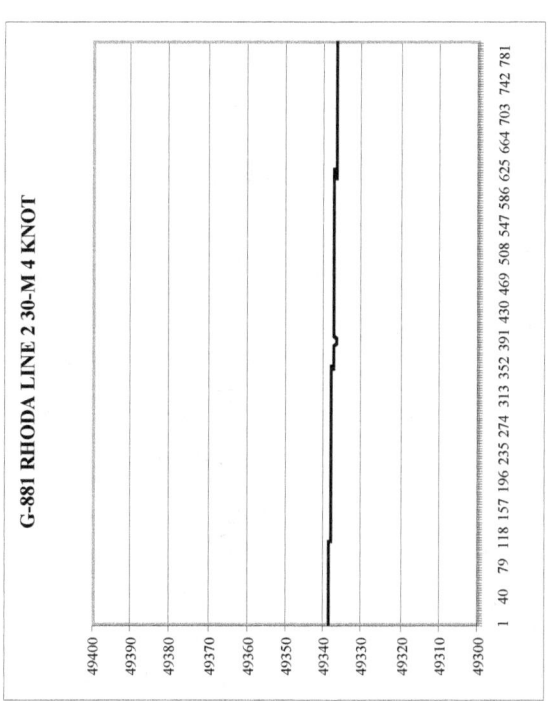

Rhoda 30-Meter Survey Interval 4-Knot Grid Strip charts. Y-axis is the gamma scale, X-axis is the sampling rate.

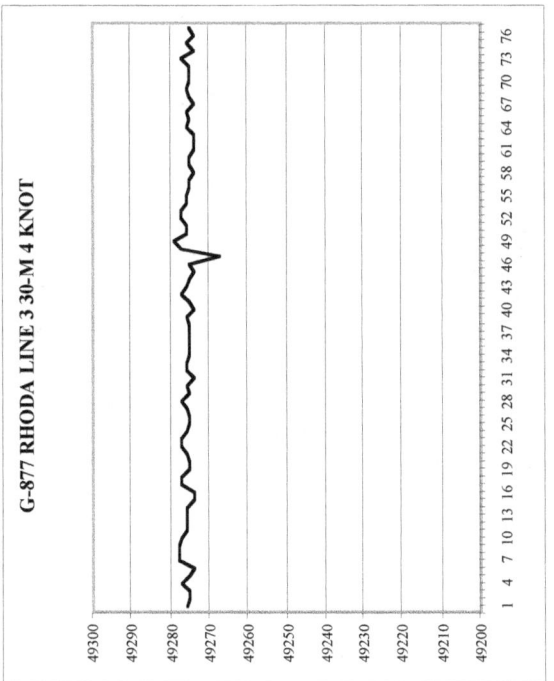

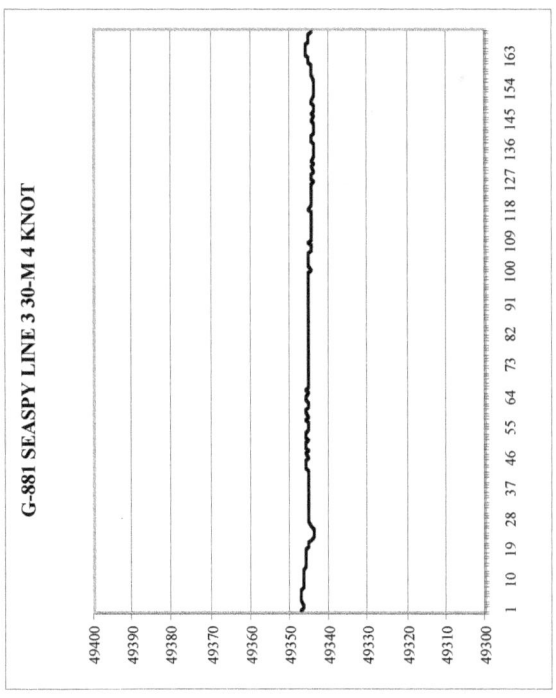

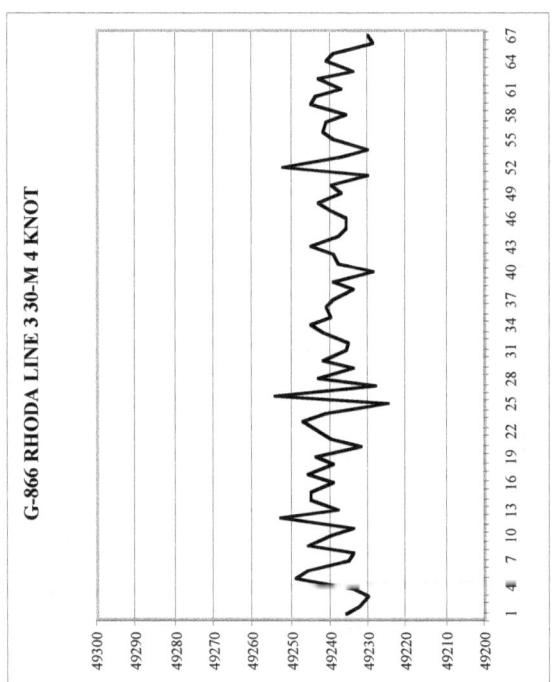

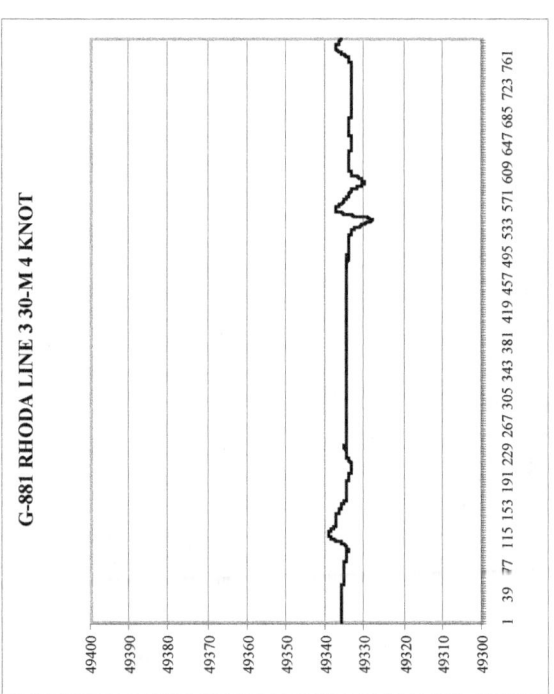

Rhoda 30-Meter Survey Interval 4-Knot Grid Strip charts. Y-axis is the gamma scale, X-axis is the sampling rate.

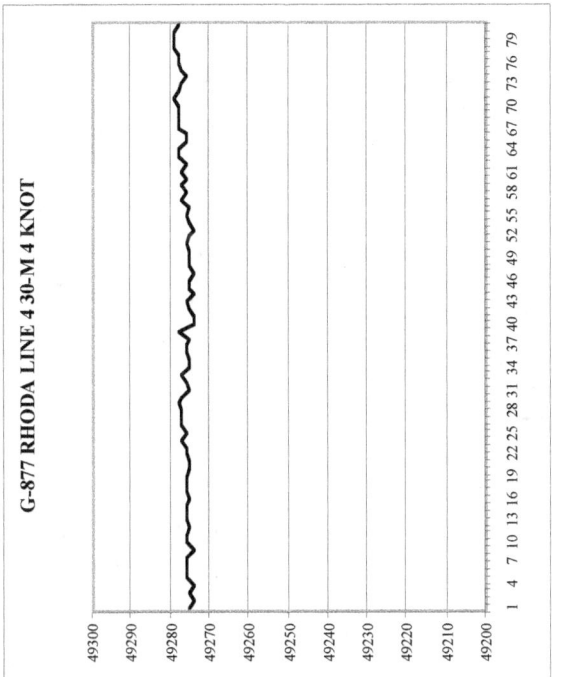

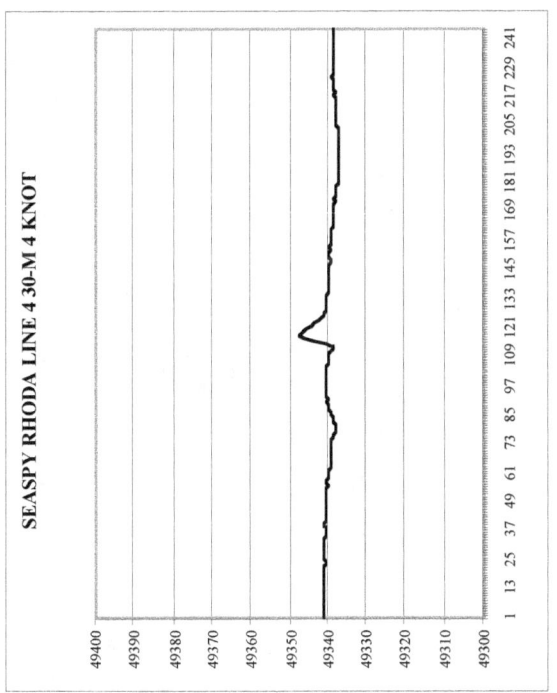

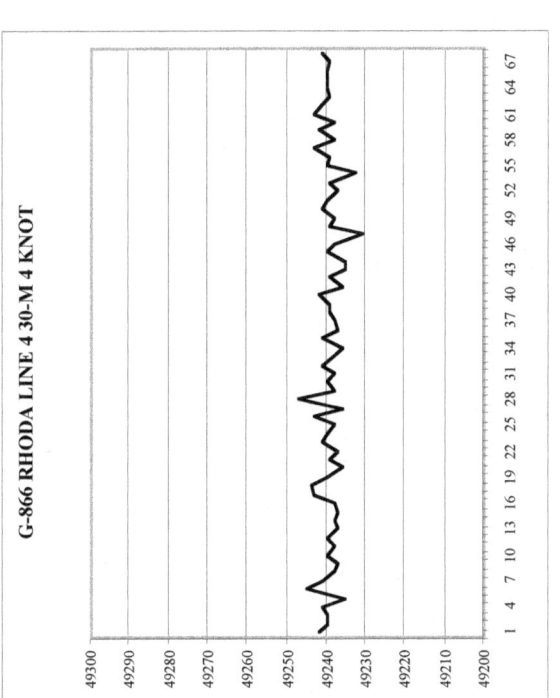

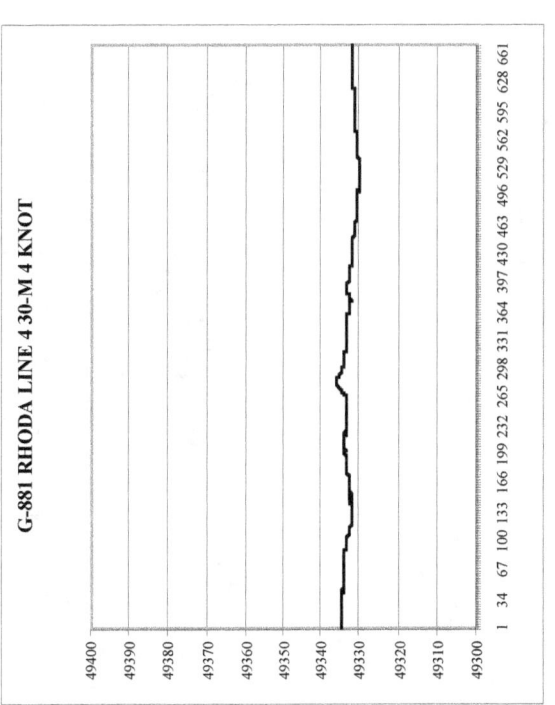

Rhoda 30-Meter Survey Interval 4-Knot Grid Strip charts. Y-axis is the gamma scale, X-axis is the sampling rate.

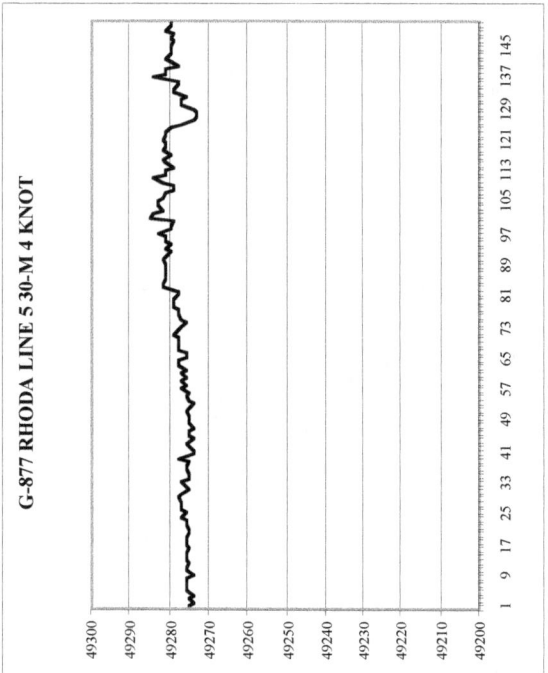

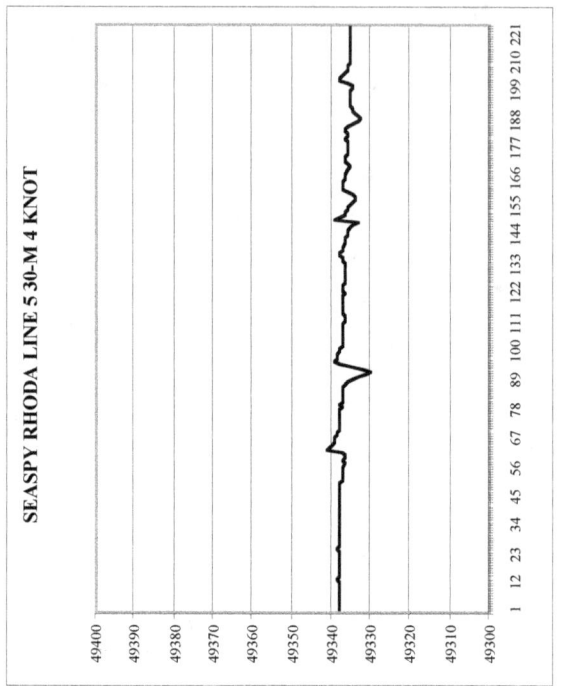

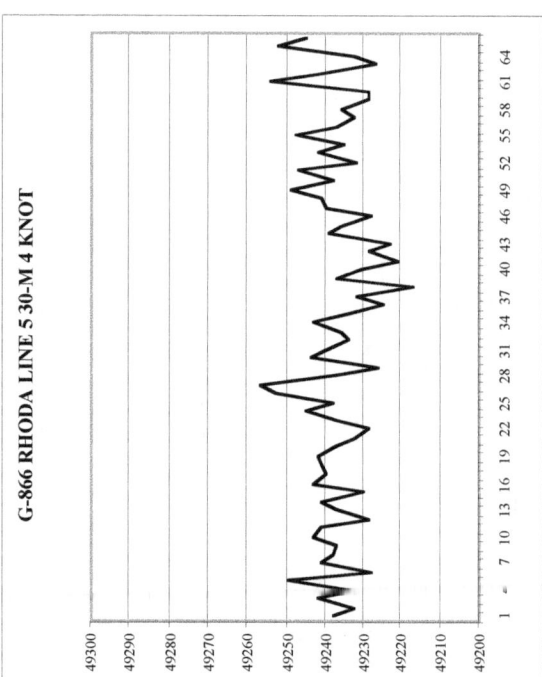

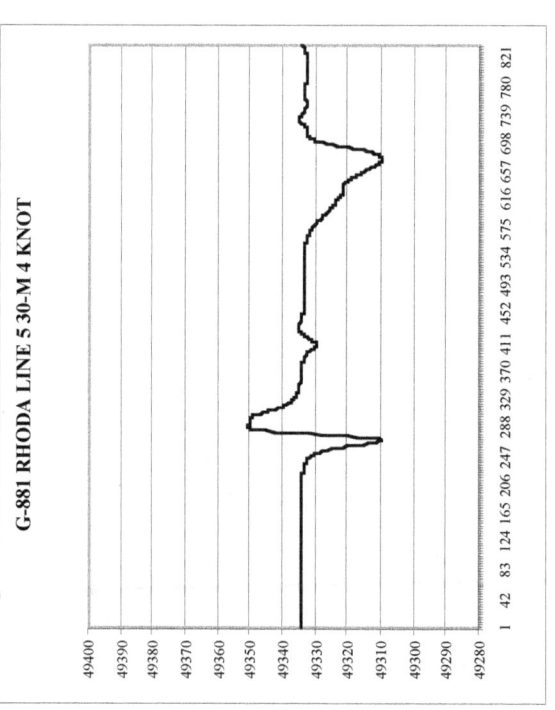

Rhoda **30-Meter Survey Interval 4-Knot Grid Strip charts. Y-axis is the gamma scale, X-axis is the sampling rate.**

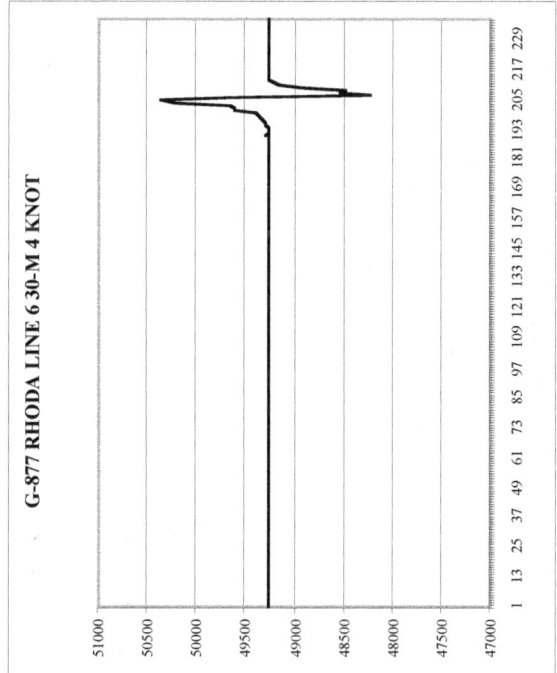

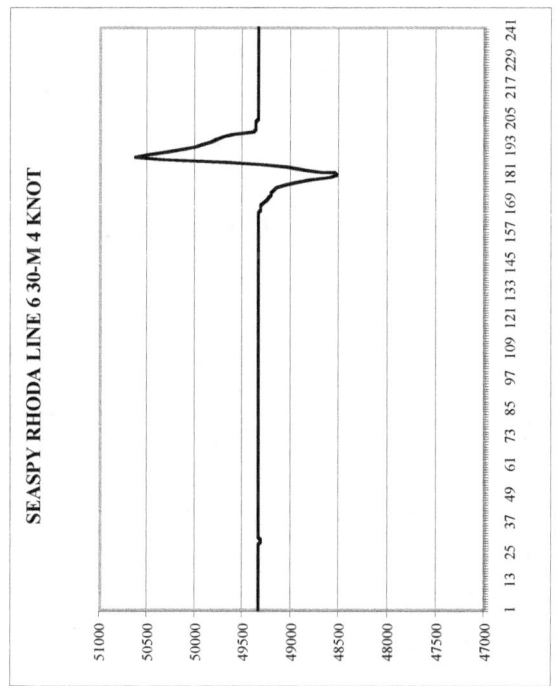

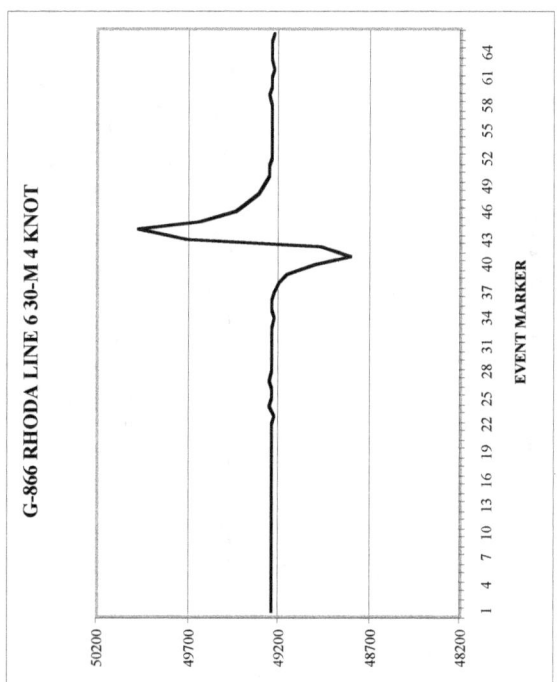

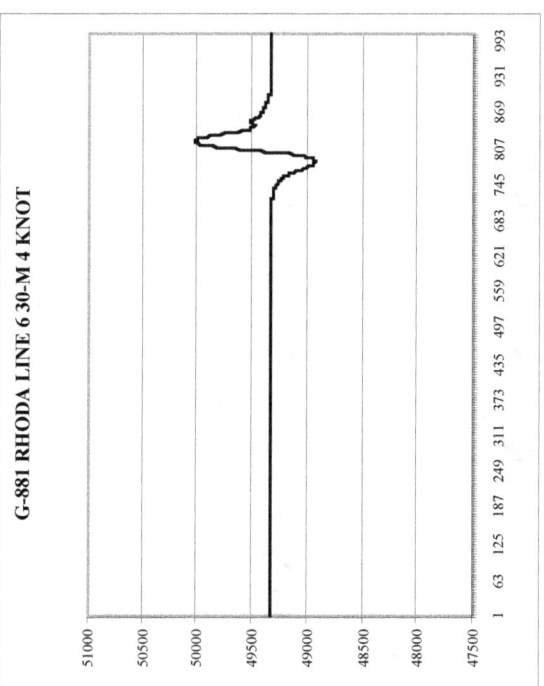

Rhoda 30-Meter Survey Interval 4-Knot Grid Strip charts. Y-axis is the gamma scale, X-axis is the sampling rate.

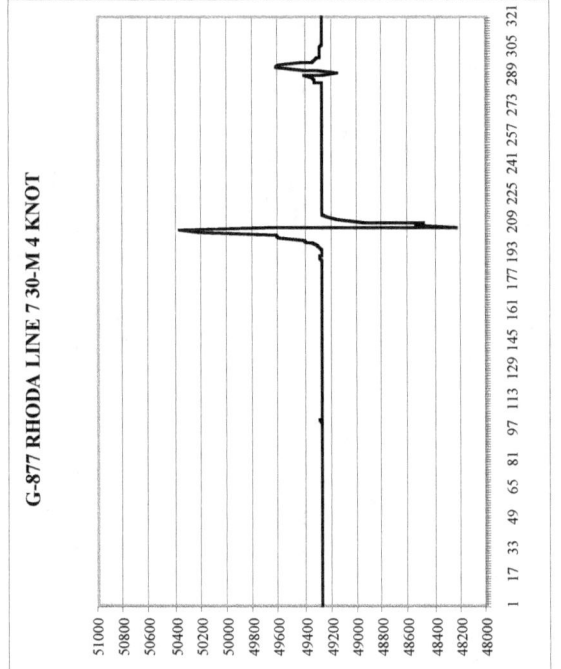

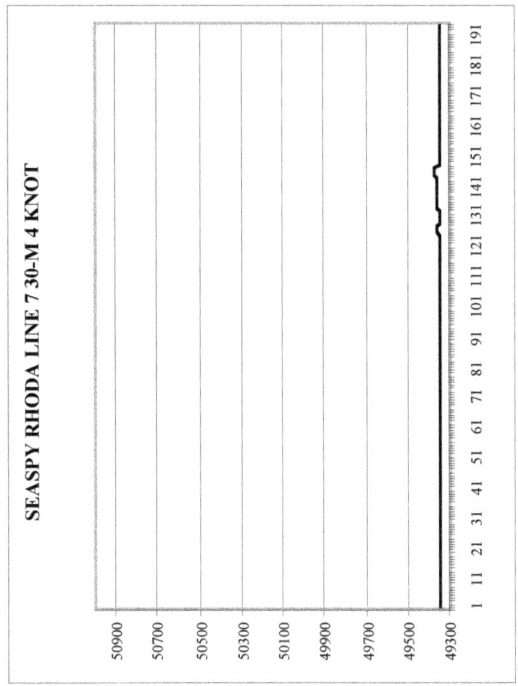

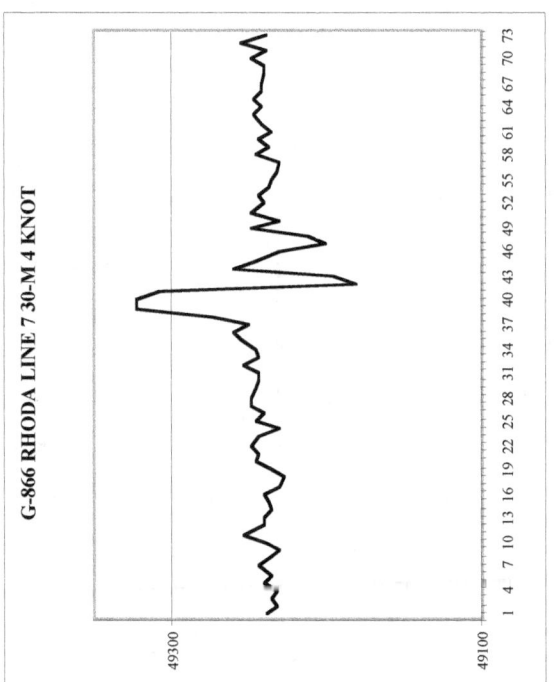

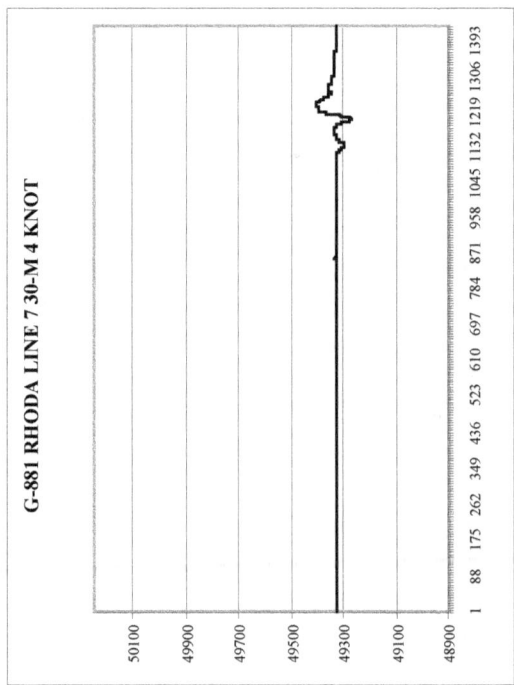

Rhoda 30-Meter Survey Interval 4-Knot Grid Strip charts. Y-axis is the gamma scale, X-axis is the sampling rate.

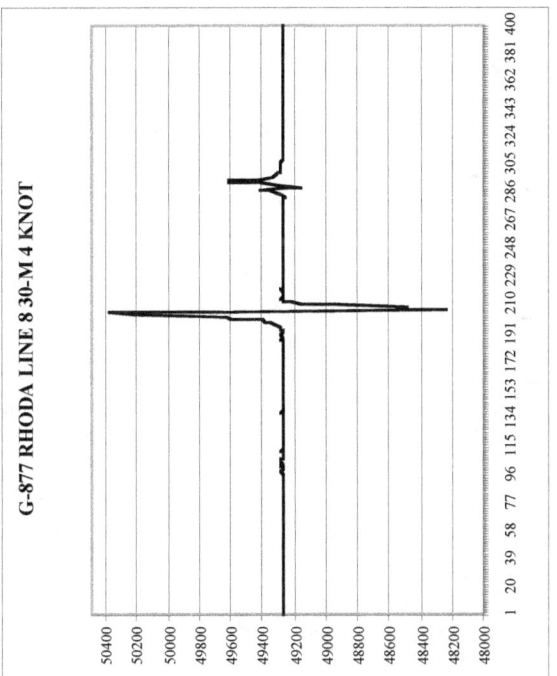

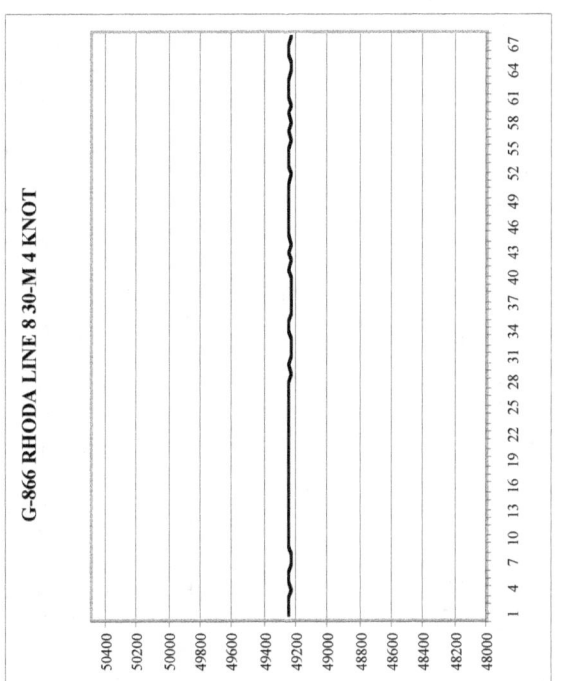

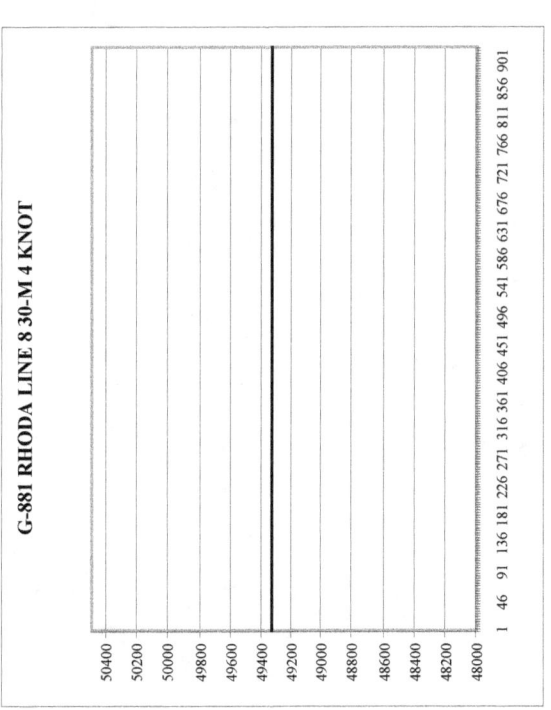

Rhoda 30-Meter Survey Interval 4-Knot Grid Strip charts. Y-axis is the gamma scale, X-axis is the sampling rate.

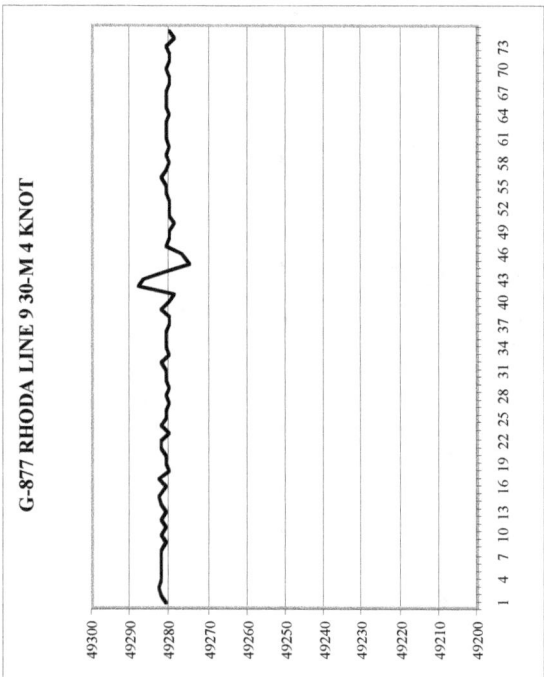

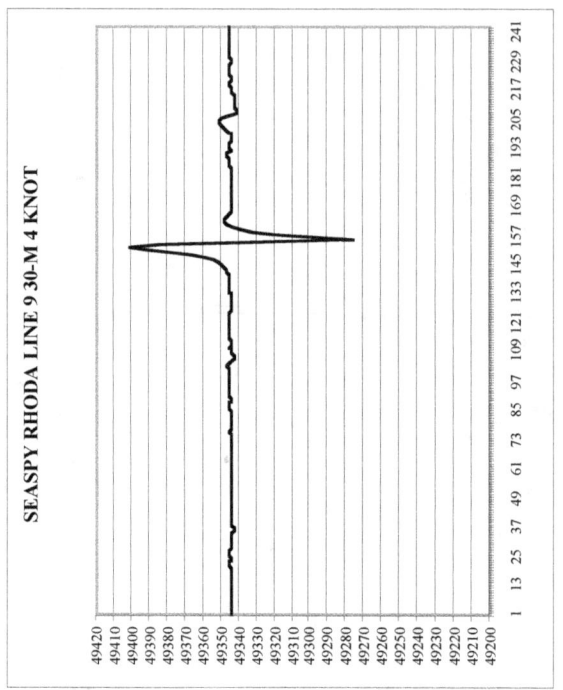

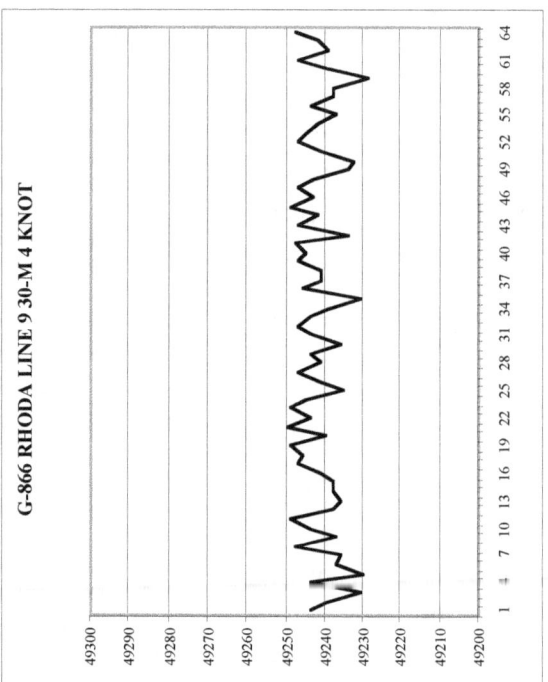

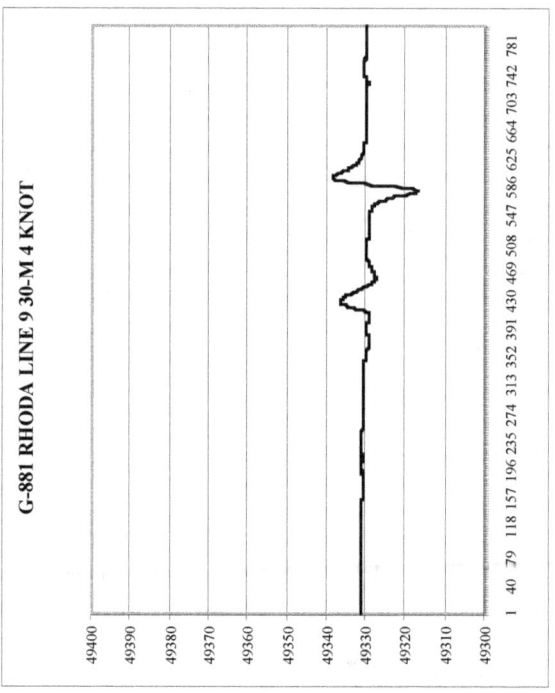

Rhoda **30-Meter Survey Interval 4-Knot Grid Strip charts. Y-axis is the gamma scale, X-axis is the sampling rate.**

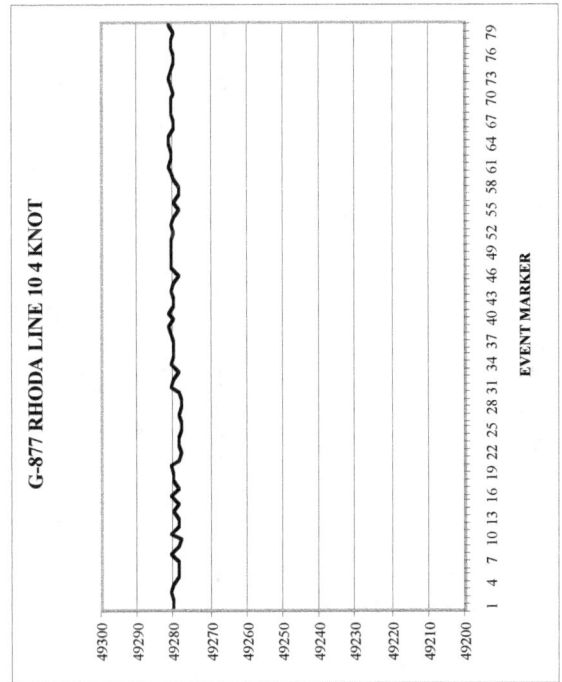

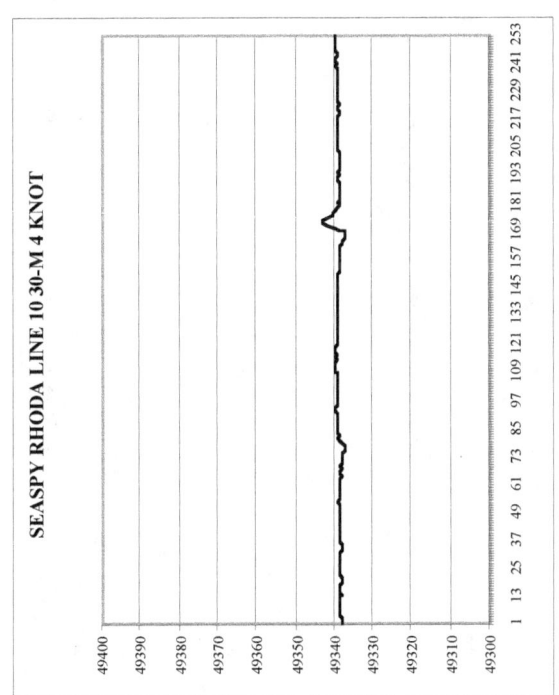

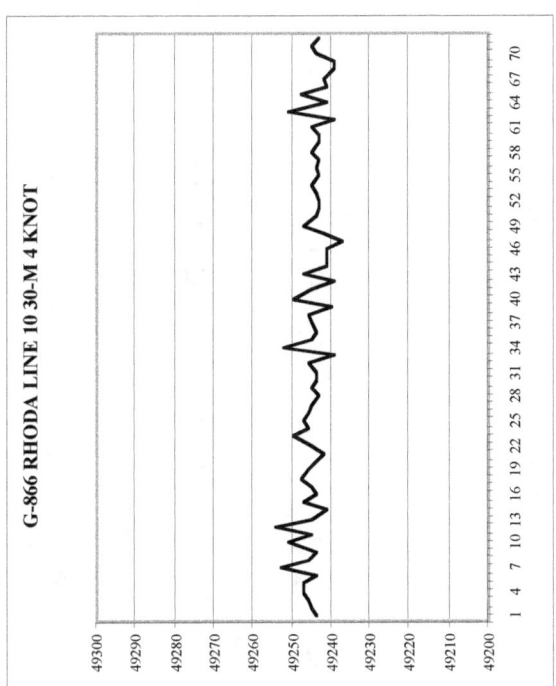

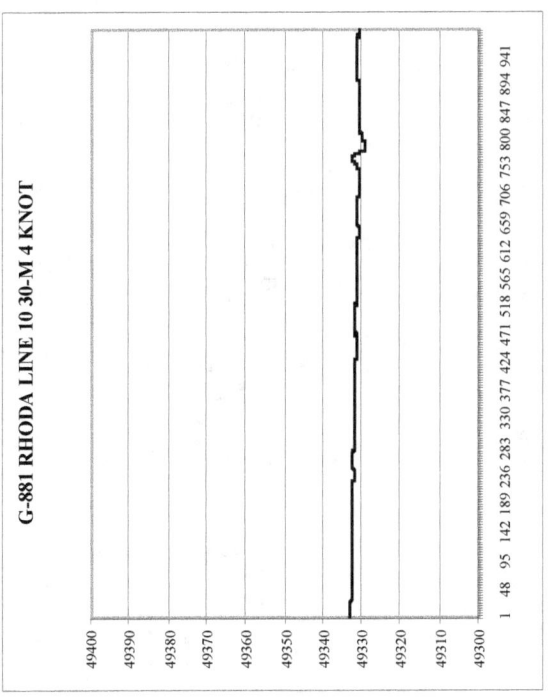

Rhoda 30-Meter Survey Interval 4-Knot Grid Strip charts. Y-axis is the gamma scale, X-axis is the sampling rate.

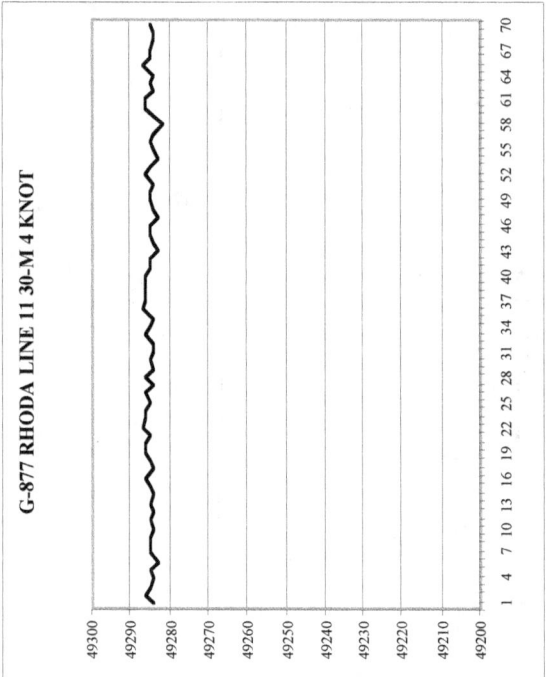

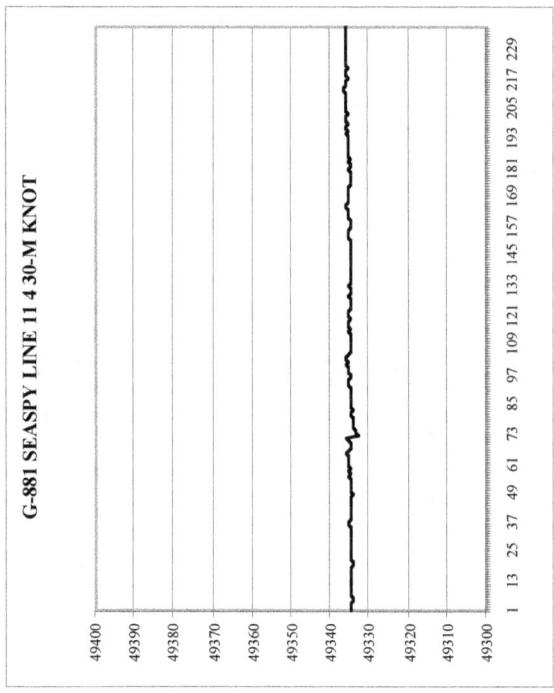

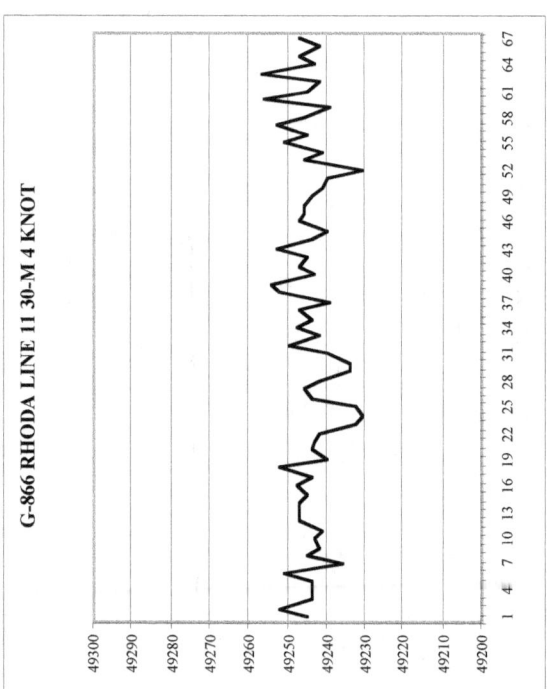

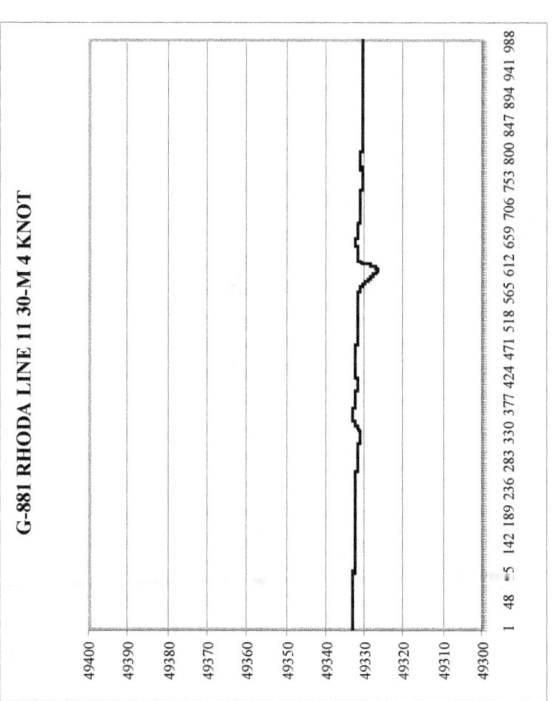

Rhoda 30-Meter Survey Interval 4-Knot Grid Strip charts. Y-axis is the gamma scale, X-axis is the sampling rate.

APPENDIX N

STRIPCHARTS BY LINE FOR EACH INSTRUMENT
***RHODA* 30-METER SURVEY INTERVAL 7-KNOT GRID**

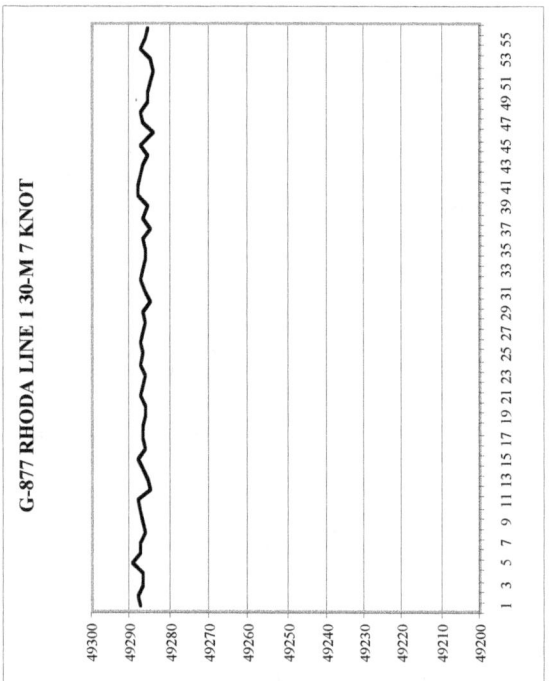

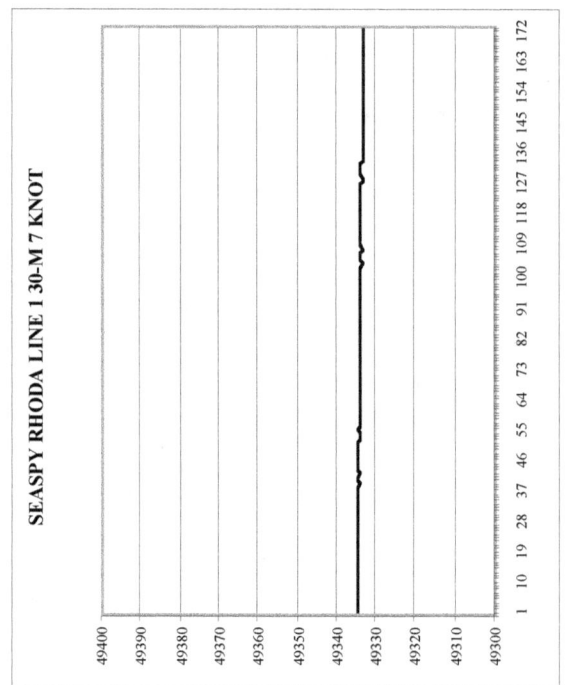

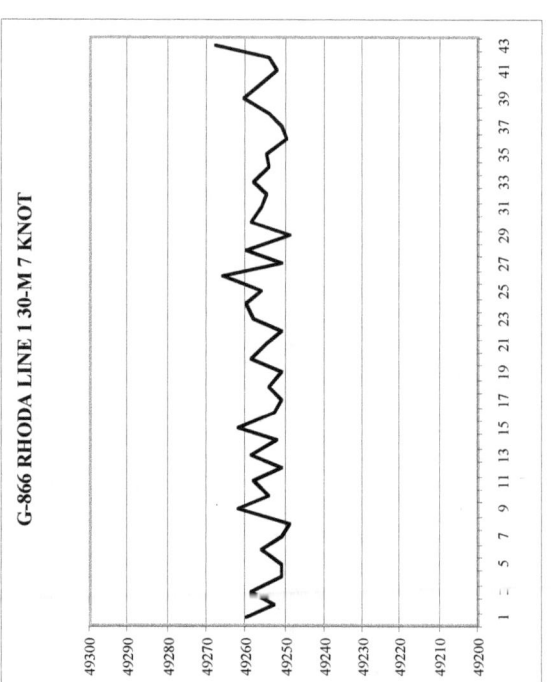

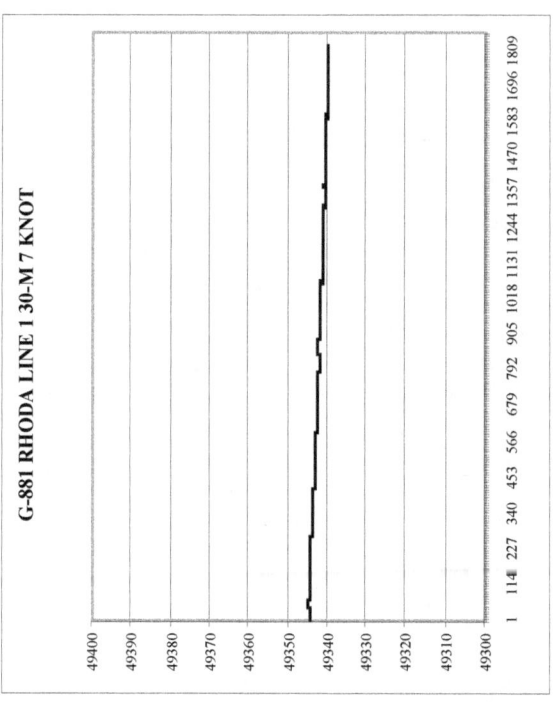

Rhoda 30-Meter Survey Interval 7-Knot Grid Strip charts. Y-axis is the gamma scale, X-axis is the sampling rate.

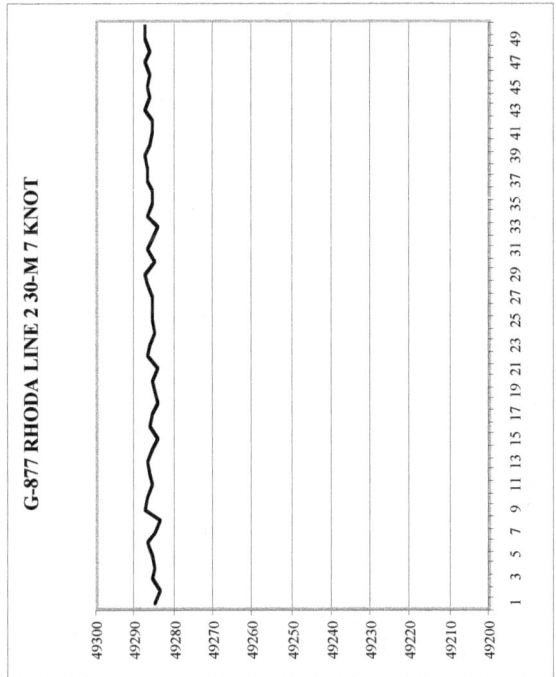

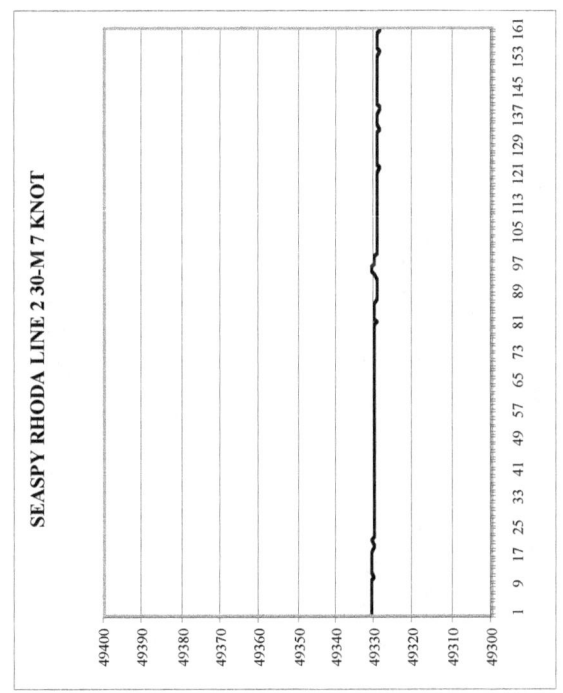

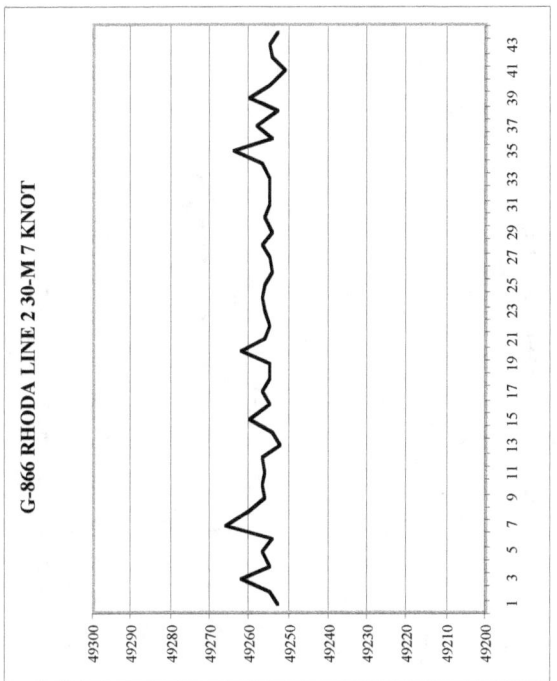

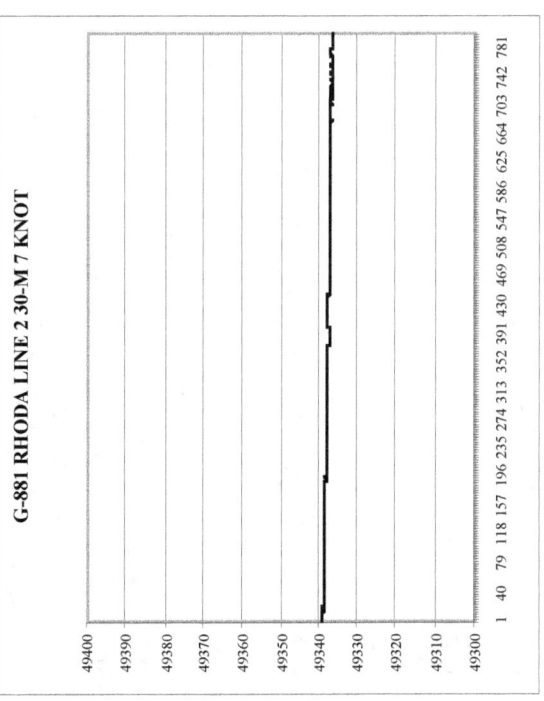

Rhoda 30-Meter Survey Interval 7-Knot Grid Strip charts. Y-axis is the gamma scale, X-axis is the sampling rate.

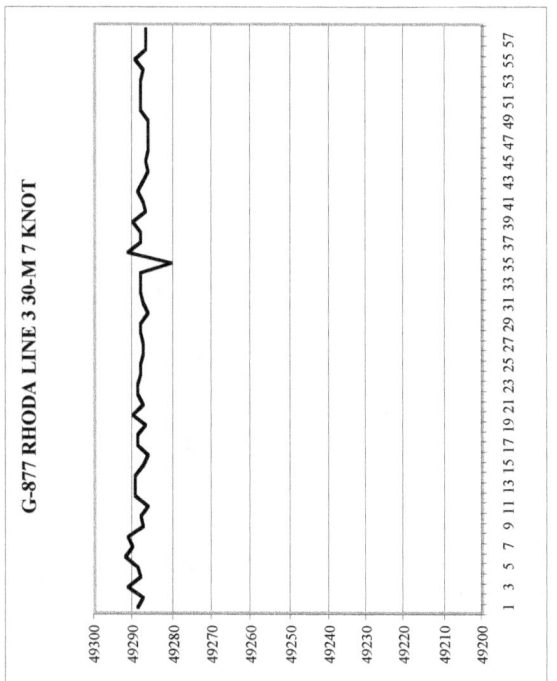

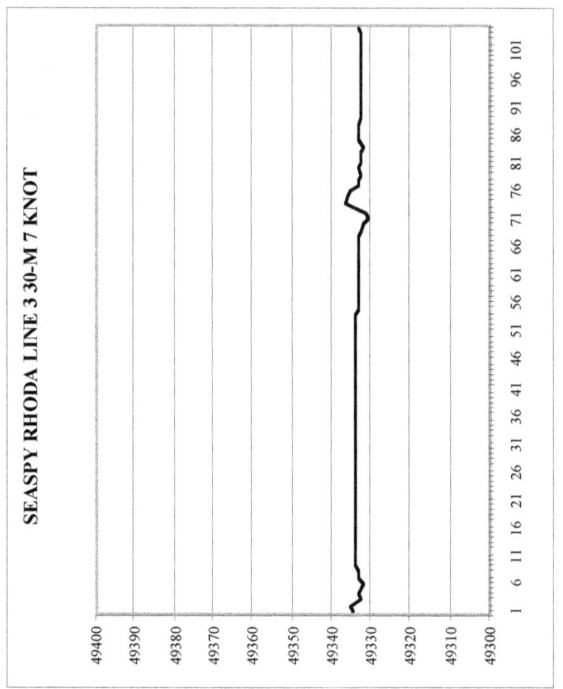

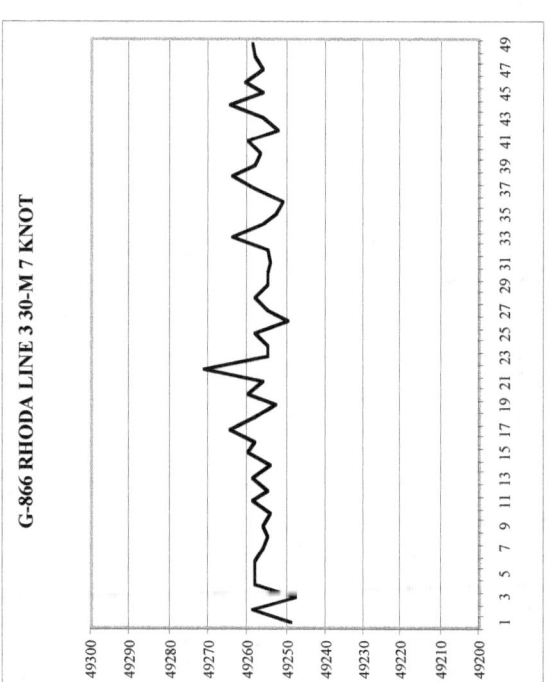

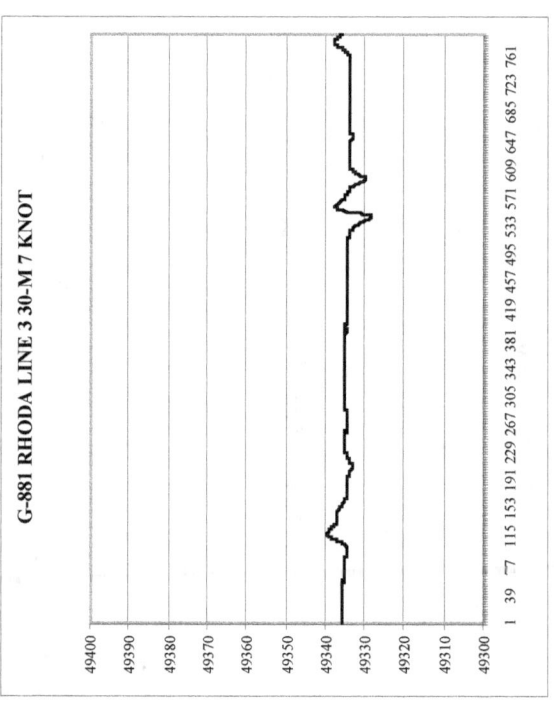

Rhoda 30-Meter Survey Interval 7-Knot Grid Strip charts. Y-axis is the gamma scale, X-axis is the sampling rate.

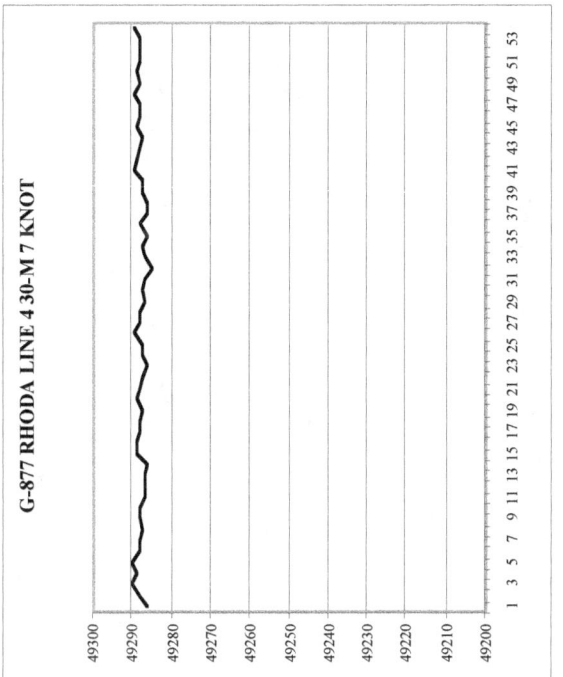

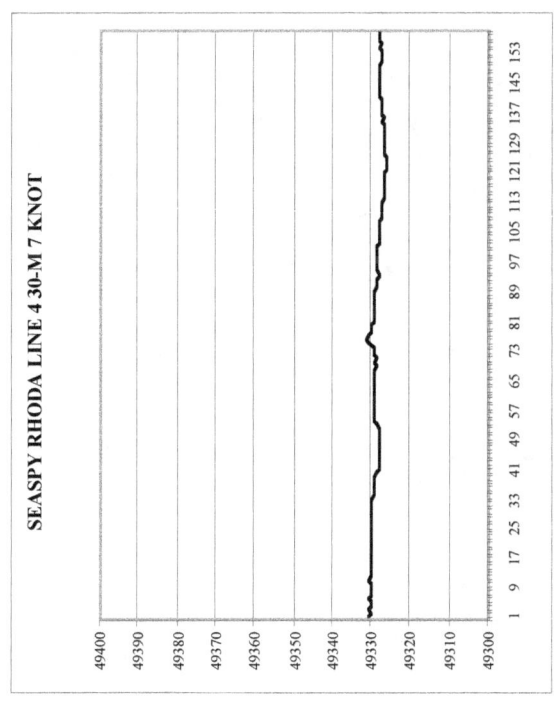

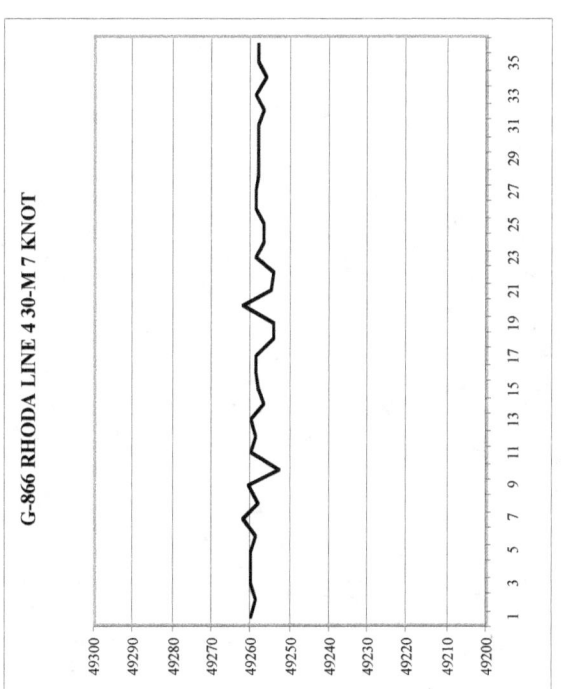

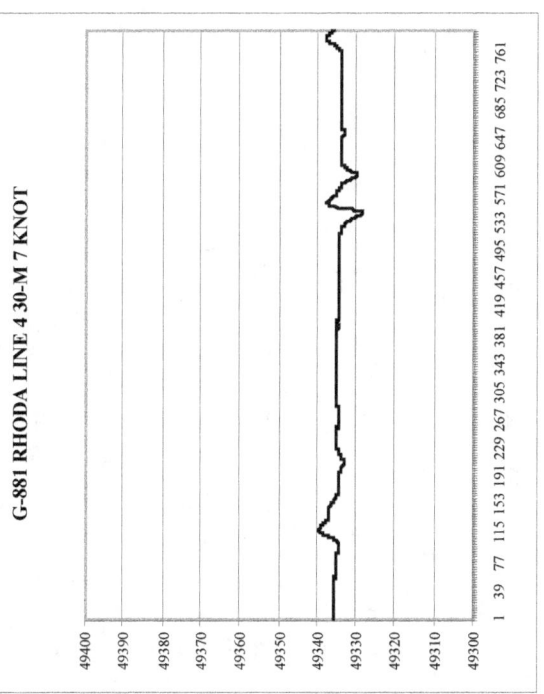

Rhoda **30-Meter Survey Interval 7-Knot Grid Strip charts. Y-axis is the gamma scale, X-axis is the sampling rate.**

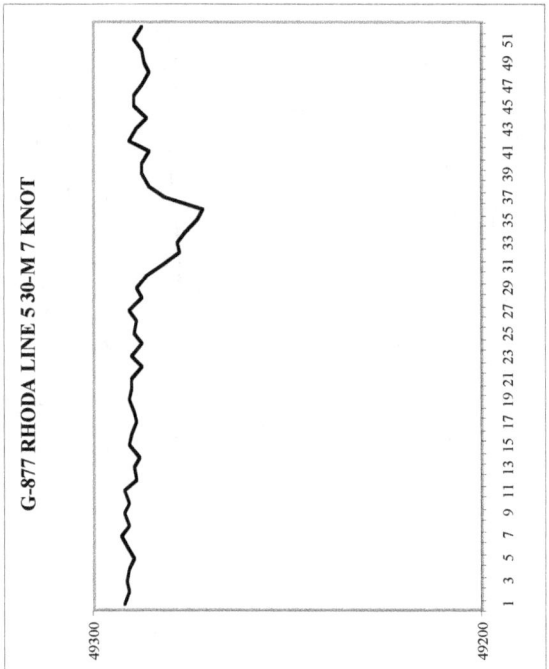

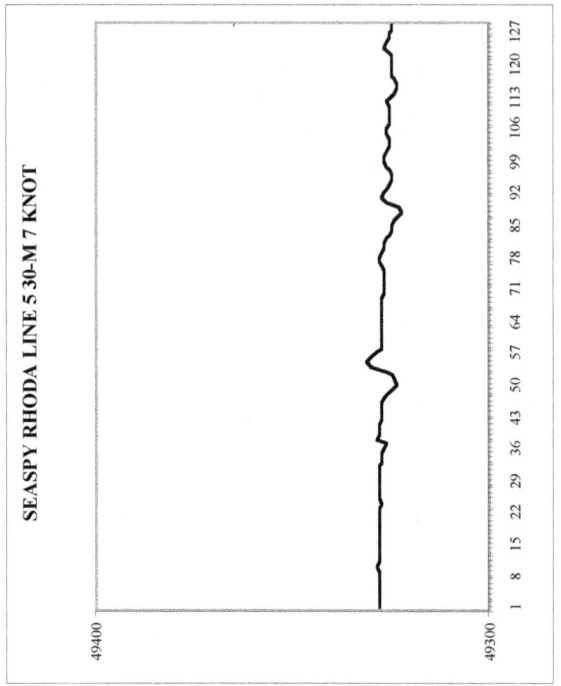

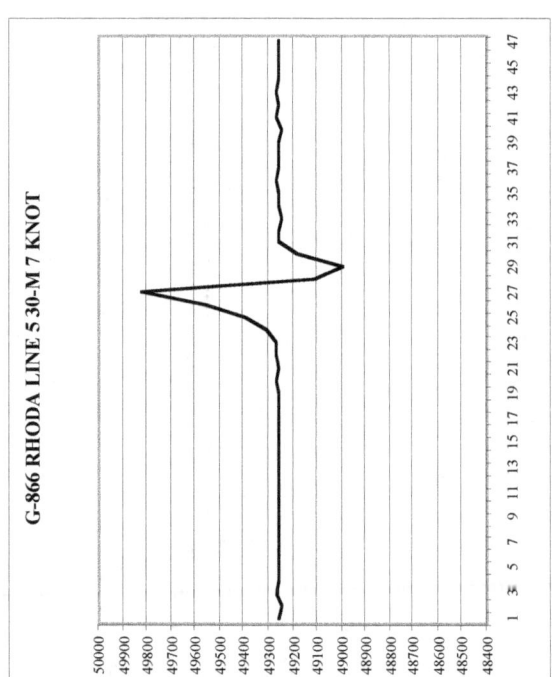

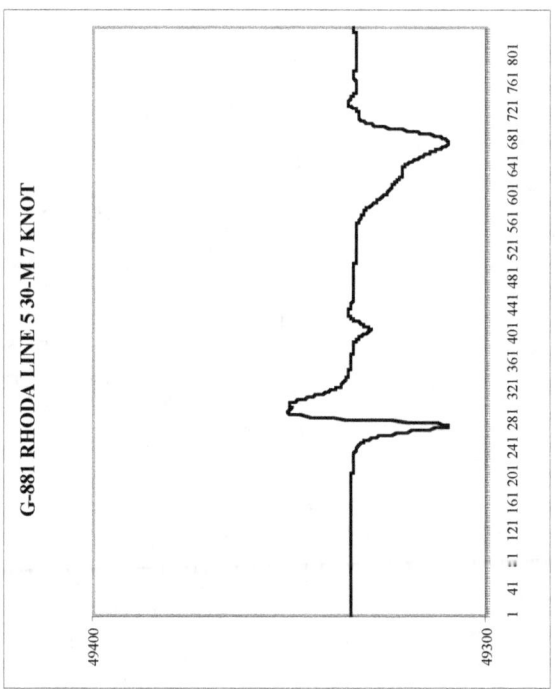

Rhoda 30-Meter Survey Interval 7-Knot Grid Strip charts. Y-axis is the gamma scale, X-axis is the sampling rate.

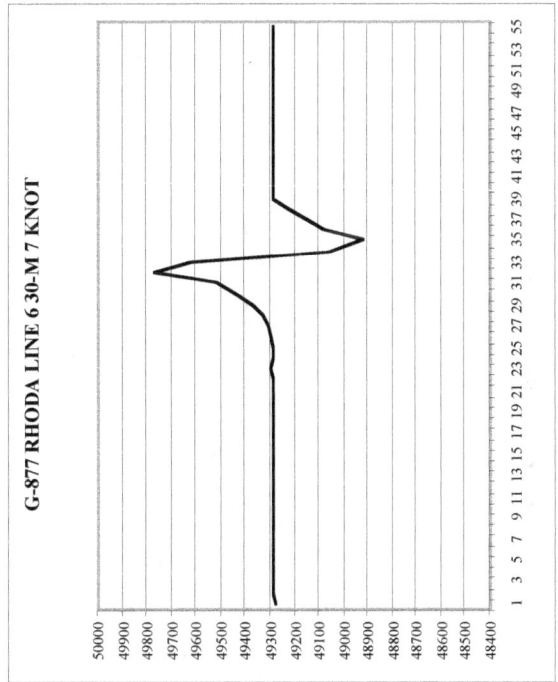

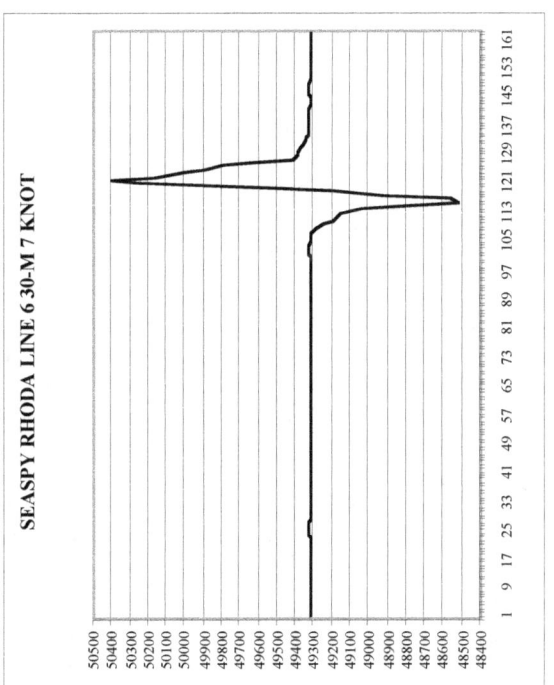

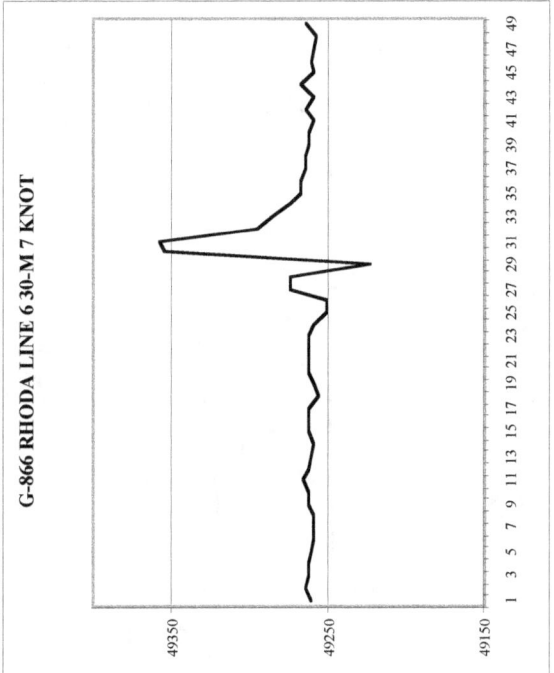

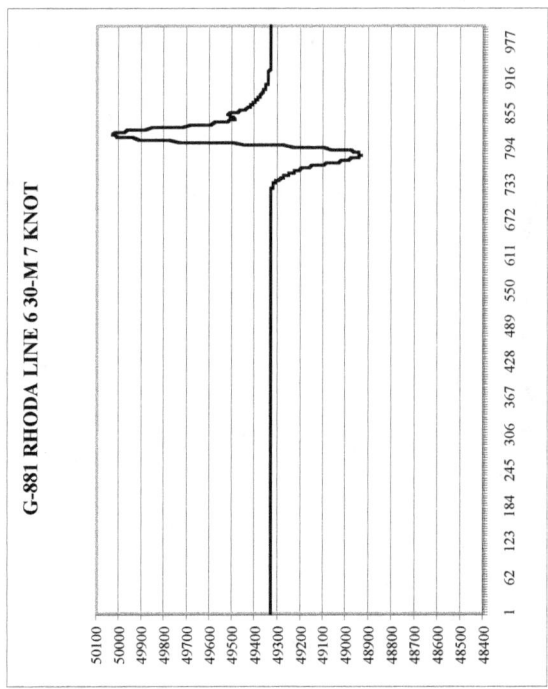

Rhoda **30-Meter Survey Interval 7-Knot Grid Strip charts. Y-axis is the gamma scale, X-axis is the sampling rate.**

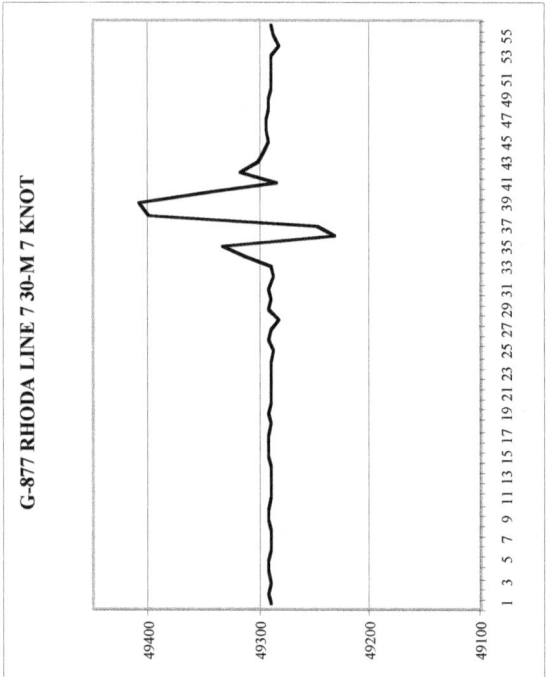

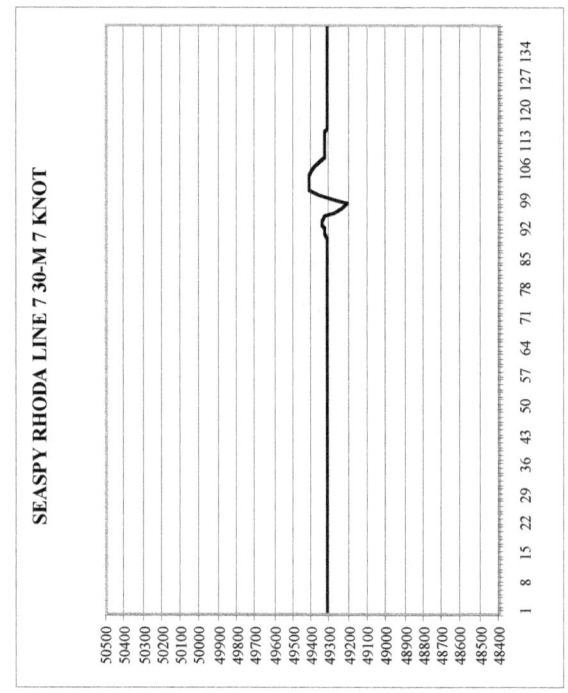

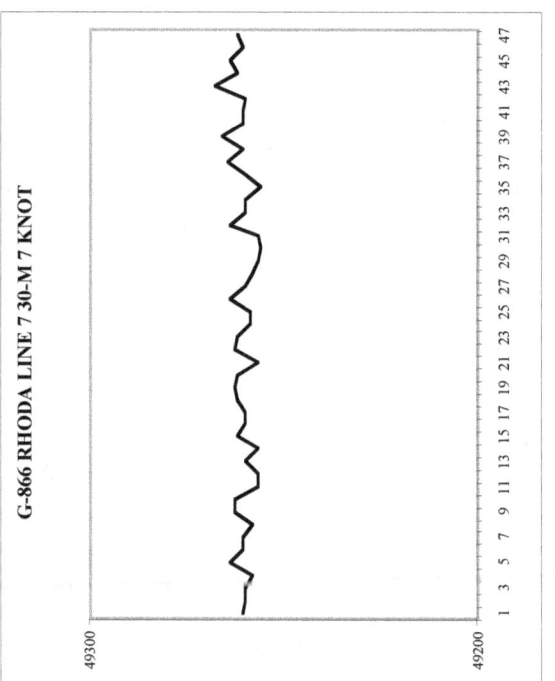

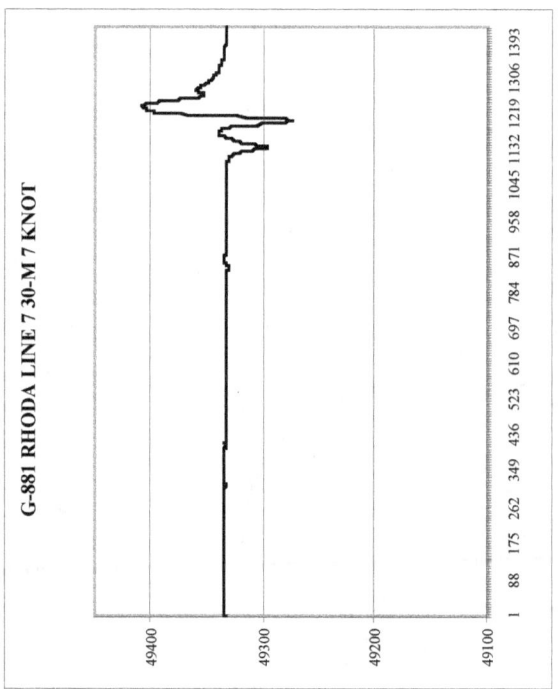

Rhoda **30-Meter Survey Interval 7-Knot Grid Strip charts. Y-axis is the gamma scale, X-axis is the sampling rate.**

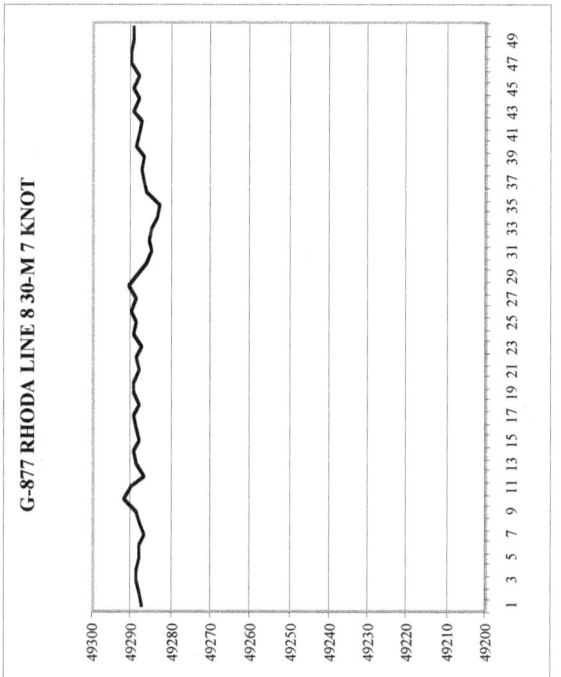

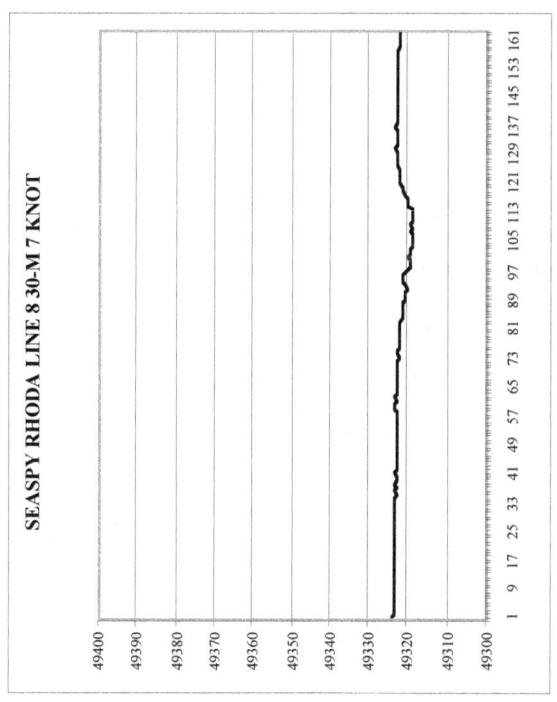

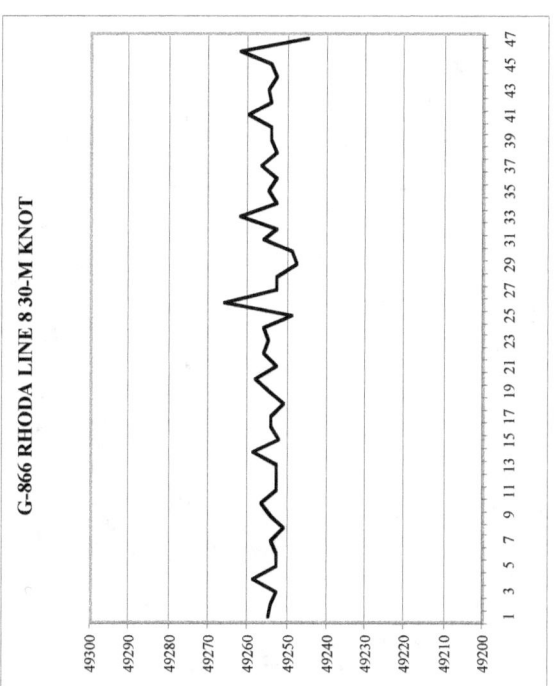

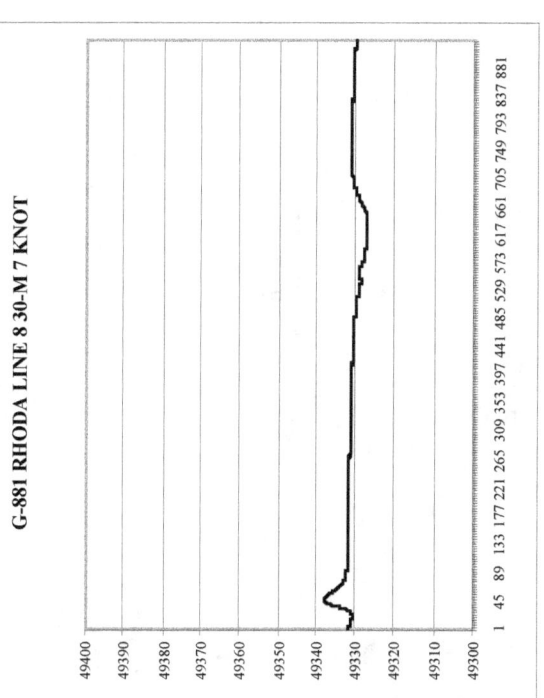

Rhoda 30-Meter Survey Interval 7-Knot Grid Strip charts. Y-axis is the gamma scale, X-axis is the sampling rate.

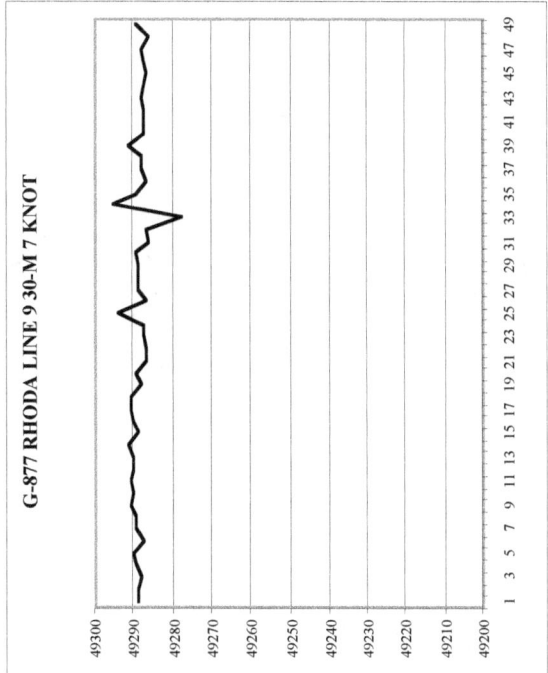

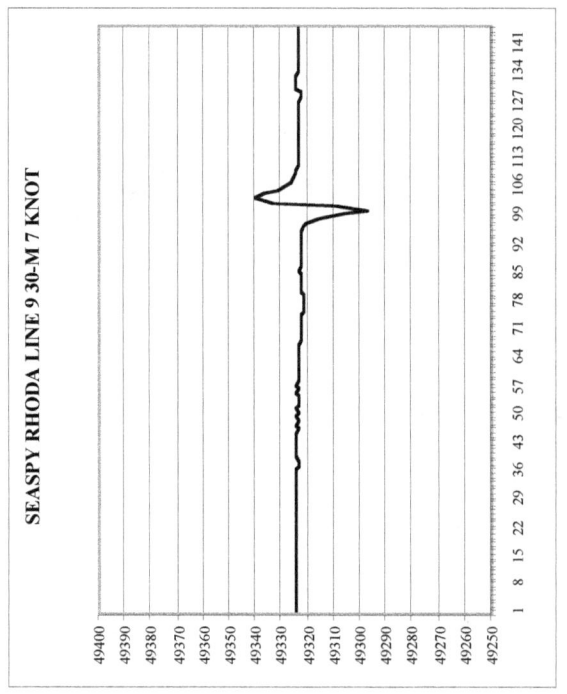

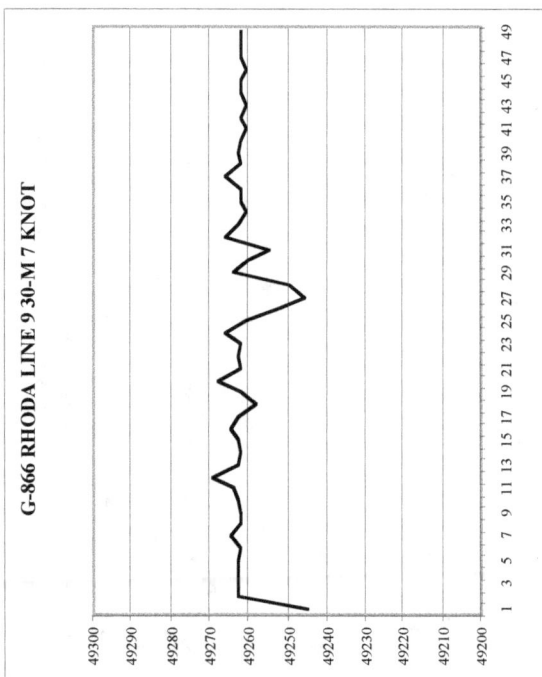

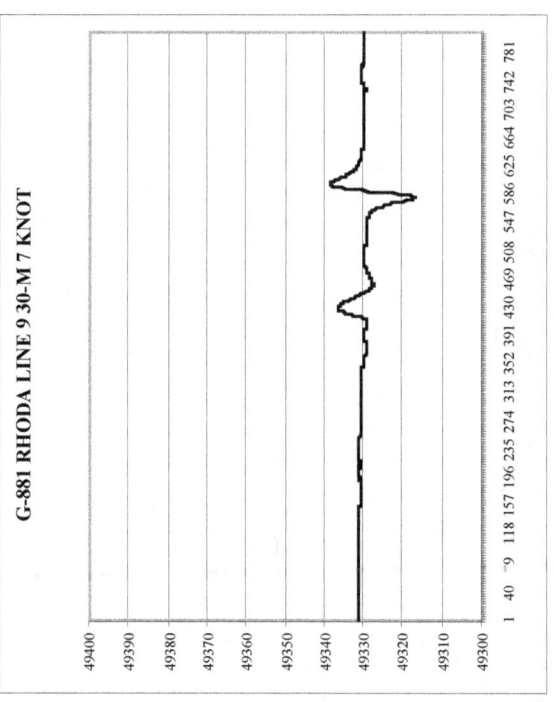

Rhoda 30-Meter Survey Interval 7-Knot Grid Strip charts. Y-axis is the gamma scale, X-axis is the sampling rate.

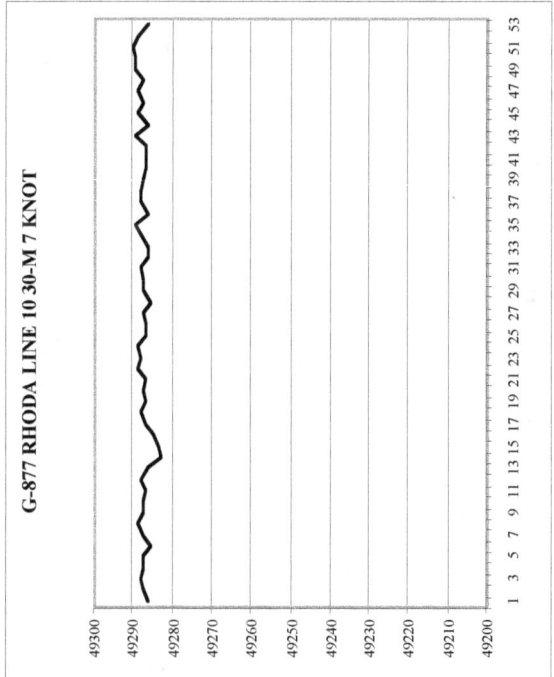

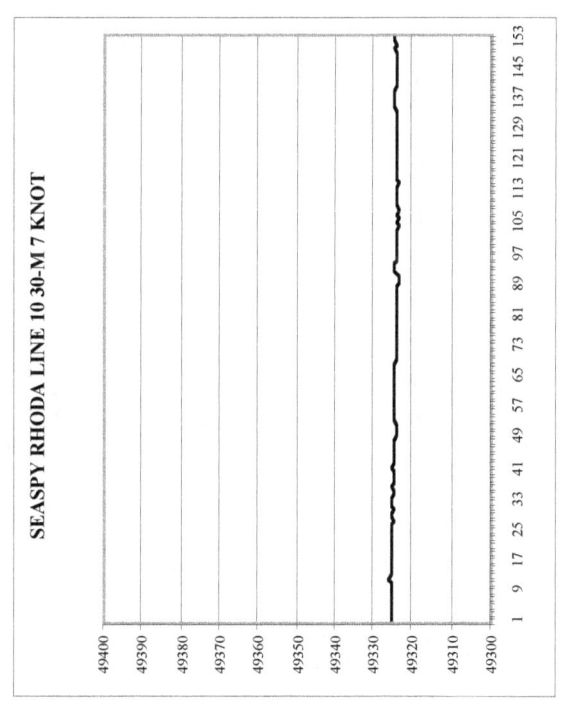

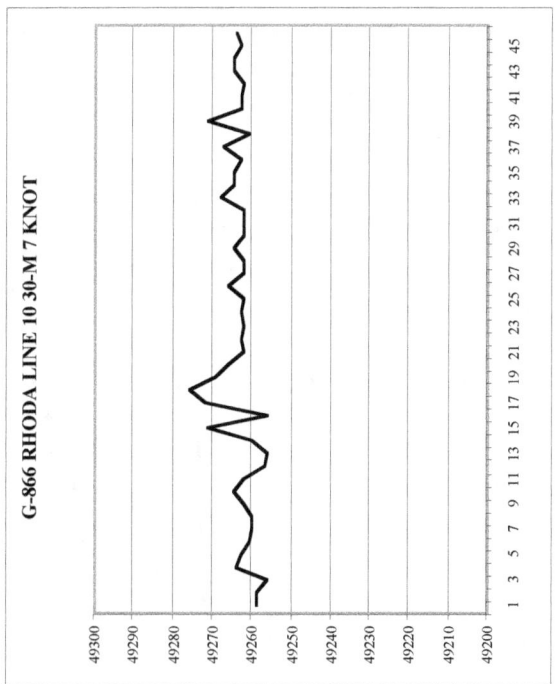

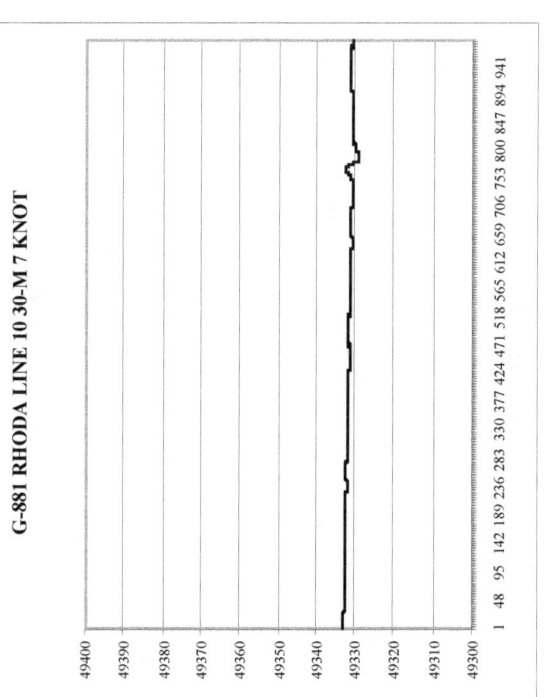

Rhoda 30-Meter Survey Interval 7-Knot Grid Strip charts. Y-axis is the gamma scale, X-axis is the sampling rate.

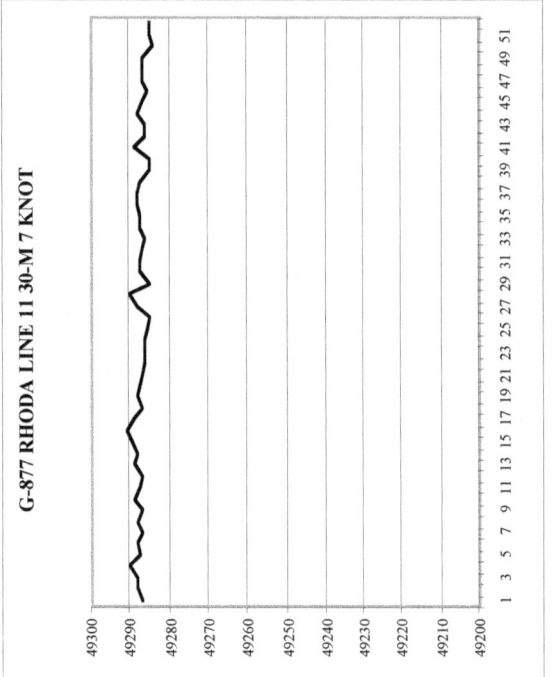

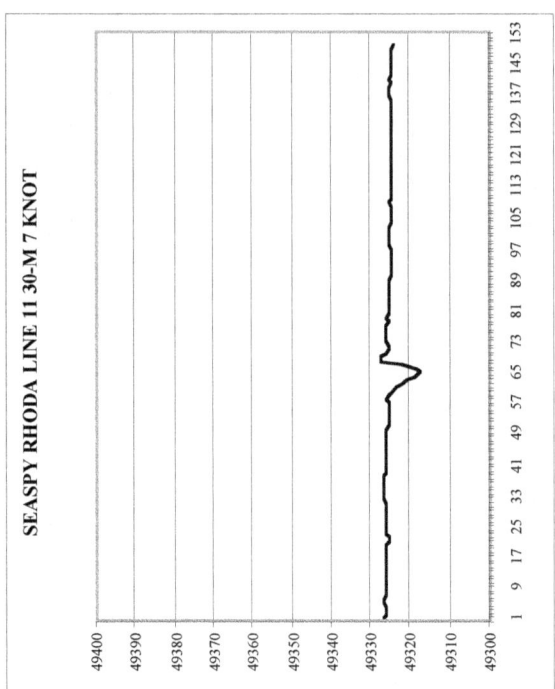

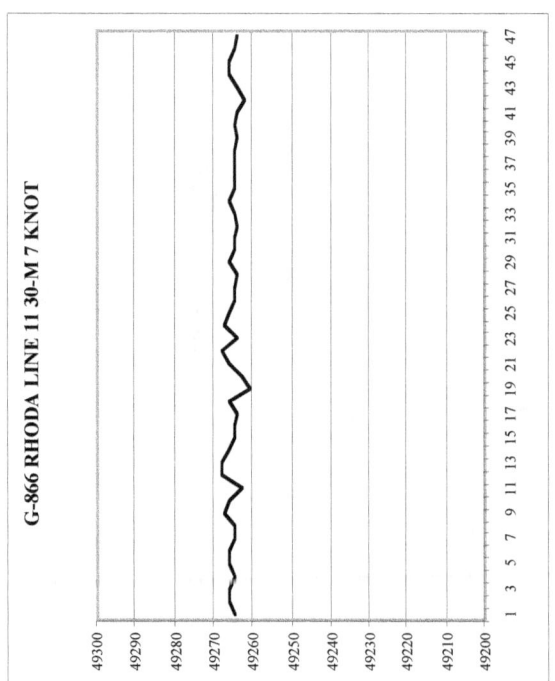

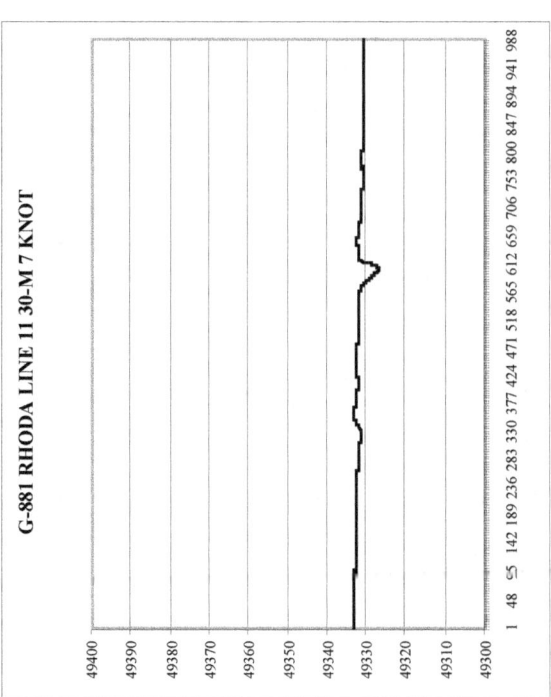

Rhoda 30-Meter Survey Interval 7-Knot Grid Strip charts. Y-axis is the gamma scale, X-axis is the sampling rate.

The Department of the Interior Mission

As the Nation's principal conservation agency, the Department of the Interior has responsibility for most of our nationally owned public lands and natural resources. This includes fostering sound use of our land and water resources; protecting our fish, wildlife, and biological diversity; preserving the environmental and cultural values of our national parks and historical places; and providing for the enjoyment of life through outdoor recreation. The Department assesses our energy and mineral resources and works to ensure that their development is in the best interests of all our people by encouraging stewardship and citizen participation in their care. The Department also has a major responsibility for American Indian reservation communities and for people who live in island territories under U.S. administration.

The Minerals Management Service Mission

As a bureau of the Department of the Interior, the Minerals Management Service's (MMS) primary responsibilities are to manage the mineral resources located on the Nation's Outer Continental Shelf (OCS), collect revenue from the Federal OCS and onshore Federal and Indian lands, and distribute those revenues.

Moreover, in working to meet its responsibilities, the **Offshore Minerals Management Program** administers the OCS competitive leasing program and oversees the safe and environmentally sound exploration and production of our Nation's offshore natural gas, oil and other mineral resources. The MMS **Minerals Revenue Management** meets its responsibilities by ensuring the efficient, timely and accurate collection and disbursement of revenue from mineral leasing and production due to Indian tribes and allottees, States and the U.S. Treasury.

The MMS strives to fulfill its responsibilities through the general guiding principles of: (1) being responsive to the public's concerns and interests by maintaining a dialogue with all potentially affected parties and (2) carrying out its programs with an emphasis on working to enhance the quality of life for all Americans by lending MMS assistance and expertise to economic development and environmental protection.